First Across The Contin
By Noah Brooks

Chapter I — A Great Transaction in Land

The people of the young Republic of the United States were greatly astonished, in the summer of 1803, to learn that Napoleon Bonaparte, then First Consul of France, had sold to us the vast tract of land known as the country of Louisiana. The details of this purchase were arranged in Paris (on the part of the United States) by Robert R. Livingston and James Monroe. The French government was represented by Barbe-Marbois, Minister of the Public Treasury.

The price to be paid for this vast domain was fifteen million dollars. The area of the country ceded was reckoned to be more than one million square miles, greater than the total area of the United States, as the Republic then existed. Roughly described, the territory comprised all that part of the continent west of the Mississippi River, bounded on the north by the British possessions and on the west and south by dominions of Spain. This included the region in which now lie the States of Louisiana, Arkansas, Missouri, Kansas, parts of Colorado, Minnesota, the States of Iowa, Nebraska, South Dakota, North Dakota, Wyoming, a part of Idaho, all of Montana and Territory of Oklahoma. At that time, the entire population of the region, exclusive of the Indian tribes that roamed over its trackless spaces, was barely ninety thousand persons, of whom forty thousand were negro slaves. The civilized inhabitants were principally French, or descendants of French, with a few Spanish, Germans, English, and Americans.

The purchase of this tremendous slice of territory could not be complete without an approval of the bargain by the United States Senate. Great opposition to this was immediately excited by people in various parts of the Union, especially in New England, where there was a very bitter feeling against the prime mover in this business,—Thomas Jefferson, then President of the United States. The scheme was ridiculed by persons who insisted that the region was not only wild and unexplored, but uninhabitable and worthless. They derided "The Jefferson Purchase," as they called it, as a useless piece of extravagance and folly; and, in addition to its being a foolish bargain, it was urged that President Jefferson had no right, under the constitution of the United States, to add any territory to the area of the Republic.

Nevertheless, a majority of the people were in favor of the purchase, and the bargain was duly approved by the United States Senate; that body, July 31, 1803, just three months after the execution of the treaty of cession, formally ratified the important agreement between the two governments. The dominion of the United States was now extended across the entire continent of North America, reaching from the Atlantic to the Pacific. The Territory of Oregon was already ours.

This momentous transfer took place one hundred years ago, when almost nothing was known of the region so summarily handed from the government of France to the government of the American Republic. Few white men had ever traversed those trackless plains, or scaled the frowning ranges of mountains that barred the way across the continent. There were living in the fastnesses of the mysterious interior of the Louisiana Purchase many tribes of Indians who had never looked in the face of the white man.

Nor was the Pacific shore of the country any better known to civilized man than was the region lying between that coast and the Big Muddy, or Missouri River. Spanish voyagers, in

1602, had sailed as far north as the harbors of San Diego and Monterey, in what is now California; and other explorers, of the same nationality, in 1775, extended their discoveries as far north as the fifty-eighth degree of latitude. Famous Captain Cook, the great navigator of the Pacific seas, in 1778, reached and entered Nootka Sound, and, leaving numerous harbors and bays unexplored, he pressed on and visited the shores of Alaska, then called Unalaska, and traced the coast as far north as Icy Cape. Cold weather drove him westward across the Pacific, and he spent the next winter at Owyhee, where, in February of the following year, he was killed by the natives.

All these explorers were looking for chances for fur-trading, which was at that time the chief industry of the Pacific coast. Curiously enough, they all passed by the mouth of the Columbia without observing that there was the entrance to one of the finest rivers on the American continent.

Indeed, Captain Vancouver, a British explorer, who has left his name on the most important island of the North Pacific coast, baffled by the deceptive appearances of the two capes that guard the way to a noble stream (Cape Disappointment and Cape Deception), passed them without a thought. But Captain Gray, sailing the good ship "Columbia," of Boston, who coasted those shores for more than two years, fully convinced that a strong current which he observed off those capes came from a river, made a determined effort; and on the 11th of May, 1792, he discovered and entered the great river that now bears the name of his ship. At last the key that was to open the mountain fastnesses of the heart of the continent had been found. The names of the capes christened by Vancouver and re-christened by Captain Gray have disappeared from our maps, but in the words of one of the numerous editors(1) of the narrative of the exploring expedition of Lewis and Clark: "The name of the good ship 'Columbia,' it is not hard to believe, will flow with the waters of the bold river as long as grass grows or water runs in the valleys of the Rocky Mountains."

(1) Dr. Archibald McVickar.

It appears that the attention of President Jefferson had been early attracted to the vast, unexplored domain which his wise foresight was finally to add to the territory of the United States. While he was living in Paris, as the representative of the United States, in 1785-89, he made the acquaintance of John Ledyard, of Connecticut, the well-known explorer, who had then in mind a scheme for the establishment of a fur-trading post on the western coast of America. Mr. Jefferson proposed to Ledyard that the most feasible route to the coveted fur-bearing lands would be through the Russian possessions and downward somewhere near to the latitude of the then unknown sources of the Missouri River, entering the United States by that route. This scheme fell through on account of the obstacles thrown in Ledyard's way by the Russian Government. A few years later, in 1792, Jefferson, whose mind was apparently fixed on carrying out his project, proposed to the American Philosophical Society of Philadelphia that a subscription should be opened for the purpose of raising money "to engage some competent person to explore that region in the opposite direction (from the Pacific coast),—that is, by ascending the Missouri, crossing the Stony (Rocky) Mountains, and descending the nearest river to the Pacific." This was the hint from which originated the famous expedition of Lewis and Clark.

But the story-teller should not forget to mention that hardy and adventurous explorer, Jonathan Carver. This man, the son of a British officer, set out from Boston, in 1766, to explore the wilderness north of Albany and lying along the southern shore of the Great Lakes. He was absent two years and seven months, and in that time he collected a vast amount of useful and strange information, besides learning the language of the Indians among whom he lived. He conceived the bold plan of travelling up a branch of the Missouri (or "Messorie"), till, having discovered the source of the traditional "Oregon, or River of the West," on the western side of the lands that divide the continent, "he would have sailed down that river to the place where it is said to empty itself, near the Straits of Anian."

By the Straits of Anian, we are to suppose, were meant some part of Behring's Straits, separating Asia from the American continent. Carver's fertile imagination, stimulated by what he knew of the remote Northwest, pictured that wild region where, according to a modern poet, "rolls the Oregon and hears no sound save his own dashing." But Carver died without the sight; in his later years, he said of those who should follow his lead: "While their spirits are elated by their success, perhaps they may bestow some commendations and blessings on the person who first pointed out to them the way."

Chapter II — Beginning a Long Journey

In 1803, availing himself of a plausible pretext to send out an exploring expedition, President Jefferson asked Congress to appropriate a small sum of money ($2,500) for the execution of his purpose. At that time the cession of the Louisiana Territory had not been completed; but matters were in train to that end, and before the expedition was fairly started on its long journey across the continent, the Territory was formally ceded to the United States.

Meriwether Lewis, a captain in the army, was selected by Jefferson to lead the expedition. Captain Lewis was a native of Virginia, and at that time was only twenty-nine years old. He had been Jefferson's private secretary for two years and was, of course, familiar with the President's plans and expectations as these regarded the wonder-land which Lewis was to enter. It is pleasant to quote here Mr. Jefferson's words concerning Captain Lewis. In a memoir of that distinguished young officer, written after his death, Jefferson said: "Of courage undaunted; possessing a firmness and perseverance of purpose which nothing but impossibilities could divert from its direction; careful as a father of those committed to his charge, yet steady in the maintenance of order and discipline; intimate with the Indian character, customs and principles; habituated to the hunting life; guarded, by exact observation of the vegetables and animals of his own country, against losing time in the description of objects already possessed; honest, disinterested, liberal, of sound understanding, and a fidelity to truth so scrupulous that whatever he should report would be as certain as if seen by ourselves—with all these qualifications, as if selected and implanted by nature in one body for this express purpose, I could have no hesitation in confiding the enterprise to him."

Before we have finished the story of Meriwether Lewis and his companions, we shall see that this high praise of the youthful commander was well deserved.

For a coadjutor and comrade Captain Lewis chose William Clark,(1) also a native of Virginia, and then about thirty-three years old. Clark, like Lewis, held a commission in the military service of the United States, and his appointment as one of the leaders of the expedition with which his name and that of Lewis will ever be associated, made the two men equal in rank. Exactly how there could be two captains commanding the same expedition, both of the same military and actual rank, without jar or quarrel, we cannot understand; but it is certain that the two young men got on together harmoniously, and no hint or suspicion of any serious disagreement between the two captains during their long and arduous service has come down to us from those distant days.

(1) It is a little singular that Captain Clark's name has
    been so persistently misspelled by historians and
    biographers. Even in most of the published versions of the
    story of the Lewis and Clark expedition, the name of one of
    the captains is spelled Clarke. Clark's own signature, of
    which many are in existence, is without the final and
    superfluous vowel; and the family name, for generations
    past, does not show it.

As finally organized, the expedition was made up of the two captains (Lewis and Clark) and twenty-six men. These were nine young men from Kentucky, who were used to life on the frontier among Indians; fourteen soldiers of the United States Army, selected from many who eagerly volunteered their services; two French voyageurs, or watermen, one of whom was an interpreter of Indian language, and the other a hunter; and one black man, a servant of Captain Clark. All these, except the negro servant, were regularly enlisted as privates in the military service of the United States during the expedition; and three of them were by the captains appointed sergeants. In addition to this force, nine voyageurs and a corporal and six private soldiers were detailed to act as guides and assistants until the explorers should reach the country of the Mandan Indians, a region lying around the spot where is now situated the flourishing city of Bismarck, the capital of North Dakota. It was expected that if hostile Indians should attack the explorers anywhere within the limits of the little-known parts through which they were to make their way, such attacks were more likely to be made below the Mandan country than elsewhere.

The duties of the explorers were numerous and important. They were to explore as thoroughly as possible the country through which they were to pass; making such observations of latitude and longitude as would be needed when maps of the region should be prepared by the War Department; observing the trade, commerce, tribal relations, manners and customs, language, traditions, and monuments, habits and industrial pursuits, diseases and laws of the Indian nations with whom they might come in contact; note the floral, mineral, and animal characteristics of the country, and, above all, to report whatever might be of interest to citizens who might thereafter be desirous of opening trade relations with those wild tribes of which almost nothing was then distinctly known.

The list of articles with which the explorers were provided, to aid them in establishing peaceful relations with the Indians, might amuse traders of the present day. But in those primitive times, and among peoples entirely ignorant of the white man's riches and resources, coats richly laced with gilt braid, red trousers, medals, flags, knives, colored handkerchiefs, paints, small looking-glasses, beads and tomahawks were believed to be so attractive to the simple-minded red man that he would gladly do much and give much of his own to win such prizes. Of these fine things there were fourteen large bales and one box. The stores of the expedition were clothing, working tools, fire-arms, food supplies, powder, ball, lead for bullets, and flints for the guns then in use, the old-fashioned flint-lock rifle and musket being still in vogue in our country; for all of this was at the beginning of the present century.

As the party was to begin their long journey by ascending the Missouri River, their means of travel were provided in three boats. The largest, a keel-boat, fifty-five feet long and drawing three feet of water, carried a big square sail and twenty-two seats for oarsmen. On board this craft was a small swivel gun. The other two boats were of that variety of open craft known as pirogue, a craft shaped like a flat-iron, square-sterned, flat-bottomed, roomy, of light draft, and usually provided with four oars and a square sail which could be used when the wind was aft, and which also served as a tent, or night shelter, on shore. Two horses, for hunting or other occasional service, were led along the banks of the river.

As we have seen, President Jefferson, whose master mind organized and devised this expedition, had dwelt longingly on the prospect of crossing the continent from the headwaters of the Missouri to the headwaters of the then newly-discovered Columbia. The route thus explored was more difficult than that which was later travelled by the first emigrants across the continent to California. That route lies up the Platte River, through what is known as the South Pass of the Rocky Mountains, by Great Salt Lake and down the valley of the Humboldt into California, crossing the Sierra Nevada at any one of several points leading into the valley of the Sacramento. The route, which was opened by the gold-seekers, was followed by the first railroads built across the continent. The route that lay so firmly in Jefferson's mind, and which was followed up with incredible hardships by the Lewis and Clark expedition, has since been traversed by two railroads, built after the first transcontinental rails were laid. If Jefferson had desired to find the shortest and most feasible route across the continent, he would have pointed to the South Pass and Utah basin trails. But these would have led the explorers into California, then and long afterwards a Spanish possession. The entire line finally traced over the Great Divide lay within the territory of the United States.

But it must be remembered that while the expedition was being organized, the vast Territory of Louisiana was as yet a French possession. Before the party were brought together and their supplies collected, the territory passed under the jurisdiction of the United States. Nevertheless, that jurisdiction was not immediately acknowledged by the officials who, up to that time, had been the representatives of the French and Spanish governments. Part of the territory was transferred from Spain to France and then from France to the United States. It was intended that the exploring party should pass the winter of 1803-4 in St. Louis, then a mere village which had been commonly known as Pain Court. But the Spanish governor of the province had not been officially told that the country had been transferred to the United States, and, after the Spanish manner, he forbade the passage of the Americans through his jurisdiction. In those days communication between frontier posts and points lying far to the eastward of the Mississippi was very difficult; it required six weeks to carry the mails between New York, Philadelphia, and Washington to St. Louis; and this was the reason why a treaty, ratified in July, was not officially heard of in St. Louis as late as December of that year. The explorers, shut out of Spanish territory, recrossed the Mississippi and wintered at the mouth of Wood River, just above St. Louis, on the eastern side of the great river, in United States territory. As a matter of record, it may be said here that the actual transfer of the lower part of the territory—commonly known as Orleans—took place at New Orleans, December 20, 1803, and the transfer of the upper part was effected at St. Louis, March 10, 1804, before the Lewis and Clark expedition had started on its long journey to the northwestward.

All over the small area of the United States then existed a deep interest in the proposed explorations of the course and sources of the Missouri River. The explorers were about to plunge into vast solitudes of which white people knew less than we know now about the North Polar country. Wild and extravagant stories of what was to be seen in those trackless regions were circulated in the States. For example, it was said that Lewis and Clark expected to find the mammoth of prehistoric times still living and wandering in the Upper Missouri region; and it was commonly reported that somewhere, a thousand miles or so up the river, was a solid mountain of rock salt, eighty miles long and forty-five miles wide, destitute of vegetation and glittering in the sun! These, and other tales like these, were said to be believed and doted upon by the great Jefferson himself. The Federalists, or "Feds," as they were called, who hated Jefferson, pretended to believe that he had invented some of these foolish yarns, hoping thereby to make his Louisiana purchase more popular in the Republic.

In his last letter to Captain Lewis, which was to reach the explorers before they started, Jefferson said: "The acquisition of the country through which you are to pass has inspired the country generally with a great deal of interest in your enterprise. The inquiries are perpetual as to your progress. The Feds alone still treat it as a philosophism, and would rejoice at its failure. Their bitterness increases with the diminution of their numbers and despair of a resurrection. I hope you will take care of yourself, and be a living witness of their malice and folly." Indeed, after the explorers were lost sight of in the wilderness which they were to traverse, many people in the States declaimed bitterly against the folly that had sent these unfortunate men to perish miserably in the fathomless depths of the continent. They no longer treated it "as a philosophism," or wild prank, but as a wicked scheme to risk life and property in a search for the mysteries of the unknown and unknowable.

As a striking illustration of this uncertainty of the outcome of the expedition, which exercised even the mind of Jefferson, it may be said that in his instructions to Captain Lewis he said: "Our Consuls, Thomas Hewes, at Batavia in Java, William Buchanan in the isles of France and Bourbon, and John Elmslie at the Cape of Good Hope, will be able to supply your necessities by drafts on us." All this seems strange enough to the young reader of the present day; but this was said and done one hundred years ago.

Chapter III — From the Lower to the Upper River

The party finally set sail up the Missouri River on Monday, May 21, 1804, but made only a few miles, owing to head winds. Four days later they camped near the last white settlement on the Missouri,—La Charrette, a little village of seven poor houses. Here lived Daniel Boone, the famous Kentucky backwoodsman, then nearly seventy years old, but still vigorous, erect, and strong of limb. Here and above this place the explorers began to meet with unfamiliar Indian tribes and names. For example, they met two canoes loaded with furs "from the Mahar nation." The writer of the Lewis and Clark journal, upon whose notes we rely for our story, made many slips of this sort. By "Mahars" we must understand that the Omahas were meant. We shall come across other such instances in which the strangers mistook the pronunciation of Indian names. For example, Kansas was by them misspelled as "Canseze" and "Canzan;" and there appear some thirteen or fourteen different spellings of Sioux, of which one of the most far-fetched is "Scouex."

The explorers were now in a country unknown to them and almost unknown to any white man. On the thirty-first of May, a messenger came down the Grand Osage River bringing a letter from a person who wrote that the Indians, having been notified that the country had been ceded to the Americans, burned the letter containing the tidings, refusing to believe the report. The Osage Indians, through whose territory they were now passing, were among the largest and finest-formed red men of the West. Their name came from the river along which they warred and hunted, but their proper title, as they called themselves, was "the Wabashas," and from them, in later years, we derive the familiar name of Wabash. A curious tradition of this people, according to the journal of Lewis and Clark, is that the founder of the nation was a snail, passing a quiet existence along the banks of the Osage, till a high flood swept him down to the Missouri, and left him exposed on the shore. The heat of the sun at length ripened him into a man; but with the change of his nature he had not forgotten his native seats on the Osage, towards which he immediately bent his way. He was, however, soon overtaken by hunger and fatigue, when happily, the Great Spirit appeared, and, giving him a bow and arrow, showed him how to kill and cook deer, and cover himself with the skin. He then proceeded to his original residence; but as he approached the river he was met by a beaver, who inquired haughtily who he was, and by what authority he came to disturb his possession. The Osage answered that the river was his own, for he had once lived on its borders. As they stood disputing, the daughter of the beaver came, and having, by her entreaties, reconciled her father to this young stranger, it was proposed that the Osage should marry the young beaver, and share with her family the enjoyment of the river. The Osage readily consented, and from this happy union there soon came the village and the nation of the Wabasha, or Osages, who have ever since preserved a pious reverence for their ancestors, abstaining from the chase of the beaver, because in killing that animal they killed a brother of the Osage. Of late years, however, since the trade with the whites has rendered beaver-skins more valuable, the sanctity of these maternal relatives has been visibly reduced, and the poor animals have lost all the privileges of kindred.

Game was abundant all along the river as the explorers sailed up the stream. Their hunters killed numbers of deer, and at the mouth of Big Good Woman Creek, which empties into the

Missouri near the present town of Franklin, Howard County, three bears were brought into the camp. Here, too, they began to find salt springs, or "salt licks," to which many wild animals resorted for salt, of which they were very fond. Saline County, Missouri, perpetuates the name given to the region by Lewis and Clark. Traces of buffalo were also found here, and occasional wandering traders told them that the Indians had begun to hunt the buffalo now that the grass had become abundant enough to attract this big game from regions lying further south.

By the tenth of June the party had entered the country of the Ayauway nation. This was an easy way of spelling the word now familiar to us as "Iowa." But before that spelling was reached, it was Ayaway, Ayahwa, Iawai, Iaway, and so on. The remnants of this once powerful tribe now number scarcely two hundred persons. In Lewis and Clark's time, they were a large nation, with several hundred warriors, and were constantly at war with their neighbors. Game here grew still more abundant, and in addition to deer and bear the hunters brought in a raccoon. One of these hunters brought into camp a wild tale of a snake which, he said, "made a guttural noise like a turkey." One of the French voyageurs confirmed this story; but the croaking snake was never found and identified.

On the twenty-fourth of June the explorers halted to prepare some of the meat which their hunters brought in. Numerous herds of deer were feeding on the abundant grass and young willows that grew along the river banks. The meat, cut in small strips, or ribbons, was dried quickly in the hot sun. This was called "jirked" meat. Later on the word was corrupted into "jerked," and "jerked beef" is not unknown at the present day. The verb "jerk" is corrupted from the Chilian word, charqui, meaning sun-dried meat; but it is not easy to explain how the Chilian word got into the Northwest.

As the season advanced, the party found many delicious wild fruits, such as currants, plums, raspberries, wild apples, and vast quantities of mulberries. Wild turkeys were also found in large numbers, and the party had evidently entered a land of plenty. Wild geese were abundant, and numerous tracks of elk were seen. But we may as well say here that the so-called elk of the Northwest is not the elk of ancient Europe; a more correct and distinctive name for this animal is wapiti, the name given the animal by the Indians. The European elk more closely resembles the American moose. Its antlers are flat, low, and palmated like our moose; whereas the antlers of the American elk, so-called, are long, high, and round-shaped with many sharp points or tines. The mouth of the great Platte River was reached on the twenty-first of July. This famous stream was then regarded as a sort of boundary line between the known and unknown regions. As mariners crossing the equator require all their comrades, who have not been "over the line" to submit to lathering and shaving, so the Western voyagers merrily compelled their mates to submit to similar horse-play. The great river was also the mark above which explorers entered upon what was called the Upper Missouri.

The expedition was now advancing into a region inhabited by several wandering tribes of Indians, chief of which were the Ottoes, Missouris, and Pawnees. It was determined, therefore, to call a council of some of the chiefs of these bands and make terms of peace with them. After some delay, the messengers sent out to them brought in fourteen representative Indians, to whom the white men made presents of roast meat, pork, flour, and corn-meal, in return for which their visitors brought them quantities of delicious watermelons. "Next day, August 3," says the journal, "the Indians, with their six chiefs, were all assembled under an awning formed with the mainsail, in presence of all our party, paraded for the occasion. A speech was then made, announcing to them the change in the government, our promises of protection, and advice as to their future conduct. All the six chiefs replied to our speech, each in his turn, according to rank. They expressed their joy at the change in the government; their hopes that we would recommend them to their Great Father (the president), that they might obtain trade and necessaries: they wanted arms as well for hunting as for defence, and asked our mediation between them and the Mahas, with whom they are now at war. We promised to do so, and wished some of them to accompany us to that nation, which they declined, for fear of being killed by them. We then proceeded to distribute our presents. The grand chief of the nation not being of the party, we sent him a flag, a medal, and some ornaments for clothing. To the six chiefs who were present, we gave a medal of the second grade to one Ottoe chief and one Missouri chief; a medal of the third grade to two inferior chiefs of each nation; the customary mode of recognizing a chief being to place a medal round his neck, which is considered among his tribe as a proof of his consideration abroad. Each of these medals was accompanied by a present of paint, garters, and cloth ornaments of dress; and to this we added a canister of powder, a bottle of whiskey, and a few presents to the whole, which appeared to make them perfectly satisfied. The air-gun, too, was fired, and astonished them greatly. The absent grand chief was an Ottoe, named Weahrushhah, which, in English, degenerates into Little Thief. The two principal chieftains present were Shongotongo, or Big Horse, and Wethea, or Hospitality; also Shosguscan, or White Horse, an Ottoe; the first an Ottoe, the second a Missouri. The incidents just related induced us to give to this place the name of the Council Bluffs: the situation of it is exceedingly favorable for a fort and trading factory, as the soil is well calculated for bricks, and there is an abundance of wood in the neighborhood, and the air being pure and healthy."

Of course the reader will recognize, in the name given to this place by Lewis and Clark, the flourishing modern city of Council Bluffs, Iowa. Nevertheless, as a matter of fact, the council took place on the Nebraskan or western side of the river, and the meeting-place was at some distance above the site of the present city of Council Bluffs.

Above Council Bluffs the explorers found the banks of the river to be high and bluffy, and on one of the highlands which they passed they saw the burial-place of Blackbird, one of the great men of the Mahars, or Omahas, who had died of small-pox. A mound, twelve feet in diameter and six feet high, had been raised over the grave, and on a tall pole at the summit the party fixed a flag of red, white, and blue. The place was regarded as sacred by the Omahas, who kept the dead chieftain well supplied with provisions. The small-pox had caused great mortality among the Indians; and a few years before the white men's visit, when the fell disease had destroyed four hundred men, with a due proportion of women and children, the survivors burned their village and fled.

"They had been a military and powerful people; but when these warriors saw their strength wasting before a malady which they could not resist, their frenzy was extreme; they burned their village, and many of them put to death their wives and children, to save them from so cruel an affliction, and that all might go together to some better country."

In Omaha, or Mahar Creek, the explorers made their first experiment in dragging the stream for fish. With a drag of willows, loaded with stones, they succeeded in catching a great variety of fine fish, over three hundred at one haul, and eight hundred at another. These were pike, bass, salmon-trout, catfish, buffalo fish, perch, and a species of shrimp, all of which proved an acceptable addition to their usual flesh bill-of-fare.

Desiring to call in some of the surrounding Indian tribes, they here set fire to the dry prairie grass, that being the customary signal for a meeting of different bands of roving peoples. In the afternoon of August 18, a party of Ottoes, headed by Little Thief and Big Horse, came in, with six other chiefs and a French interpreter. The journal says:—

"We met them under a shade, and after they had finished a repast with which we supplied them, we inquired into the origin of the war between them and the Mahas, which they related with great frankness. It seems that two of the Missouris went to the Mahas to steal horses, but were detected and killed; the Ottoes and Missouris thought themselves bound to avenge their companions, and the whole nations were at last obliged to share in the dispute. They are also in fear of a war from the Pawnees, whose village they entered this summer, while the inhabitants were hunting, and stole their corn. This ingenuous confession did not make us the less desirous of negotiating a peace for them; but no Indians have as yet been attracted by our fire. The evening was closed by a dance; and the next day, the chiefs and warriors being assembled at ten o'clock, we explained the speech we had already sent from the Council Bluffs, and renewed our advice. They all replied in turn, and the presents were then distributed. We exchanged the small medal we had formerly given to the Big Horse for one of the same size with that of Little Thief: we also gave a small medal to a third chief, and a kind of certificate or letter of acknowledgment to five of the warriors expressive of our favor and their good intentions. One of them, dissatisfied, returned us the certificate; but the chief, fearful of our being offended, begged that it might be restored to him; this we declined, and rebuked them severely for having in view mere traffic instead of peace with their neighbors. This displeased them at first; but they at length all petitioned that it should be given to the warrior, who then came forward and made an apology to us; we then delivered it to the chief to be given to the most worthy, and he bestowed it on the same warrior, whose name was Great Blue Eyes. After a more substantial present of small articles and tobacco, the council was ended with a dram to the Indians. In the evening we exhibited different objects of curiosity, and particularly the air-gun, which gave them great surprise. Those people are almost naked, having no covering except a sort of breech-cloth round the middle, with a loose blanket or buffalo robe, painted, thrown over them. The names of these warriors, besides those already mentioned, were Karkapaha, or Crow's Head, and Nenasawa, or Black Cat, Missouris; and Sananona, or Iron Eyes, Neswaunja, or Big Ox, Stageaunja, or Big Blue Eyes, and Wasashaco, or Brave Man, all Ottoes."

Chapter IV — Novel Experiences among the Indians

About this time (the nineteenth and twentieth of August), the explorers lost by death the only member of their party who did not survive the journey. Floyd River, which flows into the Upper Missouri, in the northwest corner of Iowa, still marks the last resting-place of Sergeant Charles Floyd, who died there of bilious colic and was buried by his comrades near the mouth of the stream. Near here was a quarry of red pipestone, dear to the Indian fancy as a mine of material for their pipes; traces of this deposit still remain. So fond of this red rock were the Indians that when they went there to get the stuff, even lifelong and vindictive enemies declared a truce while they gathered the material, and savage hostile tribes suspended their wars for a time.

On the north side of the Missouri, at a point in what is now known as Clay County, South Dakota, Captains Lewis and Clark, with ten men, turned aside to see a great natural curiosity, known to the Indians as the Hill of Little Devils. The hill is a singular mound in the midst of a flat prairie, three hundred yards long, sixty or seventy yards wide, and about seventy feet high. The top is a smooth level plain. The journal says:—

"The Indians have made it a great article of their superstition: it is called the Mountain of Little People, or Little Spirits; and they believe that it is the abode of little devils, in the human form, of about eighteen inches high, and with remarkably large heads; they are armed with sharp arrows, with which they are very skilful, and are always on the watch to kill those who should have the hardihood to approach their residence. The tradition is, that many have suffered from these little evil spirits, and, among others, three Maha Indians fell a sacrifice to them a few years since. This has inspired all the neighboring nations, Sioux, Mahas, and Ottoes, with such terror, that no consideration could tempt them to visit the hill. We saw none of these wicked little spirits, nor any place for them, except some small holes scattered over the top; we were happy enough to escape their vengeance, though we remained some time on the mound to enjoy the delightful prospect of the plain, which spreads itself out till the eye rests upon the northwest hills at a great distance, and those of the northeast, still farther off, enlivened by large herds of buffalo feeding at a distance."

The present residents of the region, South Dakota, have preserved the Indian tradition, and Spirit Mound may be seen on modern maps of that country.

Passing on their way up the Missouri, the explorers found several kinds of delicious wild plums and vast quantities of grapes; and here, too, they passed the mouth of the Yankton River, now known as the Dakota, at the mouth of which is the modern city of Yankton, South Dakota. The Yankton-Sioux Indians, numbering about one thousand people, inhabited this part of the country, and near here the white men were met by a large band of these Sioux who had come in at the invitation of Lewis and Clark. The messengers from the white men reported that they had been well received by the Indians, who, as a mark of respect, presented their visitors with "a fat dog, already cooked, of which they partook heartily and found it well-flavored." From this time, according to the journal, the explorers tasted occasionally of roast dog, and later on they adopted this dish as a regular feature of their bill-of-fare. They do tell us, however, that they had some difficulty in getting used to so novel an article of food.

The Sioux and the white men held a grand council under an oak-tree, from the top of which was flying the American flag. The head chief was presented with a gold-laced uniform of the United States artillery, a cocked hat and red feather. The lesser chiefs were also presented with suitable gifts of lesser value. Various festivities followed the conference. Next day another powwow was held at which the head chief, Weucha, or Shake Hand, said:—

"'I see before me my great father's two sons. You see me and the rest of our chiefs and warriors. We are very poor; we have neither powder, nor ball, nor knives; and our women and children at the village have no clothes. I wish that, as my brothers have given me a flag and a medal, they would give something to those poor people, or let them stop and trade with the first boat which comes up the river. I will bring the chiefs of the Pawnees and Mahas together, and make peace between them; but it is better that I should do it than my great father's sons, for they will listen to me more readily. I will also take some chiefs to your country in the spring; but before that time I cannot leave home. I went formerly to the English, and they gave me a medal and some clothes: when I went to the Spaniards they gave me a medal, but nothing to keep it from my skin: but now you give me a medal and clothes. But still we are poor; and I wish, brothers, you would give us something for our squaws.'"

When he sat down, Mahtoree, or White Crane, rose:

"'I have listened,' said he, 'to what our father's words were yesterday; and I am to-day glad to see how you have dressed our old chief. I am a young man, and do not wish to take much; my fathers have made me a chief; I had much sense before, but now I think I have more than ever. What the old chief has declared I will confirm, and do whatever he and you please; but I wish that you would take pity on us, for we are very poor.'

"Another chief, called Pawnawneahpahbe, then said:

"'I am a young man, and know but little; I cannot speak well, but I have listened to what you have told the old chief, and will do whatever you agree.'

"The same sentiments were then repeated by Aweawechache.

"We were surprised," the journal says, "at finding that the first of these titles means Struck by the Pawnee, and was occasioned by some blow which the chief had received in battle from one of the Pawnee tribe. The second is in English Half Man, which seemed a singular name for a warrior, till it was explained to have its origin, probably, in the modesty of the chief, who, on being told of his exploits, would say, 'I am no warrior, I am only half a man.' The other chiefs spoke very little; but after they had finished, one of the warriors delivered a speech, in which he declared he would support them. They promised to make peace with the Ottoes and Missouris, the only nations with whom they are at war. All these harangues concluded by describing the distress of the nation: they begged us to have pity on them; to send them traders; that they wanted powder and ball; and seemed anxious that we should supply them with some of their great father's milk, the name by which they distinguish ardent spirits. We gave some tobacco to each of the chiefs, and a certificate to two of the warriors who attended the chief We prevailed on M. Durion (interpreter) to remain here, and accompany as many of the Sioux chiefs as he could collect to the seat of government. We also gave his son a flag, some clothes, and provisions, with directions to bring about a peace between the surrounding tribes, and to convey some of their chiefs to see the President.

"The Indians who have just left us are the Yanktons, a tribe of the great nation of Sioux. These Yanktons are about two hundred men in number, and inhabit the Jacques, Des Moines, and Sioux Rivers. In person they are stout, well proportioned, and have a certain air of dignity and boldness. In their dress they differ nothing from the other bands of the nation whom we met afterwards."

Of the Sioux let us say here, there are many bands, or subdivisions. Some writers make eighteen of these principal branches. But the first importance is given to the Sioux proper, or Dakotas. The name "Sioux" is one of reproach, given by their enemies, and signifies "snake;" whereas "Dakota" means "friend" or "ally." The Lewis and Clark journal says of the Yankton-Sioux:—

"What struck us most was an institution peculiar to them and to the Kite (Crow) Indians further to the westward, from whom it is said to have been copied. It is an association of the most active and brave young men, who are bound to each other by attachment, secured by a vow, never to retreat before any danger, or give way to their enemies. In war they go forward without sheltering themselves behind trees, or aiding their natural valor by any artifice. Their punctilious determination not to be turned from their course became heroic, or ridiculous, a short time since, when the Yanktons were crossing the Missouri on the ice. A hole lay immediately in their course, which might easily have been avoided by going around. This the foremost of the band disdained to do, but went straight forward and was lost. The others would have followed his example, but were forcibly prevented by the rest of the tribe. These young men sit, camp, and dance together, distinct from the rest of the nation; they are generally about thirty or thirty-five years old, and such is the deference paid to courage that their seats in council are superior to those of the chiefs and their persons more respected. But, as may be supposed, such indiscreet bravery will soon diminish the numbers of those who practise it; so that the band is now reduced to four warriors, who were among our visitors. These were the remains of twenty-two who composed the society not long ago; but, in a battle with the Kite (Crow) Indians of the Black Mountains, eighteen of them were killed, and these four were dragged from the field by their companions."

Just above the site of the city of Yankton, and near what is still known as Bon Homme Island, Captain Clark explored a singular earth formation in a bend of the river. This had all the appearance of an ancient fortification, stretching across the bend and furnished with redoubts and other features of a great fort. In the journal is given a glowing account of the work and an elaborate map of the same. Modern research, however, has proved that this strange arrangement of walls and parapets is only a series of sand ridges formed by the currents of the river and driftings of sand. Many of these so-called earthworks are situated on the west bank of the Upper Missouri, in North Dakota and South Dakota.

A few days later, the party saw a species of animal which they described as "goats,"—very fleet, with short pronged horns inclining backward, and with grayish hair, marked with white on the rump. This creature, however, was the American antelope, then unknown to science, and first described by Lewis and Clark. While visiting a strange dome-shaped mountain, "resembling a cupola," and now known as "the Tower," the explorers found the abode of another animal, heretofore unknown to them. "About four acres of ground," says the journal, "was covered with small holes." The account continues: "These are the residence of a little animal, called by the French petit chien (little dog), which sit erect near the mouth, and make a whistling noise, but, when alarmed, take refuge in their holes. In order to bring them out we poured into one of the holes five barrels of water without filling it, but we dislodged and caught the owner. After digging down another of the holes for six feet, we found, on running a pole into it, that we had not yet dug half-way to the bottom: we discovered, however, two frogs in the hole, and near it we killed a dark rattlesnake, which had swallowed a small prairie dog. We were also informed, though we never witnessed the fact, that a sort of lizard and a snake live habitually with these animals. The petit chien are justly named, as they resemble a small dog in some particulars, although they have also some points of similarity to the squirrel. The head resembles the squirrel in every respect, except that the ear is shorter; the tail like that of the ground squirrel; the toe nails are long, the fur is fine, and the long hair is gray."

Great confusion has been caused in the minds of readers on account of there being another burrowing animal, called by Lewis and Clark "the burrowing squirrel," which resembles the petit chien in some respects. But the little animal described here is now well known as the prairie-dog,—an unfortunate and misleading name. It is in no sense a species of dog. The creature commonly weighs about three pounds, and its note resembles that of a toy-dog. It is a species of marmot; it subsists on grass roots and other vegetable products; its flesh is delicate and, when fat, of good flavor. The writer of these lines, when crossing the great plains, in early times, found the "prairie-dogs" excellent eating, but difficult to kill; they are expert at diving into their holes at the slightest signal of danger.

The following days they saw large herds of buffalo, and the copses of timber appeared to contain elk and deer, "just below Cedar Island," adds the journal, "on a hill to the south, is the backbone of a fish, forty-five feet long, tapering towards the tail, and in a perfect state of petrifaction, fragments of which were collected and sent to Washington." This was not a fish, but the fossil remains of a reptile of one of the earliest geological periods. Here, too, the party saw immense herds of buffalo, thousands in number, some of which they killed for their meat and skins. They also saw elk, deer, turkeys, grouse, beaver, and prairie-dogs. The journal bitterly complains of the "moschetoes," which were very troublesome. As mosquitoes we now know them.

Oddly enough, the journal sometimes speaks of "goats" and sometimes of "antelopes," and the same animal is described in both instances. Here is a good story of the fleetness of the beautiful creature:—

"Of all the animals we had seen, the antelope seems to possess the most wonderful fleetness. Shy and timorous, they generally repose only on the ridges, which command a view of all the approaches of an enemy: the acuteness of their sight distinguishes the most distant danger; the delicate sensibility of their smell defeats the precautions of concealment; and, when alarmed, their rapid career seems more like the flight of birds than the movements of a quadruped. After many unsuccessful attempts, Captain Lewis at last, by winding around the ridges, approached a party of seven, which were on an eminence towards which the wind was unfortunately blowing. The only male of the party frequently encircled the summit of the hill, as if to announce any danger to the females, which formed a group at the top. Although they did not see Captain Lewis, the smell alarmed them, and they fled when he was at the distance of two hundred yards: he immediately ran to the spot where they had been; a ravine concealed them from him; but the next moment they appeared on a second ridge, at the distance of three miles. He doubted whether they could be the same; but their number, and the extreme rapidity with which they continued their course, convinced him that they must have gone with a speed equal to that of the most distinguished race-horse. Among our acquisitions to-day were a mule-deer, a magpie, a common deer, and buffalo: Captain Lewis also saw a hare, and killed a rattlesnake near the burrows of the barking squirrels."

By "barking squirrels" the reader must understand that the animal better known as the prairie-dog is meant; and the mule-deer, as the explorers called it, was not a hybrid, but a deer with very long ears, better known afterwards as the black-tailed deer.

At the Big Bend of the Missouri, in the heart of what is now South Dakota, while camped on a sand-bar, the explorers had a startling experience. "Shortly after midnight," says the journal, "the sleepers were startled by the sergeant on guard crying out that the sand-bar was sinking, and the alarm was timely given; for scarcely had they got off with the boats before the bank under which they had been lying fell in; and by the time the opposite shore was reached, the ground on which they had been encamped sunk also. A man who was sent to step off the distance across the head of the bend, made it but two thousand yards, while its circuit is thirty miles."

The next day, three Sioux boys swam the river and told them that two parties of their nation, one of eighty lodges, and one of sixty lodges, were camped up the river, waiting to have a palaver with the white explorers. These were Teton Sioux, and the river named for them still bears that title.

Chapter V — From the Tetons to the Mandans

"On the morning of September 25th," says the journal, "we raised a flagstaff and an awning, under which we assembled, with all the party parading under arms. The chiefs and warriors, from the camps two miles up the river, met us, about fifty or sixty in number, and after smoking we delivered them a speech; but as our Sioux interpreter, M. Durion, had been left with the Yanktons, we were obliged to make use of a Frenchman who could not speak fluently, and therefore we curtailed our harangue. After this we went through the ceremony of acknowledging the chiefs, by giving to the grand chief a medal, a flag of the United States, a laced uniform coat, a cocked hat and feather; to the two other chiefs, a medal and some small presents; and to two warriors of consideration, certificates. The name of the great chief is Untongasabaw, or Black Buffalo; the second, Tortohonga, or the Partisan; the third, Tartongawaka, or Buffalo Medicine; the name of one of the warriors was Wawzinggo; that of the second, Matocoquepa, or Second Bear. We then invited the chiefs on board, and showed them the boat, the air-gun, and such curiosities as we thought might amuse them. In this we succeeded too well; for, after giving them a quarter of a glass of whiskey, which they seemed to like very much, and sucked the bottle, it was with much difficulty that we could get rid of them. They at last accompanied Captain Clark on shore, in a pirogue with five men; but it seems they had formed a design to stop us; for no sooner had the party landed than three of the Indians seized the cable of the pirogue, and one of the soldiers of the chief put his arms round the mast. The second chief, who affected intoxication, then said that we should not go on; that they had not received presents enough from us. Captain Clark told him that he would not be prevented from going on; that we were not squaws, but warriors; that we were sent by our great father, who could in a moment exterminate them. The chief replied that he too had warriors, and was proceeding to offer personal violence to Captain Clark, who immediately drew his sword, and made a signal to the boat to prepare for action. The Indians, who surrounded him, drew their arrows from their quivers, and were bending their bows, when the swivel in the boat was instantly pointed towards them, and twelve of our most determined men jumped into the pirogue and joined Captain Clark. This movement made an impression on them, for the grand chief ordered the young men away from the pirogue, and they withdrew and held a short council with the warriors. Being unwilling to irritate them, Captain Clark then went forward, and offered his hand to the first and second chiefs, who refused to take it. He then turned from them and got into the pirogue; but he had not got more than ten paces, when both the chiefs and two of the warriors waded in after him, and he brought them on board. We then proceeded on for a mile, and anchored off a willow island, which, from the circumstances which had just occurred, we called Bad-humored Island."

The policy of firmness and gentleness, which Lewis and Clark always pursued when treating with the Indians, had its good results at this time. What might have been a bloody encounter was averted, and next day the Indians contritely came into camp and asked that their squaws and children might see the white men and their boats, which would be to them a novel sight. This was agreed to, and after the expedition had sailed up the river and had been duly admired by a great crowd of men, women, and children, the Tetons invited the white men to a dance. The journal adds:—

"Captains Lewis and Clark, who went on shore one after the other, were met on landing by ten well-dressed young men, who took them up in a robe highly decorated and carried them to a large council-house, where they were placed on a dressed buffalo-skin by the side of the grand chief. The hall or council-room was in the shape of three-quarters of a circle, covered at the top and sides with skins well dressed and sewed together. Under this shelter sat about seventy men, forming a circle round the chief, before whom were placed a Spanish flag and the one we had given them yesterday. This left a vacant circle of about six feet diameter, in which the pipe of peace was raised on two forked sticks, about six or eight inches from the ground, and under it the down of the swan was scattered. A large fire, in which they were cooking provisions, stood near, and in the centre about four hundred pounds of buffalo meat as a present for us. As soon as we were seated, an old man got up, and after approving what we had done, begged us take pity on their unfortunate situation. To this we replied with assurances of protection. After he had ceased, the great chief rose and delivered a harangue to the same effect; then with great solemnity he took some of the most delicate parts of the dog which was cooked for the festival, and held it to the flag by way of sacrifice; this done, he held up the pipe of peace, and first pointed it toward the heavens, then to the four quarters of the globe, then to the earth, made a short speech, lighted the pipe, and presented it to us. We smoked, and he again harangued his people, after which the repast was served up to us. It consisted of the dog which they had just been cooking, this being a great dish among the Sioux, and used on all festivals; to this were added pemitigon, a dish made of buffalo meat, dried or jerked, and then pounded and mixed raw with grease and a kind of ground potato, dressed like the preparation of Indian corn called hominy, to which it is little inferior. Of all these luxuries, which were placed before us in platters with horn spoons, we took the pemitigon and the potato, which we found good, but we could as yet partake but sparingly of the dog."

The "pemitigon" mentioned here is better known as pemmican, a sort of dried meat, which may be eaten as prepared, or pounded fine and cooked with other articles of food. This festival concluded with a grand dance, which at midnight wound up the affair.

As the description of these Tetons, given by Lewis and Clark, will give the reader a good idea of the manners, customs, and personal appearance of most of the Sioux nation, we will copy the journal in full. It is as follows:

"The tribe which we this day saw are a part of the great Sioux nation, and are known by the name of the Teton Okandandas: they are about two hundred men in number, and their chief residence is on both sides of the Missouri, between the Chayenne and Teton Rivers. In their persons they are rather ugly and ill-made, their legs and arms being too small, their cheek-bones high, and their eyes projecting. The females, with the same character of form, are more handsome; and both sexes appear cheerful and sprightly; but in our intercourse with them we discovered that they were cunning and vicious.

"The men shave the hair off their heads, except a small tuft on the top, which they suffer to grow, and wear in plaits over the shoulders; to this they seem much attached, as the loss of it is the usual sacrifice at the death of near relations. In full dress, the men of consideration wear a hawk's feather, or calumet feather worked with porcupine quills, and fastened to the top of the head, from which it falls back. The face and body are generally painted with a mixture of grease and coal. Over the shoulders is a loose robe or mantle of buffalo skin dressed white, adorned with porcupine quills, loosely fixed, so as to make a jingling noise when in motion, and painted with various uncouth figures, unintelligible to us, but to them emblematic of military exploits or any other incident: the hair of the robe is worn next the skin in fair weather, but when it rains the hair is put outside, and the robe is either thrown over the arm or wrapped round the body, all of which it may cover. Under this, in the winter season, they wear a kind of shirt resembling ours, made either of skin or cloth, and covering the arms and body. Round the middle is fixed a girdle of cloth, or procured dressed elk-skin, about an inch in width, and closely tied to the body; to this is attached a piece of cloth, or blanket, or skin, about a foot wide, which passes between the legs, and is tucked under the girdle both before and behind. From the hip to the ankle is covered by leggins of dressed antelope skins, with seams at the sides two inches in width, and ornamented by little tufts of hair, the produce of the scalps they have made in war, which are scattered down the leg. The winter moccasins are of dressed buffalo skin, the hair being worn inward, and soled with thick elk-skin parchment; those for summer are of deer or elk-skin, dressed without the hair, and with soles of elk-skin. On great occasions, or whenever they are in full dress, the young men drag after them the entire skin of a polecat fixed to the heel of the moccasin. Another skin of the same animal, either tucked into the girdle or carried in the hand, serves as a pouch for their tobacco, or what the French traders call bois roule.(1) This is the inner bark of a species of red willow, which, being dried in the sun or over the fire, is, rubbed between the hands and broken into small pieces, and used alone or mixed with tobacco. The pipe is generally of red earth, the stem made of ash, about three or four feet long, and highly decorated with feathers, hair, and porcupine-quills. . . .

(1) This is bois roule, or "rolled wood," a poor kind of tobacco rolled with various kinds of leaves, such as the sumach and dogwood. The Indian name is kinnikinick.

"While on shore to-day we witnessed a quarrel between two squaws, which appeared to be growing every moment more boisterous, when a man came forward, at whose approach every one seemed terrified and ran. He took the squaws and without any ceremony whipped them severely. On inquiring into the nature of such summary justice, we learned that this man was an officer well known to this and many other tribes. His duty is to keep the peace, and the whole interior police of the village is confided to two or three of these officers, who are named by the chief and remain in power some days, at least till the chief appoints a successor. They seem to be a sort of constable or sentinel, since they are always on the watch to keep tranquillity during the day and guard the camp in the night. The short duration of the office is compensated by its authority. His power is supreme, and in the suppression of any riot or disturbance no resistance to him is suffered; his person is sacred, and if in the execution of his duty he strikes even a chief of the second class, he cannot be punished for this salutary insolence. In general he accompanies the person of the chief, and when ordered to any duty, however dangerous, it is a point of honor rather to die than to refuse obedience. Thus, when they attempted to stop us yesterday, the chief ordered one of these men to take possession of the boat; he immediately put his arms around the mast, and, as we understood, no force except the command of the chief would have induced him to release his hold. Like the other men his body is blackened, but his distinguishing mark is a collection of two or three raven-skins fixed to the girdle behind the back in such a way that the tails stick out horizontally from the body. On his head, too, is a raven-skin split into two parts, and tied so as to let the beak project from the forehead."

When the party of explorers subsequently made ready to leave, signs of reluctance to have them go were apparent among the Indians. Finally, several of the chief warriors sat on the rope that held the boat to the shore. Irritated by this, Captain Lewis got ready to fire upon the warriors, but, anxious to avoid bloodshed, he gave them more tobacco, which they wanted, and then said to the chief, "You have told us that you were a great man, and have influence; now show your influence by taking the rope from those men, and we will then go on without further trouble." This appeal to the chieftain's pride had the desired effect. The warriors were compelled to give up the rope, which was delivered on board, and the party set sail with a fresh breeze from the southeast.

The explorers were soon out of the country of the Teton Sioux and into that of the Ricaras, or, as these Indians are more commonly called, the Rickarees.

On the first day of October they passed the mouth of a river incorrectly known as Dog River, as if corrupted from the French word chien. But the true name is Cheyenne, from the Indians who bear that title. The stream rises in the region called the Black Mountains by Lewis and Clark, on account of the great quantity of dark cedar and pine trees that covered the hills. This locality is now known as the Black Hills, in the midst of which is the famous mining district of Deadwood. In these mountains, according to Lewis and Clark, were to be found "great quantities of goats, white bear, prairie cocks, and a species of animal which resembled a small elk, with large circular horns." By the "white bear" the reader must understand that the grizzly bear is meant. Although this animal, which was first discovered and described by Lewis and Clark, is commonly referred to in the earlier pages of the journal as "white," the error naturally came from a desire to distinguish it from the black and the cinnamon-colored bears. Afterwards, the journal refers to this formidable creature as the grizzly, and again as the grisly. Certainly, the bear was a grizzled gray; but the name "grisly," that is to say, horrible, or frightful, fitted him very well. The Latin name, *ursus horribilis* is not unlike one of those of Lewis and Clark's selection. The animals with circular curled horns, which the explorers thought resembled a small elk, are now known as the Rocky Mountain sheep, or bighorn. They very little resemble sheep, however, except in color, head, horns, and feet. They are now so scarce as to be almost extinct. They were among the discoveries of Lewis and Clark. The prairie cock is known to western sportsmen as "prairie chicken;" it is a species of grouse.

It was now early in October, and the weather became very cool. So great is the elevation of those regions that, although the days might be oppressively warm, the nights were cold and white frosts were frequent. Crossing the Rocky Mountains at the South Pass, far south of Lewis and Clark's route, emigrants who suffered from intense heat during the middle of day found water in their pails frozen solid in the morning.

The Rickarees were very curious and inquisitive regarding the white men. But the journal adds: "The object which appeared to astonish the Indians most was Captain Clark's servant York, a remarkably stout, strong negro. They had never seen a being of that color, and therefore flocked round him to examine the extraordinary monster. By way of amusement, he told them that he had once been a wild animal, and been caught and tamed by his master; and to convince them, showed them feats of strength which, added to his looks, made him more terrible than we wished him to be."

"On October 10th," says the journal, "the weather was fine, and as we were desirous of assembling the whole nation at once, we despatched Mr. Gravelines (a trader)—who, with Mr. Tabeau, another French trader, had breakfasted with us—to invite the chiefs of the two upper villages to a conference. They all assembled at one o'clock, and after the usual ceremonies we addressed them in the same way in which we had already spoken to the Ottoes and Sioux. We then made or acknowledged three chiefs, one for each of the three villages; giving to each a flag, a medal, a red coat, a cocked hat and feather, also some goods, paint and tobacco, which they divided among themselves. After this the air-gun was exhibited, very much to their astonishment, nor were they less surprised at the color and manner of York. On our side we were equally gratified at discovering that these Ricaras made use of no spirituous liquors of any kind, the example of the traders who bring it to them, so far from tempting, having in fact disgusted them. Supposing that it was as agreeable to them as to the other Indians, we had at first offered them whiskey; but they refused it with this sensible remark, that they were surprised that their father should present to them a liquor which would make them fools. On another occasion they observed to Mr. Tabeau that no man could be their friend who tried to lead them into such follies."

Presents were exchanged by the Indians and the white men; among the gifts from the former was a quantity of a large, rich bean, which grows wild and is collected by mice. The Indians hunt for the mice's deposits and cook and eat them. The Rickarees had a grand powwow with the white chiefs and, after accepting presents, agreed to preserve peace with all men, red or white. On the thirteenth of the month the explorers discovered a stream which they named Stone-Idol Creek, on account of two stones, resembling human figures, which adorn its banks. The creek is now known as Spring River, and is in Campbell County, South Dakota. Concerning the stone images the Indians gave this tradition:—

"A young man was deeply enamoured with a girl whose parents refused their consent to the marriage. The youth went out into the fields to mourn his misfortunes; a sympathy of feeling led the lady to the same spot, and the faithful dog would not cease to follow his master. After wandering together and having nothing but grapes to subsist on, they were at last converted into stone, which, beginning at the feet, gradually invaded the nobler parts, leaving nothing unchanged but a bunch of grapes which the female holds in her hand to this day. Whenever the Ricaras pass these sacred stones, they stop to make some offering of dress to propitiate these deities. Such is the account given by the Ricara chief, which we had no mode of examining, except that we found one part of the story very agreeably confirmed; for on the river near where the event is said to have occurred we found a greater abundance of fine grapes than we had yet seen."

While at their last camp in the country now known as South Dakota, October 14, 1804, one of the soldiers, tried by a court-martial for mutinous conduct, was sentenced to receive seventy-five lashes on the bare back. The sentence was carried out then and there. The Rickaree chief, who accompanied the party for a time, was so affected by the sight that he cried aloud during the whole proceeding. When the reasons for the punishment were explained to him, he acknowledged the justice of the sentence, but said he would have punished the offender with death. His people, he added, never whip even their children at any age whatever.

On the eighteenth of October, the party reached Cannonball River, which rises in the Black Hills and empties in the Missouri in Morton County, North Dakota. Its name is derived from the perfectly round, smooth, black stones that line its bed and shores. Here they saw great numbers of antelope and herds of buffalo, and of elk. They killed six fallow deer; and next day they counted fifty-two herds of buffalo and three herds of elk at one view; they also observed deer, wolves, and pelicans in large numbers.

The ledges in the bluffs along the river often held nests of the calumet bird, or golden eagle. These nests, which are apparently resorted to, year after year, by the same pair of birds, are usually out of reach, except by means of ropes by which the hunters are let down from the cliffs overhead. The tail-feathers of the bird are twelve in number, about a foot long, and are pure white except at the tip, which is jet-black. So highly prized are these by the Indians that they have been known to exchange a good horse for two feathers.

The party saw here a great many elk, deer, antelope, and buffalo, and these last were dogged along their way by wolves who follow them to feed upon those that die by accident, or are too weak to keep up with the herd. Sometimes the wolves would pounce upon a calf, too young and feeble to trot with the other buffalo; and although the mother made an effort to save her calf, the creature was left to the hungry wolves, the herd moving along without delay.

On the twenty-first of October, the explorers reached a creek to which the Indians gave the name of Chisshetaw, now known as Heart River, which, rising in Stark County, North Dakota, and running circuitously through Morton County, empties into the Missouri opposite the city of Bismarck. At this point the Northern Pacific Railway now crosses the Missouri; and here, where is built the capital of North Dakota, began, in those days, a series of Mandan villages, with the people of which the explorers were to become tolerably well acquainted; for it had been decided that the increasing cold of the weather would compel them to winter in this region. But they were as yet uncertain as to the exact locality at which they would build their camp of winter. Here they met one of the grand chiefs of the Mandans, who was on a hunting excursion with his braves. This chief greeted with much ceremony the Rickaree chief who accompanied the exploring party. The Mandans and Rickarees were ancient enemies, but, following the peaceful councils of the white men, the chiefs professed amity and smoked together the pipe of peace. A son of the Mandan chief was observed to have lost both of his little fingers, and when the strangers asked how this happened, they were told that the fingers had been cut off (according to the Mandan custom) to show the grief of the young man at the loss of some of his relations.

Chapter VI — Winter among the Mandans

Before finally selecting the spot on which to build their winter quarters, Lewis and Clark held councils with the chiefs of the tribes who were to be their neighbors during the cold season. These were Mandans, Annahaways, and Minnetarees, tribes living peacefully in the same region of country. The principal Mandan chief was Black Cat; White Buffalo Robe Unfolded represented the Annahaways, and the Minnetaree chief was Black Moccasin. This last-named chief could not come to the council, but was represented by Caltahcota, or Cherry on a Bush. The palaver being over, presents were distributed. The account says:—

"One chief of each town was acknowledged by a gift of a flag, a medal with the likeness of the President of the United States, a uniform coat, hat and feather. To the second chiefs we gave a medal representing some domestic animals and a loom for weaving; to the third chiefs, medals with the impressions of a farmer sowing grain. A variety of other presents were distributed, but none seemed to give them more satisfaction than an iron corn-mill which we gave to the Mandans. . . .

"In the evening the prairie took fire, either by accident or design, and burned with great fury, the whole plain being enveloped in flames. So rapid was its progress that a man and a woman were burned to death before they could reach a place of safety; another man, with his wife and child, were much burned, and several other persons narrowly escaped destruction. Among the rest, a boy of the half white breed escaped unhurt in the midst of the flames; his safety was ascribed to the great medicine spirit, who had preserved him on account of his being white. But a much more natural cause was the presence of mind of his mother, who, seeing no hopes of carrying off her son, threw him on the ground, and, covering him with the fresh hide of a buffalo, escaped herself from the flames. As soon as the fire had passed, she returned and found him untouched, the skin having prevented the flame from reaching the grass on which he lay."

Next day, says the journal,—

"We were visited by two persons from the lower village: one, the Big White, the chief of the village; the other, the Chayenne, called the Big Man: they had been hunting, and did not return yesterday early enough to attend the council. At their request we repeated part of our speech of yesterday, and put the medal round the neck of the chief. Captain Clark took a pirogue and went up the river in search of a good wintering-place, and returned after going seven miles to the lower point of an island on the north side, about one mile in length. He found the banks on the north side high, with coal occasionally, and the country fine on all sides; but the want of wood, and the scarcity of game up the river, induced us to decide on fixing ourselves lower down during the winter. In the evening our men danced among themselves, to the great amusement of the Indians."

It may be said here that the incident of a life saved from fire by a raw-hide, originally related by Lewis and Clark, is the foundation of a great many similar stories of adventures among the Indians. Usually, however, it is a wise and well-seasoned white trapper who saves his life by this device.

Having found a good site for their winter camp, the explorers now built a number of huts, which they called Fort Mandan. The place was on the north bank of the Missouri River, in what is now McLean County, North Dakota, about sixteen hundred miles up the river from St. Louis, and seven or eight miles below the mouth of Big Knife River. On the opposite bank, years later, the United States built a military post known as Fort Clark, which may be found on some of the present-day maps. The huts were built of logs, and were arranged in two rows, four rooms in each hut, the whole number being placed in the form of an angle, with a stockade, or picket, across the two outer ends of the angle, in which was a gate, kept locked at night. The roofs of the huts slanted upward from the inner side of the rows, making the outer side of each hut eighteen feet high; and the lofts of these were made warm and comfortable with dry grass mixed with clay, Here they were continually visited during the winter by Indians from all the region around. Here, too, they secured the services of an interpreter, one Chaboneau, who continued with them to the end. This man's wife, Sacajawea, whose Indian name was translated "Bird Woman," had been captured from the Snake Indians and sold to Chaboneau, who married her. She was "a good creature, of a mild and gentle disposition, greatly attached to the whites." In the expedition she proved herself more valuable to the explorers than her husband, and Lewis and Clark always speak of her in terms of respect and admiration.

It should not be understood that all the interpreters employed by white men on such expeditions wholly knew the spoken language of the tribes among whom they travelled. To some extent they relied upon the universal language of signs to make themselves understood, and this method of talking is known to all sorts and kinds of Indians. Thus, two fingers of the right hand placed astraddle the wrist of the left hand signifies a man on horseback; and the number of men on horseback is quickly added by holding up the requisite number of fingers. Sleep is described by gently inclining the head on the hand, and the number of "sleeps," or nights, is indicated by the fingers. Killed, or dead, is described by closed eyes and a sudden fall of the head on the talker's chest; and so on, an easily understood gesture, with a few Indian words, being sufficient to tell a long story very clearly.

Lewis and Clark discovered here a species of ermine before unknown to science. They called it "a weasel, perfectly white except at the extremity of the tail, which was black." This animal, highly prized on account of its pretty fur, was not scientifically described until as late as 1829. It is a species of stoat.

The wars of some of the Indian tribes gave Lewis and Clark much trouble and uneasiness. The Sioux were at war with the Minnetarees (Gros Ventres, or Big Bellies); and the Assiniboins, who lived further to the north, continually harassed the Sioux and the Mandans, treating these as the latter did the Rickarees. The white chiefs had their hands full all winter while trying to preserve peace among these quarrelsome and thieving tribes, their favorite game being to steal each other's horses. The Indian method of caring for their horses in the cold winter was to let them shift for themselves during the day, and to take them into their own lodges at night where they were fed with the juicy, brittle twigs of the cottonwood tree. With this spare fodder the animals thrive and keep their coats fine and glossy.

Late in November, a collision between the Sioux and the Mandans became almost certain, in consequence of the Sioux having attacked a small hunting party of the Mandans, killing one, wounding two, and capturing nine horses. Captain Clark mustered and armed twenty-four of his men, crossed over into the Mandan village and offered to lead the Indians against their enemies.

The offer was declined on account of the deep snows which prevented a march; but the incident made friends for white men, and the tidings of it had a wholesome effect on the other tribes.

"The whole religion of the Mandans," like that of many other savage tribes, says the journal, "consists in the belief of one Great Spirit presiding over their destinies. This Being must be in the nature of a good genius, since it is associated with the healing art, and 'great spirit' is synonymous with 'great medicine,' a name applied to everything which they do not comprehend. Each individual selects for himself the particular object of his devotion, which is termed his medicine, and is either some invisible being, or more commonly some animal, which thenceforward becomes his protector or his intercessor with the Great Spirit, to propitiate whom every attention is lavished and every personal consideration is sacrificed. 'I was lately owner of seventeen horses,' said a Mandan to us one day, 'but I have offered them all up to my medicine and am now poor.' He had in reality taken all his wealth, his horses, into the plain, and, turning them loose, committed them to the care of his medicine and abandoned them forever. The horses, less religious, took care of themselves, and the pious votary travelled home on foot."

To this day, all the Northwest Indians speak of anything that is highly useful or influential as "great medicine."

One cold December day, a Mandan chief invited the explorers to join them in a grand buffalo hunt. The journal adds:—

"Captain Clark with fifteen men went out and found the Indians engaged in killing buffalo. The hunters, mounted on horseback and armed with bows and arrows, encircle the herd and gradually drive them into a plain or an open place fit for the movements of horse; they then ride in among them, and singling out a buffalo, a female being preferred, go as close as possible and wound her with arrows till they think they have given the mortal stroke; when they pursue another, till the quiver is exhausted. If, which rarely happens, the wounded buffalo attacks the hunter, he evades his blow by the agility of his horse, which is trained for the combat with great dexterity. When they have killed the requisite number they collect their game, and the squaws and attendants come up from the rear and skin and dress the animals. Captain Clark killed ten buffalo, of which five only were brought to the fort; the rest, which could not be conveyed home, being seized by the Indians, among whom the custom is that whenever a buffalo is found dead without an arrow or any particular mark, he is the property of the finder; so that often a hunter secures scarcely any of the game he kills, if the arrow happens to fall off."

The weather now became excessively cold, the mercury often going thirty-two degrees below zero. Notwithstanding this, however, the Indians kept up their outdoor sports, one favorite game of which resembled billiards. But instead of a table, the players had an open flooring, about fifty yards long, and the balls were rings of stone, shot along the flooring by means of sticks like billiard-cues. The white men had their sports, and they forbade the Indians to visit them on Christmas Day, as this was one of their "great medicine days." The American flag was hoisted on the fort and saluted with a volley of musketry. The men danced among themselves; their best provisions were brought out and "the day passed," says the journal, "in great festivity."

The party also celebrated New Year's Day by similar festivities. Sixteen of the men were given leave to go up to the first Mandan village with their musical instruments, where they delighted the whole tribe with their dances, one of the French voyageurs being especially applauded when he danced on his hands with his head downwards. The dancers and musicians were presented with several buffalo-robes and a large quantity of Indian corn. The cold grew more intense, and on the tenth of the month the mercury stood at forty degrees below zero. Some of the men were badly frost-bitten, and a young Indian, about thirteen years old, who had been lost in the snows, came into the fort. The journal says:—

"His father, who came last night to inquire after him very anxiously, had sent him in the afternoon to the fort; he was overtaken by the night, and was obliged to sleep on the snow with no covering except a pair of antelope-skin moccasins and leggins, and a buffalo-robe. His feet being frozen, we put them into cold water, and gave him every attention in our power. About the same time an Indian who had also been missing returned to the fort. Although his dress was very thin, and he had slept on the snow without a fire, he had not suffered the slightest inconvenience. We have indeed observed that these Indians support the rigors of the season in a way which we had hitherto thought impossible. A more pleasing reflection occurred at seeing the warm interest which the situation of these two persons had excited in the village. The boy had been a prisoner, and adopted from charity; yet the distress of the father proved that he felt for him the tenderest affection. The man was a person of no distinction, yet the whole village was full of anxiety for his safety; and, when they came to us, borrowed a sleigh to bring them home with ease if they had survived, or to carry their bodies if they had perished. . . .

"January 13. Nearly one half of the Mandan nation passed down the river to hunt for several days. In these excursions, men, women, and children, with their dogs, all leave the village together, and, after discovering a spot convenient for the game, fix their tents; all the family bear their part in the labor, and the game is equally divided among the families of the tribe. When a single hunter returns from the chase with more than is necessary for his own immediate consumption, the neighbors are entitled by custom to a share of it: they do not, however, ask for it, but send a squaw, who, without saying anything, sits down by the door of the lodge till the master understands the hint, and gives her gratuitously a part for her family."

By the end of January, 1805, the weather had so far moderated that the explorers thought they might cut their boats from the ice in the river and prepare to resume their voyage; but the ice being three feet thick, they made no progress and were obliged to give up the attempt. Their stock of meat was low, although they had had good success when the cold was not too severe to prevent them from hunting deer, elk, and buffalo. The Mandans, who were careless in providing food for future supplies, also suffered for want of meat, sometimes going for days without flesh food. Captain Clark and eighteen men went down the river in search of game. The hunters, after being out nine days, returned and reported that they had killed forty deer, three buffalo, and sixteen elk. But much of the game was lean and poor, and the wolves, who devour everything left out at night, had stolen a quantity of the flesh. Four men, with sleds, were sent out to bring into camp the meat, which had been secured against wolves by being stored in pens. These men were attacked by Sioux, about one hundred in number, who robbed them of their game and two of their three horses. Captain Lewis, with twenty-four men, accompanied by some of the Mandans, set out in pursuit of the marauders. They were unsuccessful, however, but, having found a part of their game untouched, they brought it back, and this, with other game killed after their chase of the Sioux, gave them three thousand pounds of meat; they had killed thirty-six deer, fourteen elk, and one wolf.

By the latter part of February, the party were able to get their boats from the ice. These were dragged ashore, and the work of making them ready for their next voyage was begun. As the ice in the river began to break up, the Mandans had great sport chasing across the floating cakes of ice the buffalo who were tempted over by the appearance of green, growing grass on the other side. The Indians were very expert in their pursuit of the animals, which finally slipped from their insecure footing on the drifting ice, and were killed.

At this point, April 7, 1805, the escorting party, the voyageurs, and one interpreter, returned down the river in their barge. This party consisted of thirteen persons, all told, and to them were intrusted several packages of specimens for President Jefferson, with letters and official reports. The presents for Mr. Jefferson, according to the journal, "consisted of a stuffed male and female antelope, with their skeletons, a weasel, three squirrels from the Rocky Mountains, the skeleton of a prairie wolf, those of a white and gray hare, a male and female blaireau, (badger) or burrowing dog of the prairie, with a skeleton of the female, two burrowing squirrels, a white weasel, and the skin of the louservia (loup-servier, or lynx), the horns of a mountain ram, or big-horn, a pair of large elk horns, the horns and tail of a black-tailed deer, and a variety of skins, such as those of the red fox, white hare, marten, yellow bear, obtained from the Sioux; also a number of articles of Indian dress, among which was a buffalo robe representing a battle fought about eight years since between the Sioux and Ricaras against the Mandans and Minnetarees, in which the combatants are represented on horseback. . . . Such sketches, rude and imperfect as they are, delineate the predominant character of the savage nations. If they are peaceable and inoffensive, the drawings usually consist of local scenery and their favorite diversions. If the band are rude and ferocious, we observe tomahawks, scalping-knives, bows and arrows, and all the engines of destruction.—A Mandan bow, and quiver of arrows; also some Ricara tobacco-seed, and an ear of Mandan corn: to these were added a box of plants, another of insects, and three cases containing a burrowing squirrel, a prairie hen, and four magpies, all alive." . . .

The articles reached Mr. Jefferson safely and were long on view at his Virginia residence, Monticello. They were subsequently dispersed, and some found their way to Peale's Museum, Philadelphia. Dr. Cones, the zealous editor of the latest and fullest edition of Lewis and Clark's narrative, says that some of the specimens of natural history were probably extant in 1893.

Chapter VII — From Fort Mandan to the Yellowstone

Up to this time, the expedition had passed through regions from which vague reports had been brought by the few white men who, as hunters and trappers in pursuit of fur-bearing game, had dared to venture into these trackless wildernesses. Now they were to launch out into the mysterious unknown, from which absolutely no tidings had ever been brought by white men. The dim reports of Indians who had hunted through some parts of the region were unreliable, and, as they afterwards proved, were often as absurdly false as if they had been fairy tales.

Here, too, they parted from some of their comrades who were to return to "the United States," as the explorers fondly termed their native country, although the strange lands through which they were voyaging were now a part of the American Republic. The despatches sent to Washington by these men contained the first official report from Lewis and Clark since their departure from St. Louis, May 16, 1803; and they were the last word from the explorers until their return in September, 1806. During all that long interval, the adventurers were not heard of in the States. No wonder that croakers declared that the little party had been cut off to perish miserably in the pathless woods that cover the heart of the continent.

But they set out on the long journey with light hearts. In his journal, whose spelling and punctuation are not always models for the faithful imitation of school-boys, Captain Lewis set down this observation:—

"Our vessels consisted of six small canoes, and two large perogues. This little fleet altho' not quite so respectable as those of Columbus or Capt. Cook, were still viewed by us with as much pleasure as those deservedly famed adventurers ever beheld theirs; and I dare say with quite as much anxiety for their safety and preservation. We were now about to penetrate a country at least two thousand miles in width, on which the foot of civilized man had never trodden; the good or evil it had in store for us was for experiment yet to determine, and these little vessels contained every article by which we were to expect to subsist or defend ourselves. However as the state of mind in which we are, generally gives the colouring to events, when the imagination is suffered to wander into futurity, the picture which now presented itself to me was a most pleasing one. Entertaining as I do the most confident hope of succeeding in a voyage which had formed a darling project of mine for the last ten years, I could but esteem this moment of our departure as among the most happy of my life."

The barge sent down the river to St. Louis was in command of Corporal Wharfington; and with him were six private soldiers, two French voyageurs, Joseph Gravelines (pilot and interpreter), and Brave Raven, a Ricara (or Arikara) chief who was to be escorted to Washington to visit the President. The party was also intrusted with sundry gifts for the President, among them being natural history specimens, living and dead, and a number of Indian articles which would be objects of curiosity in Washington.

The long voyage of the main party began on the 8th of April, 1805, early passing the mouth of the Big Knife River, one of the five considerable streams that fall into the Missouri from the westward in this region; the other streams are the Owl, the Grand, the Cannonball, and the Heart. The large town of Stanton, Mercer County, North Dakota, is now situated at the mouth of the Big

Knife. The passage of the party up the river was slow, owing to unfavorable winds; and they observed along the banks many signs of early convulsions of nature. The earth of the bluffs was streaked with layers of coal, or carbonized wood, and large quantities of lava and pumice-stone were strewn around, showing traces of ancient volcanic action. The journal of April 9 says:—

"A great number of brants (snow-geese) pass up the river; some of them are perfectly white, except the large feathers of the first joint of the wing, which are black, though in every other characteristic they resemble common gray brant. We also saw but could not procure an animal (gopher) that burrows in the ground, and is similar in every respect to the burrowing-squirrel, except that it is only one-third of its size. This may be the animal whose works we have often seen in the plains and prairies; they resemble the labors of the salamander in the sand-hills of South Carolina and Georgia, and like him the animals rarely come above ground; they consist of a little hillock of ten or twelve pounds of loose ground, which would seem to have been reversed from a pot, though no aperture is seen through which it could have been thrown. On removing gently the earth, you discover that the soil has been broken in a circle of about an inch and a half diameter, where the ground is looser, though still no opening is perceptible. When we stopped for dinner the squaw (Sacajawea) went out, and after penetrating with a sharp stick the holes of the mice (gophers), near some drift-wood, brought to us a quantity of wild artichokes, which the mice collect and hoard in large numbers. The root is white, of an ovate form, from one to three inches long, and generally of the size of a man's finger, and two, four, and sometimes six roots are attached to a single stalk. Its flavor as well as the stalk which issues from it resemble those of the Jerusalem artichoke, except that the latter is much larger."

The weather rapidly grew so warm, although this was early in April, that the men worked half-naked during the day; and they were very much annoyed by clouds of mosquitoes. They found that the hillsides and even the banks of the rivers and sand-bars were covered with "a white substance, which appears in considerable quantities on the surface of the earth, and tastes like a mixture of common salt with Glauber's salts." "Many of the streams," the journal adds, "are so strongly impregnated with this substance that the water has an unpleasant taste and a purgative effect." This is nothing more than the so-called alkali which has since become known all over the farthest West. It abounds in the regions west of Salt Lake Valley, whitening vast areas like snow and poisoning the waters so that the traveller often sees the margins of the brown pools lined with skeletons and bodies of small animals whose thirst had led them to drink the deadly fluid. Men and animals stiffer from smaller doses of this stuff, which is largely a sulphate of soda, and even in small quantities is harmful to the system.

Here, on the twelfth of April, they were able to determine the exact course of the Little Missouri, a stream about which almost nothing was then known. Near here, too, they found the source of the Mouse River, only a few miles from the Missouri. The river, bending to the north and then making many eccentric curves, finally empties into Lake Winnipeg, and so passes into the great chain of northern lakes in British America. At this point the explorers saw great flocks of the wild Canada goose. The journal says:—

"These geese, we observe, do not build their nests on the ground or in the sand-bars, but in the tops of the lofty cottonwood trees. We saw some elk and buffalo to-day, but at too great a distance to obtain any of them, though a number of the carcasses of the latter animal are strewed along the shore, having fallen through the ice and been swept along when the river broke up. More bald eagles are seen on this part of the Missouri than we have previously met with; the small sparrow-hawk, common in most parts of the United States, is also found here. Great quantities of geese are feeding on the prairies, and one flock of white brant, or geese with black-tipped wings, and some gray brant with them, pass up the river; from their flight they seem to proceed much further to the northwest. We killed two antelopes, which were very lean, and caught last night two beavers."

Lewis and Clark were laughed at by some very knowing people who scouted the idea that wild geese build their nests in trees. But later travellers have confirmed their story; the wise geese avoid foxes and other of their four-footed enemies by fixing their homes in the tall cottonwoods. In other words, they roost high.

The Assiniboins from the north had lately been on their spring hunting expeditions through this region,—just above the Little Missouri,—and game was scarce and shy. The journal, under the date of April 14, says:—

"One of the hunters shot at an otter last evening; a buffalo was killed, and an elk, both so poor as to be almost unfit for use; two white (grizzly) bears were also seen, and a muskrat swimming across the river. The river continues wide and of about the same rapidity as the ordinary current of the Ohio. The low grounds are wide, the moister parts containing timber; the upland is extremely broken, without wood, and in some places seems as if it had slipped down in masses of several acres in surface. The mineral appearance of salts, coal, and sulphur, with the burnt hill and pumice-stone, continue, and a bituminous water about the color of strong lye, with the taste of Glauber's salts and a slight tincture of alum. Many geese were feeding in the prairies, and a number of magpies, which build their nests much like those of the blackbird, in trees, and composed of small sticks, leaves, and grass, open at the top; the egg is of a bluish-brown color, freckled with reddish-brown spots. We also killed a large hooting-owl resembling that of the United States except that it was more booted and clad with feathers. On the hills are many aromatic herbs, resembling in taste, smell, and appearance the sage, hyssop, wormwood, southernwood, juniper, and dwarf cedar; a plant also about two or three feet high, similar to the camphor in smell and taste; and another plant of the same size, with a long, narrow, smooth, soft leaf, of an agreeable smell and flavor, which is a favorite food of the antelope, whose necks are often perfumed by rubbing against it."

What the journalist intended to say here was that at least one of the aromatic herbs resembled sage, hyssop, wormwood, and southernwood, and that there were junipers and dwarf cedars. The pungent-smelling herb was the wild sage, now celebrated in stories of adventure as the sage-brush. It grows abundantly in the alkali country, and is browsed upon by a species of grouse known as the sage-hen. Junipers and dwarf cedars also grow on the hills of the alkali and sage-brush country. The sage belongs to the Artemisia family of plants.

Four days later, the journal had this interesting entry:

"The country to-day presented the usual variety of highlands interspersed with rich plains. In one of these we observed a species of pea bearing a yellow flower, which is now in blossom, the leaf and stalk resembling the common pea. It seldom rises higher than six inches, and the root is perennial. On the rose-bushes we also saw a quantity of the hair of a buffalo, which had become perfectly white by exposure and resembled the wool of the sheep, except that it was much finer and more soft and silky. A buffalo which we killed yesterday had shed his long hair, and that which remained was about two inches long, thick, fine, and would have furnished five pounds of wool, of which we have no doubt an excellent cloth may be made. Our game to-day was a beaver, a deer, an elk, and some geese. . . .

"On the hills we observed considerable quantities of dwarf juniper, which seldom grows higher than three feet. We killed in the course of the day an elk, three geese, and a beaver. The beaver on this part of the Missouri are in greater quantities, larger and fatter, and their fur is more abundant and of a darker color, than any we have hitherto seen. Their favorite food seems to be the bark of the cottonwood and willow, as we have seen no other species of tree that has been touched by them, and these they gnaw to the ground through a diameter of twenty inches."

And on the twenty-first of April the journal says:

"Last night there was a hard white frost, and this morning the weather was cold, but clear and pleasant; in the course of the day, however, it became cloudy and the wind rose. The country is of the same description as within the few last days. We saw immense quantities of buffalo, elk, deer, antelopes, geese, and some swans and ducks, out of which we procured three deer and four buffalo calves, which last are equal in flavor to the most delicious veal; also two beaver and an otter."

As the party advanced to the westward, following the crooked course of the Missouri, they were very much afflicted with inflamed eyes, occasioned by the fine, alkaline dust that blew so lightly that it sometimes floated for miles, like clouds of smoke. The dust even penetrated the works of one of their watches, although it was protected by tight, double cases. In these later days, even the double windows of the railway trains do not keep out this penetrating dust, which makes one's skin dry and rough.

On the twenty-fifth of April, the explorers believed, by the signs which they observed, that they must be near the great unknown river of which they had dimly heard as rising in the rocky passes of the Great Divide and emptying into the Missouri. Captain Lewis accordingly left the party, with four men, and struck off across the country in search of the stream. Under the next day's date the journal reports the return of Captain Lewis and says:—

"On leaving us yesterday he pursued his route along the foot of the hills, which he descended to the distance of eight miles; from these the wide plains watered by the Missouri and the Yellowstone spread themselves before the eye, occasionally varied with the wood of the banks, enlivened by the irregular windings of the two rivers, and animated by vast herds of buffalo, deer, elk, and antelope. The confluence of the two rivers was concealed by the wood, but the Yellowstone itself was only two miles distant, to the south. He therefore descended the hills and camped on the bank of the river, having killed, as he crossed the plain, four buffaloes; the deer alone are shy and retire to the woods, but the elk, antelope, and buffalo suffered him to approach them without alarm, and often followed him quietly for some distance."

The famous water-course, first described by Lewis and Clark, was named by them the Yellow Stone River. Earlier than this, however, the French voyageurs had called the Upper Missouri the Riviere Jaune, or Yellow River; but it is certain that the stream, which rises in the Yellowstone National Park, was discovered and named by Lewis and Clark. One of the party, Private Joseph Fields, was the first white man who ever ascended the Yellowstone for any considerable distance. Sent up the river by Captains Lewis and Clark, he travelled about eight miles, and observed the currents and sand-bars. Leaving the mouth of the river, the party went on their course along the Missouri. The journal, under date of April 27, says:—

"From the point of junction a wood occupies the space between the two rivers, which at the distance of a mile come within two hundred and fifty yards of each other. There a beautiful low plain commences, widening as the rivers recede, and extends along each of them for several miles, rising about half a mile from the Missouri into a plain twelve feet higher than itself. The low plain is a few inches above high water mark, and where it joins the higher plain there is a channel of sixty or seventy yards in width, through which a part of the Missouri, when at its greatest height, passes into the Yellowstone. . . .

"The northwest wind rose so high at eleven o'clock that we were obliged to stop till about four in the afternoon, when we proceeded till dusk. On the south a beautiful plain separates the two rivers, till at about six miles there is a piece of low timbered ground, and a little above it bluffs, where the country rises gradually from the river: the situations on the north are more high and open. We encamped on that side, the wind, the sand which it raised, and the rapidity of the current having prevented our advancing more than eight miles; during the latter part of the day the river became wider, and crowded with sand-bars. The game was in such plenty that we killed only what was necessary for our subsistence. For several days past we have seen great numbers of buffalo lying dead along the shore, some of them partly devoured by the wolves. They have either sunk through the ice during the winter, or been drowned in attempting to cross; or else, after crossing to some high bluff, have found themselves too much exhausted either to ascend or swim back again, and perished for want of food: in this situation we found several small parties of them. There are geese, too, in abundance, and more bald eagles than we have hitherto observed; the nests of these last being always accompanied by those of two or three magpies, who are their inseparable attendants."

Chapter VIII — In the Haunts of Grizzlies and Buffalo

Game, which had been somewhat scarce after leaving the Yellowstone, became more plentiful as they passed on to the westward, still following the winding course of the Missouri. Much of the time, baffling winds and the crookedness of the stream made sailing impossible, and the boats were towed by men walking along the banks.

Even this was sometimes difficult, on account of the rocky ledges that beset the shores, and sharp stones that lay in the path of the towing parties. On the twenty-eighth of April, however, having a favorable wind, the party made twenty-eight miles with their sails, which was reckoned a good day's journey. On that day the journal records that game had again become very abundant, deer of various kinds, elk, buffalo, antelope, bear, beaver, and geese being numerous. The beaver, it was found, had wrought much damage by gnawing down trees; some of these, not less than three feet in diameter had been gnawed clean through by the beaver. On the following day the journal has this record:—

"We proceeded early, with a moderate wind. Captain Lewis, who was on shore with one hunter, met, about eight o'clock, two white (grizzly) bears. Of the strength and ferocity of this animal the Indians had given us dreadful accounts. They never attack him but in parties of six or eight persons, and even then are often defeated with a loss of one or more of their party. Having no weapons but bows and arrows, and the bad guns with which the traders supply them, they are obliged to approach very near to the bear; as no wound except through the head or heart is mortal, they frequently fall a sacrifice if they miss their aim. He rather attacks than avoids a man, and such is the terror which he has inspired, that the Indians who go in quest of him paint themselves and perform all the superstitious rites customary when they make war on a neighboring nation. Hitherto, those bears we had seen did not appear desirous of encountering us; but although to a skilful rifleman the danger is very much diminished, yet the white bear is still a terrible animal. On approaching these two, both Captain Lewis and the hunter fired, and each wounded a bear. One of them made his escape; the other turned upon Captain Lewis and pursued him seventy or eighty yards, but being badly wounded the bear could not run so fast as to prevent him from reloading his piece, which he again aimed at him, and a third shot from the hunter brought him to the ground. He was a male, not quite full grown, and weighed about three hundred pounds. The legs are somewhat longer than those of the black bear, and the talons and tusks much larger and longer. Its color is a yellowish-brown; the eyes are small, black, and piercing; the front of the fore legs near the feet is usually black, and the fur is finer, thicker, and deeper than that of the black bear. Add to which, it is a more furious animal, and very remarkable for the wounds which it will bear without dying."

Next day, the hunter killed the largest elk which they had ever seen. It stood five feet three inches high from hoof to shoulder. Antelopes were also numerous, but lean, and not very good for food. Of the antelope the journal says:—

"These fleet and quick-sighted animals are generally the victims of their curiosity. When they first see the hunters, they run with great velocity; if he lies down on the ground, and lifts up his arm, his hat, or his foot, they return with a light trot to look at the object, and sometimes go and return two or three times, till they approach within reach of the rifle. So, too, they sometimes leave their flock to go and look at the wolves, which crouch down, and, if the antelope is frightened at first, repeat the same manoevre, and sometimes relieve each other, till they decoy it from the party, when they seize it. But, generally, the wolves take them as they are crossing the rivers; for, although swift on foot, they are not good swimmers."

Later wayfarers across the plains were wont to beguile the antelope by fastening a bright-colored handkerchief to a ramrod stuck in the ground. The patient hunter was certain to be rewarded by the antelope coming within range of his rifle; for, unless scared off by some interference, the herd, after galloping around and around and much zigzagging, would certainly seek to gratify their curiosity by gradually circling nearer and nearer the strange object until a deadly shot or two sent havoc into their ranks.

May came on cold and windy, and on the second of the month, the journal records that snow fell to the depth of an inch, contrasting strangely with the advanced vegetation.

"Our game to-day," proceeds the journal, "were deer, elk, and buffalo: we also procured three beaver. They were here quite gentle, as they have not been hunted; but when the hunters are in pursuit, they never leave their huts during the day. This animal we esteem a great delicacy, particularly the tail, which, when boiled, resembles in flavor the fresh tongues and sounds of the codfish, and is generally so large as to afford a plentiful meal for two men. One of the hunters, in passing near an old Indian camp, found several yards of scarlet cloth suspended on the bough of a tree, as a sacrifice to the deity, by the Assiniboins; the custom of making these offerings being common among that people, as, indeed, among all the Indians on the Missouri. The air was sharp this evening; the water froze on the oars as we rowed."

The Assiniboin custom of sacrificing to their deity, or "great medicine," the article which they most value themselves, is not by any means peculiar to that tribe, nor to the Indian race.

An unusual number of porcupines were seen along here, and these creatures were so free from wildness that they fed on, undisturbed, while the explorers walked around and among them. The captains named a bold and beautiful stream, which here entered the Missouri from the north,—Porcupine River; but modern geography calls the water-course Poplar River; at the mouth of the river, in Montana, is now the Poplar River Indian Agency and military post. The waters of this stream, the explorers found, were clear and transparent,—an exception to all the streams, which, discharging into the Missouri, give it its name of the Big Muddy. The journal adds:—

"A quarter of a mile beyond this river a creek falls in on the south, to which, on account of its distance from the mouth of the Missouri, we gave the name of Two-thousand-mile creek. It is a bold stream with a bed thirty yards wide. At three and one-half miles above Porcupine River, we reached some high timber on the north, and camped just above an old channel of the river, which is now dry. We saw vast quantities of buffalo, elk, deer,—principally of the long-tailed kind,—antelope, beaver, geese, ducks, brant, and some swan. The porcupines too are numerous, and so careless and clumsy that we can approach very near without disturbing them, as they are feeding on the young willows. Toward evening we also found for the first time the nest of a goose among some driftwood, all that we had hitherto seen being on the top of a broken tree on the forks, invariably from fifteen to twenty or more feet in height."

"Next day," May 4, says the journal, "we passed some old Indian hunting-camps, one of which consisted of two large lodges, fortified with a circular fence twenty or thirty feet in diameter, made of timber laid horizontally, the beams overlying each other to the height of five feet, and covered with the trunks and limbs of trees that have drifted down the river. The lodges themselves are formed by three or more strong sticks about the size of a man's leg or arm and twelve feet long, which are attached at the top by a withe of small willows, and spread out so as to form at the base a circle of ten to fourteen feet in diameter. Against these are placed pieces of driftwood and fallen timber, usually in three ranges, one on the other; the interstices are covered with leaves, bark, and straw, so as to form a conical figure about ten feet high, with a small aperture in one side for the door. It is, however, at best a very imperfect shelter against the inclemencies of the seasons."

Wolves were very abundant along the route of the explorers, the most numerous species being the common kind, now known as the coyote (pronounced kyote), and named by science the canis latrans. These animals are cowardly and sly creatures, of an intermediate size between the fox and dog, very delicately formed, fleet and active.

"The ears are large, erect, and pointed; the head is long and pointed, like that of the fox; the tail long and bushy; the hair and fur are of a pale reddish-brown color, though much coarser than that of the fox; the eye is of a deep sea-green color, small and piercing; the talons are rather longer than those of the wolf of the Atlantic States, which animal, as far as we can perceive, is not to be found on this side of the Platte. These wolves usually associate in bands of ten or twelve, and are rarely, if ever, seen alone, not being able, singly, to attack a deer or antelope. They live and rear their young in burrows, which they fix near some pass or spot much frequented by game, and sally out in a body against any animal which they think they can overpower; but on the slightest alarm retreat to their burrows, making a noise exactly like that of a small dog.

"A second species is lower, shorter in the legs, and thicker than the Atlantic wolf; the color, which is not affected by the seasons, is of every variety of shade, from a gray or blackish-brown to a cream-colored white. They do not burrow, nor do they bark, but howl; they frequent the woods and plains, and skulk along the skirts of the buffalo herds, in order to attack the weary or wounded."

Under date of May 5, the journal has an interesting story of an encounter with a grizzly bear, which, by way of variety, is here called "brown," instead of "white." It is noticeable that the explorers dwelt with much minuteness upon the peculiar characteristics of the grizzly; this is natural enough when we consider that they were the first white men to form an intimate acquaintance with "Ursus horribilis." The account says:—

"Captain Clark and one of the hunters met, this evening, the largest brown bear we have seen. As they fired he did not attempt to attack, but fled with a most tremendous roar; and such was his extraordinary tenacity of life, that, although he had five balls passed through his lungs, and five other wounds, he swam more than half across the river to a sand-bar, and survived twenty minutes. He weighed between five and six hundred pounds at least, and measured eight feet seven inches and a half from the nose to the extremity of the hind feet, five feet ten inches and a half round the breast, three feet eleven inches round the neck, one foot eleven inches round the middle of the fore leg, and his claws five on each foot, were four inches and three-eighths in length. This animal differs from the common black bear in having his claws much longer and more blunt; his tail shorter; his hair of a reddish or bay brown, longer, finer, and more abundant; his liver, lungs, and heart much larger even in proportion to his size, the heart, particularly, being equal to that of a large ox; and his maw ten times larger. Besides fish and flesh, he feeds on roots and every kind of wild fruit."

On May 8 the party discovered the largest and most important of the northern tributaries of the Upper Missouri. The journal thus describes the stream:—

"Its width at the entrance is one hundred and fifty yards; on going three miles up, Captain Lewis found it to be of the same breadth and sometimes more; it is deep, gentle, and has a large quantity of water; its bed is principally of mud; the banks are abrupt, about twelve feet in height, and formed of a dark, rich loam and blue clay; the low grounds near it are wide and fertile, and possess a considerable proportion of cottonwood and willow. It seems to be navigable for boats and canoes; by this circumstance, joined to its course and quantity of water, which indicates that it passes through a large extent of country, we are led to presume that it may approach the Saskaskawan (Saskatchewan) and afford a communication with that river. The water has a peculiar whiteness, such as might be produced by a tablespoonful of milk in a dish of tea, and this circumstance induced us to call it Milk River."

Modern geography shows that the surmise of Captain Lewis was correct. Some of the tributaries of Milk River (the Indian name of which signifies "The River that Scolds at all Others") have their rise near St. Mary's River, which is one of the tributaries of the Saskatchewan, in British America.

The explorers were surprised to find the bed of a dry river, as deep and as wide as the Missouri itself, about fifteen miles above Milk River. Although it had every appearance of a water-course, it did not discharge a drop of water. Their journal says:—

"It passes through a wide valley without timber; the surrounding country consists of waving low hills, interspersed with some handsome level plains; the banks are abrupt, and consist of a black or yellow clay, or of a rich sandy loam; though they do not rise more than six or eight feet above the bed, they exhibit no appearance of being overflowed; the bed is entirely composed of a light brown sand, the particles of which, like those of the Missouri, are extremely fine. Like the dry rivers we passed before, this seemed to have discharged its waters recently, but the watermark indicated that its greatest depth had not been more than two feet. This stream, if it deserve the name, we called Bigdry (Big Dry) River."

And Big Dry it remains on the maps unto this day. In this region the party recorded this observation:—

"The game is now in great quantities, particularly the elk and buffalo, which last is so gentle that the men are obliged to drive them out of the way with sticks and stones. The ravages of the beaver are very apparent; in one place the timber was entirely prostrated for a space of three acres in front on the river and one in depth, and great part of it removed, though the trees were in large quantities, and some of them as thick as the body of a man."

Yet so great have been the ravages of man among these gentle creatures, that elk are now very rarely found in the region, and the buffalo have almost utterly disappeared from the face of the earth. Just after the opening of the Northern Pacific Railway, in 1883, a band of sixty buffaloes were heard of, far to the southward of Bismarck, and a party was organized to hunt them. The *bold* hunters afterwards boasted that they killed every one of this little band of survivors of their race.

The men were now (in the middle of May) greatly troubled with boils, abscesses, and inflamed eyes, caused by the poison of the alkali that covered much of the ground and corrupted the water. Here is an entry in the journal of May 11:—

"About five in the afternoon one of our men (Bratton), who had been afflicted with boils and suffered to walk on shore, came running to the boats with loud cries, and every symptom of terror and distress. For some time after we had taken him on board he was so much out of breath as to be unable to describe the cause of his anxiety; but he at length told us that about a mile and a half below he had shot a brown bear, which immediately turned and was in close pursuit of him; but the bear being badly wounded could not overtake him. Captain Lewis, with seven men, immediately went in search of him; having found his track they followed him by the blood for a mile, found him concealed in some thick brushwood, and shot him with two balls through the skull. Though somewhat smaller than that killed a few days ago, he was a monstrous animal, and a most terrible enemy. Our man had shot him through the centre of the lungs; yet he had pursued him furiously for half a mile, then returned more than twice that distance, and with his talons prepared himself a bed in the earth two feet deep and five feet long; he was perfectly alive when they found him, which was at least two hours after he had received the wound. The wonderful power of life which these animals possess renders them dreadful; their very track in the mud or sand, which we have sometimes found eleven inches long and seven and one-fourth wide, exclusive of the talons, is alarming; and we had rather encounter two Indians than meet a single brown bear. There is no chance of killing them by a single shot unless the ball goes through the brain, and this is very difficult on account of two large muscles which cover the side of the forehead and the sharp projection of the centre of the frontal bone, which is also thick.

"Our camp was on the south, at the distance of sixteen miles from that of last night. The fleece and skin of the bear were a heavy burden for two men, and the oil amounted to eight gallons."

The name of the badly-scared Bratton was bestowed upon a creek which discharges into the Missouri near the scene of this encounter. Game continued to be very abundant. On the fourteenth, according to the journal, the hunters were hunted, to their great discomfiture. The account says:—

"Toward evening the men in the hindmost canoes discovered a large brown (grizzly) bear lying in the open grounds, about three hundred paces from the river. Six of them, all good hunters, immediately went to attack him, and concealing themselves by a small eminence came unperceived within forty paces of him. Four of the hunters now fired, and each lodged a ball in his body, two of them directly through the lungs. The furious animal sprang up and ran open-mouthed upon them.

"As he came near, the two hunters who had reserved their fire gave him two wounds, one of which, breaking his shoulder, retarded his motion for a moment; but before they could reload he was so near that they were obliged to run to the river, and before they had reached it he had almost overtaken them. Two jumped into the canoe; the other four separated, and, concealing themselves in the willows, fired as fast as they could reload. They struck him several times, but, instead of weakening the monster, each shot seemed only to direct him towards the hunters, till at last he pursued two of them so closely that they threw aside their guns and pouches, and jumped down a perpendicular bank of twenty feet into the river: the bear sprang after them, and was within a few feet of the hindmost, when one of the hunters on shore shot him in the head, and finally killed him. They dragged him to the shore, and found that eight balls had passed through him in different directions. The bear was old, and the meat tough, so that they took the skin only, and rejoined us at camp, where we had been as much terrified by an accident of a different kind.

"This was the narrow escape of one of our canoes, containing all our papers, instruments, medicine, and almost every article indispensable for the success of our enterprise. The canoe being under sail, a sudden squall of wind struck her obliquely and turned her considerably. The man at the helm, who was unluckily the worst steersman of the party, became alarmed, and, instead of putting her before the wind, luffed her up into it. The wind was so high that it forced the brace of the square-sail out of the hand of the man who was attending it, and instantly upset the canoe, which would have been turned bottom upward but for the resistance made by the awning. Such was the confusion on board, and the waves ran so high, that it was half a minute before she righted, and then nearly full of water, but by bailing her out she was kept from sinking until they rowed ashore. Besides the loss of the lives of three men, who, not being able to swim, would probably have perished, we should have been deprived of nearly everything necessary for our purposes, at a distance of between two and three thousand miles from any place where we could supply the deficiency."

Fortunately, there was no great loss from this accident, which was caused by the clumsiness and timidity of the steersman, Chaboneau. Captain Lewis's account of the incident records that the conduct of Chaboneau's wife, Sacajawea, was better than that of her cowardly husband. He says:—

"The Indian woman, to whom I ascribe equal fortitude and resolution with any person on board at the time of the accident, caught and preserved most of the light articles which were washed overboard."

Chapter IX — In the Solitudes of the Upper Missouri

Under date of May 17, the journal of the party has the following interesting entries:—

"We set out early and proceeded on very well; the banks being firm and the shore bold, we were enabled to use the towline, which, whenever the banks will permit it, is the safest and most expeditious mode of ascending the river, except under sail with a steady breeze. At the distance of ten and one-half miles we came to the mouth of a small creek on the south, below which the hills approach the river, and continue near it during the day. Three miles further is a large creek on the north; and again, six and three-quarters miles beyond this, is another large creek, to the south; both containing a small quantity of running water, of a brackish taste. The last we called Rattlesnake Creek, from our seeing that animal near it. Although no timber can be observed on it from the Missouri, it throws out large quantities of driftwood, among which were some pieces of coal brought down by the stream. . . .

"The game is in great quantities, but the buffalo are not so numerous as they were some days ago; two rattlesnakes were seen to-day, and one of them was killed. It resembles those of the Middle Atlantic States, being about thirty inches long, of a yellowish brown on the back and sides, variegated with a row of oval dark brown spots lying transversely on the back from the neck to the tail, and two other rows of circular spots of the same color on the sides along the edge of the scuta; there are one hundred and seventy-six scuta on the belly, and seventeen on the tail."

Two days later, the journal records that one of the party killed a grizzly bear, "which, though shot through the heart, ran at his usual pace nearly a quarter of a mile before he fell."

The mouth of the Musselshell River, which was one of the notable points that marked another stage in the journey, was reached on the twentieth of May. This stream empties into the Missouri two thousand two hundred and seventy miles above its mouth, and is still known by the name given it by its discoverers. The journal says:

"It is one hundred and ten yards wide, and contains more water than streams of that size usually do in this country; its current is by no means rapid, and there is every appearance of its being susceptible of navigation by canoes for a considerable distance. Its bed is chiefly formed of coarse sand and gravel, with an occasional mixture of black mud; the banks are abrupt and nearly twelve feet high, so that they are secure from being overflowed; the water is of a greenish-yellow cast, and much more transparent than that of the Missouri, which itself, though clearer than below, still retains its whitish hue and a portion of its sediment. Opposite the point of junction the current of the Missouri is gentle, and two hundred and twenty-two yards in width; the bed is principally of mud, the little sand remaining being wholly confined to the points, and the water is still too deep to use the setting-pole.

"If this be, as we suppose, the Musselshell, our Indian information is that it rises in the first chain of the Rocky mountains not far from the sources of the Yellowstone, whence in its course to this place it waters a high broken country, well timbered, particularly on its borders, and interspersed with handsome fertile plains and meadows. We have reason, however, to believe, from their giving a similar account of the timber where we now are, that the timber of which they speak is similar to that which we have seen for a few days past, which consists of nothing more than a few straggling small pines and dwarf cedars on the summits of the hills, nine-tenths of the ground being totally destitute of wood, and covered with short grass, aromatic herbs, and an immense quantity of prickly-pear; though the party who explored it for eight miles represented the low grounds on the river to be well supplied with cottonwood of a tolerable size, and of an excellent soil. They also report that the country is broken and irregular, like that near our camp; and that about five miles up, a handsome river, about fifty yards wide, which we named after Chaboneau's wife, Sacajawea's or the Bird-woman's River, discharges into the Musselshell on the north or upper side."

Later explorations have shown that the Musselshell rises in the Little Belt Mountains, considerably to the north of the sources of the Yellowstone. Modern geography has also taken from the good Sacajawea the honor of having her name bestowed on one of the branches of the Musselshell. The stream once named for her is now known as Crooked Creek: it joins the river near its mouth, in the central portion of Montana. The journal, under date of May 22, has this entry:—

"The river (the Missouri) continues about two hundred and fifty yards wide, with fewer sand-bars, and the current more gentle and regular. Game is no longer in such abundance since leaving the Musselshell. We have caught very few fish on this side of the Mandans, and these were the white catfish, of two to five pounds. We killed a deer and a bear. We have not seen in this quarter the black bear, common in the United States and on the lower parts of the Missouri, nor have we discerned any of their tracks. They may easily be distinguished by the shortness of the talons from the brown, grizzly, or white bear, all of which seem to be of the same species, which assumes those colors at different seasons of the year. We halted earlier than usual, and camped on the north, in a point of woods, at the distance of sixteen and one half miles (thus past the site of Fort Hawley, on the south)."

Notwithstanding the advance of the season, the weather in those great altitudes grew more and more cold. Under date of May 23, the journal records the fact that ice appeared along the edges of the river, and water froze upon their oars. But notwithstanding the coolness of the nights and mornings, mosquitoes were very troublesome.

The explorers judged that the cold was somewhat unusual for that locality, inasmuch as the cottonwood trees lost their leaves by the frost, showing that vegetation, generally well suited to the temperature of its country, or habitat, had been caught by an unusual nip of the frost. The explorers noticed that the air of those highlands was so pure and clear that objects appeared to be much nearer than they really were. A man who was sent out to explore the country attempted to reach a ridge (now known as the Little Rocky Mountains), apparently about fifteen miles from the river. He travelled about ten miles, but finding himself not halfway to the object of his search, he returned without reaching it.

The party was now just westward of the site of the present town of Carroll, Montana, on the Missouri. Their journal says:—

"The low grounds are narrow and without timber; the country is high and broken; a large portion of black rock and brown sandy rock appears in the face of the hills, the tops of which are covered with scattered pine, spruce, and dwarf cedar; the soil is generally poor, sandy near the tops of the hills, and nowhere producing much grass, the low grounds being covered with little else than the hyssop, or southernwood, and the pulpy-leaved thorn. Game is more scarce, particularly beaver, of which we have seen but few for several days, and the abundance or scarcity of which seems to depend on the greater or less quantity of timber. At twenty-four and one-half miles we reached a point of woodland on the south, where we observed that the trees had no leaves, and camped for the night."

The "hyssop, or southernwood," the reader now knows to be the wild sage, or sage-brush. The "pulpy-leaved thorn" mentioned in the journal is the greasewood; and both of these shrubs flourish in the poverty-stricken, sandy, alkaline soil of the far West and Northwest. The woody fibre of these furnished the only fuel available for early overland emigrants to the Pacific.

The character of this country now changed considerably as the explorers turned to the northward, in their crooked course, with the river. On the twenty-fifth of May the journal records this:—

"The country on each side is high, broken, and rocky; the rock being either a soft brown sandstone, covered with a thin stratum of limestone, or else a hard, black, rugged granite, both usually in horizontal strata, and the sand-rock overlaying the other. Salts and quartz, as well as some coal and pumice-stone, still appear. The bars of the river are composed principally of gravel; the river low grounds are narrow, and afford scarcely any timber; nor is there much pine on the hills. The buffalo have now become scarce; we saw a polecat (skunk) this evening, which was the first for several days; in the course of the day we also saw several herds of the bighorned animals among the steep cliffs on the north, and killed several of them."

The bighorned animals, the first of which were killed here, were sometimes called "Rocky Mountain sheep." But sheep they were not, bearing hair and not wool. As we have said, they are now more commonly known as bighorns.

The patience of the explorers was rewarded, on Sunday, May 26, 1806, by their first view of the Rocky Mountains. Here is the journal's record on that date:—

"It was here (Cow Creek, Mont.) that, after ascending the highest summit of the hills on the north side of the river, Captain Lewis first caught a distant view of the Rock mountains—the object of all our hopes, and the reward of all our ambition. On both sides of the river, and at no great distance from it, the mountains followed its course. Above these at the distance of fifty miles from us, an irregular range of mountains spread from west to northwest from his position. To the north of these, a few elevated points, the most remarkable of which bore N. 65'0 W., appeared above the horizon; and as the sun shone on the snows of their summits, he obtained a clear and satisfactory view of those mountains which close on the Missouri the passage to the Pacific."

As they continued to ascend the Missouri they found themselves confronted by many considerable rapids which sometimes delayed their progress. They also set forth this observation: "The only animals we have observed are the elk, the bighorn, and the hare common to this country." Wayfarers across the plains now call this hare the jack-rabbit. The river soon became very rapid with a marked descent, indicating their nearness to its mountain sources. The journal says:—

"Its general width is about two hundred yards; the shoals are more frequent, and the rocky points at the mouths of the gullies more troublesome to pass. Great quantities of stone lie in the river and on its bank, and seem to have fallen down as the rain washed away the clay and sand in which they were imbedded. The water is bordered by high, rugged bluffs, composed of irregular but horizontal strata of yellow and brown or black clay, brown and yellowish-white sand, soft yellowish-white sandstone, and hard dark brown freestone; also, large round kidney-formed irregular separate masses of a hard black ironstone, imbedded in the clay and sand; some coal or carbonated wood also makes its appearance in the cliffs, as do its usual attendants, the pumice-stone and burnt earth. The salts and quartz are less abundant, and, generally speaking, the country is, if possible, more rugged and barren than that we passed yesterday; the only growth of the hills being a few pine, spruce, and dwarf cedar, interspersed with an occasional contrast, once in the course of some miles, of several acres of level ground, which supply a scanty subsistence for a few little cottonwoods."

But, a few days later, the party passed out of this inhospitable region, and, after passing a stream which they named Thompson's (now Birch) Creek, after one of their men, they were glad to make this entry in their diary:

"Here the country assumed a totally different aspect: the hills retired on both sides from the river, which spreads to more than three times its former size, and is filled with a number of small handsome islands covered with cottonwood. The low grounds on its banks are again wide, fertile, and enriched with trees: those on the north are particularly wide, the hills being comparatively low, and opening into three large valleys, which extend themselves for a considerable distance towards the north. These appearances of vegetation are delightful after the dreary hills among which we have passed; and we have now to congratulate ourselves at having escaped from the last ridges of the Black Mountains. On leaving Thompson's Creek we passed two small islands, and at twenty-three miles' distance encamped among some timber; on the north, opposite to a small creek, which we named Bull Creek. The bighorn are in great quantities, and must bring forth their young at a very early season, as they are now half grown. One of the party saw a large bear also; but, being at a distance from the river, and having no timber to conceal him, he would not venture to fire."

A curious adventure happened on the twenty-eighth, of which the journal, next day, makes this mention:—

"Last night we were alarmed by a new sort of enemy. A buffalo swam over from the opposite side, and to the spot where lay one of our canoes, over which he clambered to the shore: then, taking fright, he ran full speed up the bank towards our fires, and passed within eighteen inches of the heads of some of the men before the sentinel could make him change his course. Still more alarmed, he ran down between four fires, and within a few inches of the heads of a second row of the men, and would have broken into our lodge if the barking of the dog had not stopped him. He suddenly turned to the right, and was out of sight in a moment, leaving us all in confusion, every one seizing his rifle and inquiring the cause of the alarm. On learning what had happened, we had to rejoice at suffering no more injury than some damage to the guns that were in the canoe which the buffalo crossed. . . .

"We passed an island and two sand-bars, and at the distance of two and a half miles came to a handsome river, which discharges itself on the South, and which we ascended to the distance of a mile and a half: we called it Judith's River. It rises in the Rocky Mountains, in about the same place with the Musselshell, and near the Yellowstone River. Its entrance is one hundred yards wide from one bank to the other, the water occupying about seventy-five yards, and being in greater quantity than that of the Musselshell River. . . . There were great numbers of the argalea, or bighorned animals, in the high country through which it passes, and of beaver in its waters. Just above the entrance of it we saw the ashes of the fires of one hundred and twenty-six lodges, which appeared to have been deserted about twelve or fifteen days."

Leaving Judith's River, named for a sweet Virginia lass, the explorers sailed, or were towed, seventeen miles up the river, where they camped at the mouth of a bold, running river to which they gave the name of Slaughter River. The stream is now known as the Arrow; the appropriateness of the title conferred on the stream by Lewis and Clark appears from the story which they tell of their experience just below "Slaughter River," as follows:

"On the north we passed a precipice about one hundred and twenty feet high, under which lay scattered the fragments of at least one hundred carcasses of buffaloes, although the water which had washed away the lower part of the hill must have carried off many of the dead. These buffaloes had been chased down the precipice in a way very common on the Missouri, by which vast herds are destroyed in a moment. The mode of hunting is to select one of the most active and fleet young men, who is disguised by a buffalo-skin round his body; the skin of the head with the ears and horns being fastened on his own head in such a way as to deceive the buffalo. Thus dressed, he fixes himself at a convenient distance between a herd of buffalo and any of the river precipices, which sometimes extend for some miles. His companions in the mean time get in the rear and side of the herd, and at a given signal show themselves and advance toward the buffaloes. These instantly take the alarm, and finding the hunters beside them, they run toward the disguised Indian or decoy, who leads them on at full speed toward the river; when, suddenly securing himself in some crevice of the cliff which he had previously fixed on, the herd is left on the brink of the precipice. It is then in vain for the foremost buffaloes to retreat or even to stop; they are pressed on by the hindmost rank, which, seeing no danger but from the hunters, goad on those before them till the whole are precipitated, and the shore is strewn with their dead bodies. Sometimes, in this perilous seduction, the Indian is himself either trodden under foot by the rapid movements of the buffaloes, or missing his footing in the cliff is urged down the precipice by the falling herd. The Indians then select as much meat as they wish; the rest is abandoned to the wolves, and creates a most dreadful stench. The wolves which had been feasting on these carcasses were very fat, and so gentle that one of them was killed with an espontoon." (1)

(1) A short spear.

The dryness and purity of the air roused the admiration of the explorers, who noticed that the woodwork of the cases of their instruments shrank, and the joints opened, although the wood was old and perfectly seasoned. A tablespoonful of water, exposed to the air in an open saucer, would wholly evaporate in thirty-six hours, when the thermometer did not mark higher than the "Temperate" point at the warmest hour of the day. Contrary to their expectations, they had not yet met with any Indians, although they saw many signs of their having recently been in that vicinity. The journal says:

"In the course of the day (May 30) we passed several encampments of Indians, the most recent of which seemed to have been evacuated about five weeks since; and, from the several apparent dates, we supposed that they were formed by a band of about one hundred lodges, who were travelling slowly up the river. Although no part of the Missouri from the Minnetarees to this place exhibits signs of permanent settlements, yet none seem exempt from the transient visits of

44

hunting-parties. We know that the Minnetarees of the Missouri extend their excursions on the south side of the river as high as the Yellowstone, and the Assiniboins visit the northern side, most probably as high as Porcupine River. All the lodges between that place and the Rocky Mountains we supposed to belong to the Minnetarees of Fort de Prairie, who live on the south fork of the Saskashawan."

The party now entered upon some of the natural wonders of the West, which have since become famous. Their journal says:—

"These hills and river-cliffs exhibit a most extraordinary and romantic appearance. They rise in most places nearly perpendicular from the water, to the height of between two hundred and three hundred feet, and are formed of very white sandstone, so soft as to yield readily to the impression of water, in the upper part of which lie imbedded two or three thin horizontal strata of white freestone, insensible to the rain; on the top is a dark rich loam, which forms a gradually ascending plain, from a mile to a mile and a half in extent, when the hills again rise abruptly to the height of about three hundred feet more. In trickling down the cliffs, the water has worn the soft sandstone into a thousand grotesque figures, among which, with a little fancy, may be discerned elegant ranges of freestone buildings, with columns variously sculptured, and supporting long and elegant galleries, while the parapets are adorned with statuary. On a nearer approach they represent every form of elegant ruins—columns, some with pedestals and capitals entire, others mutilated and prostrate, and some rising pyramidally over each other till they terminate in a sharp point. These are varied by niches, alcoves, and the customary appearances of desolated magnificence. The illusion is increased by the number of martins, which have built their globular nests in the niches, and hover over these columns, as in our country they are accustomed to frequent large stone structures. As we advance there seems no end to the visionary enchantment which surrounds us.

"In the midst of this fantastic scenery are vast ranges of walls, which seem the productions of art, so regular is the workmanship. They rise perpendicularly from the river, sometimes to the height of one hundred feet, varying in thickness from one to twelve feet, being as broad at the top as below. The stones of which they are formed are black, thick, durable, and composed of a large portion of earth, intermixed and cemented with a small quantity of sand and a considerable proportion of talk (talc) or quartz. These stones are almost invariably regular parallelopipeds of unequal sizes in the wall, but equally deep and laid regularly in ranges over each other like bricks, each breaking and covering the interstice of the two on which it rests; but though the perpendicular interstice be destroyed, the horizontal one extends entirely through the whole work. The stones are proportioned to the thickness of the wall in which they are employed, being largest in the thickest walls. The thinner walls are composed of a single depth of the parallelopiped, while the thicker ones consist of two or more depths. These walls pass the river at several places, rising from the water's edge much above the sandstone bluffs, which they seem to penetrate; thence they cross in a straight line, on either side of the river, the plains, over which they tower to the height of from ten to seventy feet, until they lose themselves in the second range of hills. Sometimes they run parallel in several ranges near to each other, sometimes intersect each other at right angles, and have the appearance of walls of ancient houses or gardens."

The wall-like, canyon formations were charted by Lewis and Clark as "The Stone Walls." Their fantastic outlines have been admired and described by modern tourists, and some of them have been named "Cathedral Rocks," "Citadel Rock," "Hole in the Wall," and so on.

Passing out of this wonderful region, the expedition entered upon a more level country, here and there broken by bluffy formations which extended along the river, occasionally interspersed with low hills. Their journal says:

"In the plains near the river are the choke-cherry, yellow and red currant bushes, as well as the wild rose and prickly pear, both of which are now in bloom. From the tops of the river-hills, which are lower than usual, we enjoyed a delightful view of the rich, fertile plains on both sides, in many places extending from the river-cliffs to a great distance back. In these plains we meet, occasionally, large banks of pure sand, which were driven apparently by the southwest winds and there deposited. The plains are more fertile some distance from the river than near its banks, where the surface of the earth is very generally strewed with small pebbles, which appear to be smoothed and worn by the agitation of the waters with which they were, no doubt, once covered."

Under date of June 2d, the journal says:—

"The current of the river is strong but regular, the timber increases in quantity, the low grounds become more level and extensive, and the bluffs are lower than before. As the game is very abundant, we think it necessary to begin a collection of hides for the purpose of making a leathern boat, which we intend constructing shortly. The hunters, who were out the greater part of the day, brought in six elk, two buffalo, two mule-deer, and a bear. This last animal had nearly cost us the lives of two of our hunters, who were together when he attacked them. One of them narrowly escaped being caught, and the other, after running a considerable distance, concealed himself in some thick bushes, and, while the bear was in quick pursuit of his hiding-place, his companion came up, and fortunately shot the animal through the head."

Here the party came to the mouth of a large river which entered the Missouri from the northwest, at the site of the latter-day town of Ophir, Montana. This stream they named Maria's River, in honor of another Virginia damsel. So large and important in appearance was Maria's River that the explorers were not certain which was the main stream, that which came in from the north, or that which, flowing here in a general course from southwest to northeast, was really the true Missouri. The journal says:

"It now became an interesting question, which of these two streams is what the Minnetarees call Ahmateahza, or Missouri, which they describe as approaching very near to the Columbia. On our right decision much of the fate of the expedition depends; since if, after ascending to the Rocky Mountains or beyond them, we should find that the river we were following did not come near the Columbia, and be obliged to return, we should not only lose the travelling season, two months of which have already elapsed, but probably dishearten the men so much as to induce them either to abandon the enterprise, or yield us a cold obedience, instead of the warm and zealous support which they have hitherto afforded us. We determined, therefore, to examine well before we decided on our future course. For this purpose we despatched two canoes with three men up each of the streams, with orders to ascertain the width, depth, and rapidity of the current, so as to judge of their comparative bodies of water. At the same time parties were sent out by land to penetrate the country, and discover from the rising grounds, if possible, the distant bearings of the two rivers; and all were directed to return toward evening. . . ."

Both parties returned without bringing any information that would settle the point. Which was the true Missouri still remained uncertain. Under these circumstances, it became necessary that there should be a more thorough exploration, and the next morning Captains Lewis and Clark set out at the head of two separate parties, the former to examine the north, and the latter the south fork. In his progress Captain Lewis and his party were frequently obliged to quit the course of the river and cross the plains and hills, but he did not lose sight of its general direction, and carefully took the bearings of the distant mountains. On the morning of the third day he became convinced that this river pursued a course too far north for his contemplated route to the Pacific, and he accordingly determined to return, but judged it advisable to wait till noon, that he might obtain a meridian altitude. In this, however, he was disappointed, owing to the state of the weather. Much rain had fallen, and their return was somewhat difficult, and not unattended with danger, as the following incident, which occurred on June 7th, will show:

"In passing along the side of a bluff at a narrow pass thirty yards in length, Captain Lewis slipped, and, but for a fortunate recovery by means of his spontoon, would have been precipitated into the river over a precipice of about ninety feet. He had just reached a spot where, by the assistance of his spontoon, he could stand with tolerable safety, when he heard a voice behind him cry out, 'Good God, captain, what shall I do?' He turned instantly, and found it was Windsor, who had lost his foothold about the middle of the narrow pass, and had slipped down to the very verge of the precipice, where he lay on his belly, with his right arm and leg over it, while with the other leg and arm he was with difficulty holding on, to keep himself from being dashed to pieces below. His dreadful situation was instantly perceived by Captain Lewis, who, stifling his alarm, calmly told him that he was in no danger; that he should take his knife out of his belt with his right hand, and dig a hole in the side of the bluff to receive his right foot. With great presence of mind he did this, and then raised himself on his knees. Captain Lewis then told him to take off his moccasins and come forward on his hands and knees, holding the knife in one hand and his rifle in the other. He immediately crawled in this way till he came to a secure spot. The men who had not attempted this passage were ordered to return and wade the river at the foot of the bluff, where they found the water breast-high. This adventure taught them the danger of crossing the slippery heights of the river; but as the plains were intersected by deep ravines, almost as difficult to pass, they continued down the river, sometimes in the mud of the low grounds, sometimes up to their arms in the water; and when it became too deep to wade, they cut footholds with their knives in the sides of the banks. In this way they travelled through the rain, mud, and water, and having made only eighteen miles during the whole day, camped in an old Indian lodge of sticks, which afforded them a dry shelter. Here they cooked part of six deer they had killed in the course of their walk, and having eaten the only morsel they had tasted during the whole day, slept comfortably on some willow-boughs."

Chapter X — To the Great Falls of the Missouri

Next day, June 8, the Lewis party returned to the main body of the expedition. They reported that timber was scarce along the river, except in the lowlands, where there were pretty groves and thickets. These trees, the journal says, were the haunts of innumerable birds, which, as the sun rose, sung delightfully:—

"Among these birds they distinguished the brown thrush, robin, turtle-dove, linnet, gold-finch, large and small blackbird, wren, and some others. As they came along, the whole party were of opinion that this river was the true Missouri; but Captain Lewis, being fully persuaded that it was neither the main stream, nor that which it would be advisable to ascend, gave it the name of Maria's River. After travelling all day they reached camp about five o'clock in the afternoon, and found Captain Clark and the party very anxious for their safety. As they had stayed two days longer than had been expected, and as Captain Clark had returned at the appointed time, it was feared that they had met with some accident."

As we now know, the stream that came in from the north was that which is still called Maria's (or Marais) River, and the so-called branch from the southwest was the Missouri River. Lewis and Clark, however, were in the dark as to the relations of the two streams. Which was the parent? Which was the branch? After pondering all the evidence that could be collected to bear on the important question, the two captains agreed that the southern stream was the true Missouri, and the northern stream was an important branch. The journal says:

"These observations, which satisfied our minds completely, we communicated to the party; but every one of them was of a contrary opinion. Much of their belief depended on Crusatte, an experienced waterman on the Missouri, who gave it as his decided judgment that the north fork was the genuine Missouri. The men, therefore, mentioned that, although they would most cheerfully follow us wherever we should direct, yet they were afraid that the south fork would soon terminate in the Rocky Mountains, and leave us at a great distance from the Columbia. In order that nothing might be omitted which could prevent our falling into an error, it was agreed that one of us should ascend the southern branch by land, until we reached either the falls or the mountains. In the meantime, in order to lighten our burdens as much as possible, we determined to deposit here one of the pirogues, and all the heavy baggage which we could possibly spare, as well as some provision, salt, powder, and tools. This would at once lighten the other boats, and give them the crew which had been employed on board the pirogue."

On the tenth of June, the weather being fair and pleasant, they dried all their baggage and merchandise and secreted them in places of deposits, called caches, as follows:—

"These deposits—or caches, as they are called by the Missouri traders—are very common, particularly among those who deal with the Sioux, as the skins and merchandise will keep perfectly sound for years, and are protected from robbery. Our cache was built in the usual manner. In the high plain on the north side of the Missouri, and forty yards from a steep bluff, we chose a dry situation, and then, describing a small circle of about twenty inches diameter, removed the sod as gently and carefully as possible: the hole was then sunk perpendicularly for a foot deep. It was now worked gradually wider as it descended, till at length it became six or

48

seven feet deep, shaped nearly like a kettle, or the lower part of a large still with the bottom somewhat sunk at the centre. As the earth was dug it was handed up in a vessel, and carefully laid on a skin or cloth, in which it was carried away and thrown into the river, so as to leave no trace of it. A floor of three or four inches in thickness was then made of dry sticks, on which was placed a hide perfectly dry. The goods, being well aired and dried, were laid on this floor, and prevented from touching the wall by other dried sticks, as the merchandise was stowed away. When the hole was nearly full, a skin was laid over the goods, and on this earth was thrown and beaten down, until, with the addition of the sod first removed, the whole was on a level with the ground, and there remained not the slightest appearance of an excavation. In addition to this, we made another of smaller dimensions, in which we placed all the baggage, some powder, and our blacksmith's tools, having previously repaired such of the tools as we carry with us that require mending. To guard against accident, we had two parcelss of lead and powder in the two places. The red pirogue was drawn up on the middle of a small island, at the entrance of Maria's River, and secured, by being fastened to the trees, from the effects of any floods. We now took another observation of the meridian altitude of the sun, and found that the mean latitude of Maria's River, as deduced from three observations, is 49'0 25' 17.2" N."

In order to make assurance doubly sure, Captain Lewis resolved to take four men with him and ascend the south branch (that is, the true Missouri), before committing the expedition to that route as the final one. His proposition was that his party should proceed up the river as rapidly as possible in advance of the main party. On the second day out, says the journal:—

"Captain Lewis left the bank of the river in order to avoid the steep ravines, which generally run from the shore to the distance of one or two miles in the plain. Having reached the open country he went for twelve miles in a course a little to the W. of S.W.; when, the sun becoming warm by nine o'clock, he returned to the river in quest of water, and to kill something for breakfast; there being no water in the plain, and the buffalo, discovering them before they came within gunshot, took to flight. They reached the banks in a handsome open low ground with cottonwood, after three miles' walk. Here they saw two large brown bears, and killed them both at the first fire—a circumstance which has never before occurred since we have seen that animal. Having made a meal of a part, and hung the remainder on a tree, with a note for Captain Clark, they again ascended the bluffs into the open plains. Here they saw great numbers of the burrowing-squirrel, also some wolves, antelopes, mule-deer, and vast herds of buffalo. They soon crossed a ridge considerably higher than the surrounding plains, and from its top had a beautiful view of the Rocky Mountains, which are now completely covered with snow. Their general course is from S.E. to N. of N.W., and they seem to consist of several ranges which successively rise above each other, till the most distant mingles with the clouds. After travelling twelve miles they again met the river, where there was a handsome plain of cottonwood."

Again leaving the river, Captain Lewis bore off more to the north, the stream here bearing considerably to the south, with difficult bluffs along its course. But fearful of passing the Great Falls before reaching the Rocky Mountains, he again changed his course and, leaving the bluffs to his right he turned towards the river.

The journal gives this description of what followed:—

"In this direction Captain Lewis had gone about two miles, when his ears were saluted with the agreeable sound of a fall of water, and as he advanced a spray, which seemed driven by the high southwest wind, arose above the plain like a column of smoke, and vanished in an instant. Toward this point he directed his steps; the noise increased as he approached, and soon became too tremendous to be mistaken for anything but the Great Falls of the Missouri. Having travelled seven miles after first hearing the sound, he reached the falls about twelve o'clock. The hills as he approached were difficult of access and two hundred feet high. Down these he hurried with impatience; and, seating himself on some rocks under the centre of the falls, enjoyed the sublime spectacle of this stupendous object, which since the creation had been lavishing its magnificence upon the desert, unknown to civilization.

"The river immediately at this cascade is three hundred yards wide, and is pressed in by a perpendicular cliff on the left, which rises to about one hundred feet and extends up the stream for a mile; on the right the bluff is also perpendicular for three hundred yards above the falls. For ninety or one hundred yards from the left cliff, the water falls in one smooth, even sheet, over a precipice of at least eighty feet. The remaining part of the river precipitates itself with a more rapid current, but being received as it falls by the irregular and somewhat projecting rocks below, forms a splendid prospect of perfectly white foam, two hundred yards in length and eighty in perpendicular elevation. This spray is dissipated into a thousand shapes, sometimes flying up in columns of fifteen or twenty feet, which are then oppressed by larger masses of the white foam, on all of which the sun impresses the brightest colors of the rainbow. Below the fall the water beats with fury against a ledge of rocks, which extends across the river at one hundred and fifty yards from the precipice. From the perpendicular cliff on the north to the distance of one hundred and twenty yards, the rocks are only a few feet above the water; and, when the river is high, the stream finds a channel across them forty yards wide, and near the higher parts of the ledge, which rise about twenty feet, and terminate abruptly within eighty or ninety yards of the southern side. Between them and the perpendicular cliff on the south, the whole body of water runs with great swiftness. A few small cedars grow near this ridge of rocks, which serves as a barrier to defend a small plain of about three acres, shaded with cottonwood; at the lower extremity of which is a grove of the same trees, where are several deserted Indian cabins of sticks; below which the river is divided by a large rock, several feet above the surface of the water, and extending down the stream for twenty yards. At the distance of three hundred yards from the same ridge is a second abutment of solid perpendicular rock, about sixty feet high, projecting at right angles from the small plain on the north for one hundred and thirty-four yards into the river. After leaving this, the Missouri again spreads itself to its previous breadth of three hundred yards, though with more than its ordinary rapidity."

One of Lewis's men was sent back to inform Captain Clark of this momentous discovery, which finally settled all doubt as to which was the true Missouri. The famous Great Falls of the river had been finally reached. Captain Lewis next went on to examine the rapids above the falls. The journal says:—

"After passing one continued rapid and three cascades, each three or four feet high, he reached, at the distance of five miles, a second fall. The river is here about four hundred yards wide, and for the distance of three hundred rushes down to the depth of nineteen feet, and so irregularly that he gave it the name of the Crooked Falls. From the southern shore it extends obliquely upward about one hundred and fifty yards, and then forms an acute angle downward nearly to the commencement of four small islands close to the northern side. From the perpendicular pitch to these islands, a distance of more than one hundred yards, the water glides down a sloping rock with a velocity almost equal to that of its fall: above this fall the river bends suddenly to the northward. While viewing this place, Captain Lewis heard a loud roar above him, and, crossing the point of a hill a few hundred yards, he saw one of the most beautiful objects in nature: the whole Missouri is suddenly stopped by one shelving rock, which, without a single niche, and with an edge as straight and regular as if formed by art, stretches itself from one side of the river to the other for at least a quarter of a mile. Over this it precipitates itself in an even, uninterrupted sheet, to the perpendicular depth of fifty feet, whence, dashing against the rocky bottom, it rushes rapidly down, leaving behind it a sheet of the purest foam across the river. The scene which it presented was indeed singularly beautiful; since, without any of the wild, irregular sublimity of the lower falls, it combined all the regular elegancies which the fancy of a painter would select to form a beautiful waterfall. The eye had scarcely been regaled with this charming prospect, when at the distance of half a mile Captain Lewis observed another of a similar kind. To this he immediately hastened, and found a cascade stretching across the whole river for a quarter of a mile, with a descent of fourteen feet, though the perpendicular pitch was only six feet. This, too, in any other neighborhood, would have been an object of great magnificence; but after what he had just seen, it became of secondary interest. His curiosity being, however, awakened, he determined to go on, even should night overtake him, to the head of the falls.

"He therefore pursued the southwest course of the river, which was one constant succession of rapids and small cascades, at every one of which the bluffs grew lower, or the bed of the river became more on a level with the plains. At the distance of two and one-half miles he arrived at another cataract, of twenty-six feet. The river is here six hundred yards wide, but the descent is not immediately perpendicular, though the river falls generally with a regular and smooth sheet; for about one-third of the descent a rock protrudes to a small distance, receives the water in its passage, and gives it a curve. On the south side is a beautiful plain, a few feet above the level of the falls; on the north, the country is more broken, and there is a hill not far from the river. Just below the falls is a little island in the middle of the river, well covered with timber. Here on a cottonwood tree an eagle had fixed her nest, and seemed the undisputed mistress of a spot, to contest whose dominion neither man nor beast would venture across the gulfs that surround it, and which is further secured by the mist rising from the falls. This solitary bird could not escape the observation of the Indians, who made the eagle's nest a part of their description of the falls, which now proves to be correct in almost every particular, except that they did not do justice to the height.

"Just above this is a cascade of about five feet, beyond which, as far as could be discerned, the velocity of the water seemed to abate. Captain Lewis now ascended the hill which was behind him, and saw from its top a delightful plain, extending from the river to the base of the Snowy (Rocky) Mountains to the south and southwest. Along this wide, level country the Missouri pursued its winding course, filled with water to its smooth, grassy banks, while about four miles above, it was joined by a large river flowing from the northwest, through a valley three miles in width, and distinguished by the timber which adorned its shores. The Missouri itself stretches to the south, in one unruffled stream of water, as if unconscious of the roughness it must soon encounter, and bearing on its bosom vast flocks of geese, while numerous herds of buffalo are feeding on the plains which surround it.

"Captain Lewis then descended the hill, and directed his course towards the river falling in from the west. He soon met a herd of at least a thousand buffalo, and, being desirous of providing for supper, shot one of them. The animal immediately began to bleed, and Captain Lewis, who had forgotten to reload his rifle, was intently watching to see him fall, when he beheld a large brown bear which was stealing on him unperceived, and was already within twenty steps. In the first moment of surprise he lifted his rifle; but, remembering instantly that it was not charged, and that he had no time to reload, he felt that there was no safety but in flight. It was in the open, level plain; not a bush nor a tree within three hundred yards; the bank of the river sloping, and not more than three feet high, so that there was no possible mode of concealment. Captain Lewis, therefore, thought of retreating with a quick walk, as fast as the bear advanced, towards the nearest tree; but, as soon as he turned, the bear rushed open-mouthed, and at full speed, upon him. Captain Lewis ran about eighty yards, but finding that the animal gained on him fast, it flashed on his mind that, by getting into the water to such a depth that the bear would be obliged to attack him swimming, there was still some chance of his life; he therefore turned short, plunged into the river about waist-deep, and facing about presented the point of his espontoon. The bear arrived at the water's edge within twenty feet of him; but as soon as he put himself in this posture of defence, the bear seemed frightened, and wheeling about, retreated with as much precipitation as he had pursued. Very glad to be released from this danger, Captain Lewis returned to the shore, and observed him run with great speed, sometimes looking back as if he expected to be pursued, till he reached the woods. He could not conceive the cause of the sudden alarm of the bear, but congratulated himself on his escape when he saw his own track torn to pieces by the furious animal, and learned from the whole adventure never to suffer his rifle to be a moment unloaded."

Captain Lewis now resumed his progress towards the western, or Sun, River, then more commonly known among the Indians as Medicine River. In going through the lowlands of this stream, he met an animal which he thought was a wolf, but which was more likely a wolverine, or carcajou. The journal says:—

"It proved to be some brownish yellow animal, standing near its burrow, which, when he came nigh, crouched, and seemed as if about to spring on him. Captain Lewis fired, and the beast disappeared in its burrow. From the track, and the general appearance of the animal, he supposed it to be of the tiger kind. He then went on; but, as if the beasts of the forest had conspired against him, three buffalo bulls, which were feeding with a large herd at the distance of half a mile, left their companions, and ran at full speed towards him. He turned round, and, unwilling to give up the field, advanced to meet them: when they were within a hundred yards they stopped, looked at him for some time, and then retreated as they came. He now pursued his route in the dark, reflecting on the strange adventures and sights of the day, which crowded on his mind so rapidly, that he should have been inclined to believe it all enchantment if the thorns of the prickly pear, piercing his feet, had not dispelled at every moment the illusion. He at last reached the party, who had been very anxious for his safety, and who had already decided on the route which each should take in the morning to look for him. Being much fatigued, he supped, and slept well during the night."

On awaking the next morning, Captain Lewis found a large rattlesnake coiled on the trunk of a tree under which he had been sleeping. He killed it, and found it like those he had seen before, differing from those of the Atlantic States, not in its colors, but in the form and arrangement of them. Information was received that Captain Clark had arrived five miles below, at a rapid which he did not think it prudent to ascend, and that he was waiting there for the party above to rejoin him.

After the departure of Captain Lewis, Captain Clark had remained a day at Maria's River, to complete the deposit of such articles as they could dispense with, and started on the twelfth of June.

Four days later, Captain Clark left the river, having sent his messenger to Captain Lewis, and began to search for a proper portage to convey the pirogue and canoes across to the Columbia River, leaving most of the men to hunt, make wheels and draw the canoes up a creek which they named Portage Creek, as it was to be the base of their future operations. The stream is now known as Belt Mountain Creek. But the explorers soon found that although the pirogue was to be left behind, the way was too difficult for a portage even for canoes. The journal says:—

"We found great difficulty and some danger in even ascending the creek thus far, in consequence of the rapids and rocks of the channel of the creek, which just above where we brought the canoes has a fall of five feet, with high steep bluffs beyond it. We were very fortunate in finding, just below Portage Creek, a cottonwood tree about twenty-two inches in diameter, large enough to make the carriage-wheels. It was, perhaps, the only one of the same size within twenty miles; and the cottonwood which we are obliged to employ in the other parts of the work is extremely soft and brittle. The mast of the white pirogue, which we mean to leave behind, supplied us with two axle-trees.

"There are vast quantities of buffalo feeding on the plains or watering in the river, which is also strewed with the floating carcasses and limbs of these animals. They go in large herds to water about the falls, and as all the passages to the river near that place are narrow and steep, the foremost are pressed into the river by the impatience of those behind. In this way we have seen ten or a dozen disappear over the falls in a few minutes. They afford excellent food for the wolves, bears, and birds of prey; which circumstance may account for the reluctance of the bears to yield their dominion over the neighborhood.

"The pirogue was drawn up a little below our camp, and secured in a thick copse of willow-bushes. We now began to form a cache or place of deposit, and to dry our goods and other articles which required inspection. The wagons are completed. Our hunters brought us ten deer, and we shot two out of a herd of buffalo that came to water at Sulphur Spring. There is a species of gooseberry, growing abundantly among the rocks on the sides of the cliffs. It is now ripe, of a pale red color, about the size of the common gooseberry, and like it is an ovate pericarp of soft pulp enveloping a number of small whitish seeds, and consisting of a yellowish, slimy, mucilaginous substance, with a sweet taste; the surface of the berry is covered glutinous, adhesive matter, and its fruit, though ripe, retains its withered corolla. The shrub itself seldom rises more than two feet high, is much branched, and has no thorns. The leaves resemble those of the common gooseberry, except in being smaller, and the berry is supported by separate peduncles or foot-stalks half an inch long. There are also immense quantities of grasshoppers, of a brown color, on the plains; they, no doubt, contribute to the lowness of the grass, which is not generally more than three inches high, though it is soft, narrow-leaved, and affords a fine pasture for the buffalo."

Chapter XI — A the Heart of the Continent

Captain Clark continued his observations up the long series of rapids and falls until he came to a group of three small islands to which he gave the name of White Bear Islands, from his having seen numerous white, or grizzly, bears on them. On the nineteenth of June, Captain Clark, after a careful survey of the country on both sides of the stream, decided that the best place for a portage was on the south, or lower, side of the river, the length of the portage being estimated to be about eighteen miles, over which the canoes and supplies must be carried. Next day he proceeded to mark out the exact route of the portage, or carry, by driving stakes along its lines and angles. From the survey and drawing which he made, the party now had a clear and accurate view of the falls, cascades, and rapids of the Missouri; and, it may be added, this draught, which is reproduced on another page of this book, is still so correct in all its measurements that when a Montana manufacturing company undertook to build a dam at Black Eagle Falls, nearly one hundred years afterwards, they discovered that their surveys and those of Captain Clark were precisely alike. The total fall of the river, from the White Bear Islands, as Lewis and Clark called them, to the foot of the Great Falls, is four hundred twelve and five-tenths feet; the sheer drop of the Great Fall is seventy-five and five-tenths feet. The wild, trackless prairie of Lewis and Clark's time is now the site of the thriving town of Great Falls, which has a population of ten thousand.

Here is a lucid and connected account of the falls and rapids, discovered and described by Lewis and Clark:

"This river is three hundred yards wide at the point where it receives the waters of Medicine (Sun) River, which is one hundred and thirty-seven yards in width. The united current continues three hundred and twenty-eight poles to a small rapid on the north side, from which it gradually widens to fourteen hundred yards, and at the distance of five hundred and forty-eight poles reaches the head of the rapids, narrowing as it approaches them. Here the hills on the north, which had withdrawn from the bank, closely border the river, which, for the space of three hundred and twenty poles, makes its way over the rocks, with a descent of thirty feet. In this course the current is contracted to five hundred and eighty yards, and after throwing itself over a small pitch of five feet, forms a beautiful cascade of twenty-six feet five inches; this does not, however, fall immediately or perpendicularly, being stopped by a part of the rock, which projects at about one-third of the distance. After descending this fall, and passing the cottonwood island on which the eagle has fixed her nest, the river goes on for five hundred and thirty-two poles over rapids and little falls, the estimated descent of which is thirteen and one-half feet, till it is joined by a large fountain boiling up underneath the rocks near the edge of the river, into which it falls with a cascade of eight feet. The water of this fountain is of the most perfect clearness, and of rather a bluish cast; and, even after falling into the Missouri, it preserves its color for half a mile. From the fountain the river descends with increased rapidity for the distance of two hundred and fourteen poles, during which the estimated descent is five feet; and from this, for a distance of one hundred and thirty-five poles, it descends fourteen feet seven inches, including a perpendicular fall of six feet seven inches. The Missouri has now become pressed into a space of four hundred and seventy-three yards, and here forms a grand cataract, by falling over a plain rock the whole distance across the river, to the depth of forty-seven feet eight inches. After recovering itself, it then proceeds with an estimated descent of three feet, till, at the distance of one hundred and two poles, it is precipitated down the Crooked Falls nineteen feet perpendicular. Below this, at the mouth of a deep ravine, is a fall of five feet; after which, for the distance of nine hundred and seventy poles, the descent is much more gradual, not being more than ten feet, and then succeeds a handsome level plain for the space of one hundred and seventy-eight poles, with a computed descent of three feet, the river making a bend towards the north. Thence it descends, for four hundred and eighty poles, about eighteen and one-half feet, when it makes a perpendicular fall of two feet, which is ninety poles beyond the great cataract; in approaching which, it descends thirteen feet within two hundred yards, and, gathering strength from its confined channel, which is only two hundred and eighty yards wide, rushes over the fall to the depth of eighty-seven feet.

"After raging among the rocks, and losing itself in foam, it is compressed immediately into a bed of ninety-three yards in width: it continues for three hundred and forty poles to the entrance of a run or deep ravine, where there is a fall of three feet, which, added to the decline during that distance, makes the descent six feet. As it goes on, the descent within the next two hundred and forty poles is only four feet; from this, passing a run or deep ravine, the descent in four hundred poles is thirteen feet; within two hundred and forty poles, another descent of eighteen feet; thence, in one hundred and sixty poles, a descent of six feet; after which, to the mouth of Portage Creek, a distance of two hundred and eighty poles, the descent is ten feet. From this survey and estimate, it results that the river experiences a descent of three hundred and fifty-two feet in the distance of two and three quarter miles, from the commencement of the rapids to the mouth of Portage Creek, exclusive of the almost impassable rapids which extend for a mile below its entrance."

On the twenty-first of the month, all the needed preparations having been finished, the arduous work of making the portage, or carry, was begun. All the members of the expedition were now together, and the two captains divided with their men the labor of hunting, carrying luggage, boat-building, exploring, and so on. They made three camps, the lower one on Portage Creek, the next at Willow Run (see map), and a third at a point opposite White Bear Islands. The portage was not completed until July second. They were often delayed by the breaking down of their rude carriages, and during the last stage of their journey much of their luggage was carried on the backs of the men. They were also very much annoyed with the spines of the prickly pear, a species of cactus, which, growing low on the ground, is certain to be trampled upon by the wayfarer. The spines ran through the moccasins of the men and sorely wounded their feet. Thus, under date of June twenty-fourth, the journal says (It should be understood that the portage was worked from above and below the rapids):—

"On going down yesterday Captain Clark cut off several angles of the former route, so as to shorten the portage considerably, and marked it with stakes. He arrived there in time to have two of the canoes carried up in the high plain, about a mile in advance. Here they all repaired their moccasins, and put on double soles to protect them from the prickly pear, and from the sharp points of earth which have been formed by the trampling of the buffalo during the late rains. This of itself is sufficient to render the portage disagreeable to one who has no burden; but as the men are loaded as heavily as their strength will permit, the crossing is really painful. Some are limping with the soreness of their feet; others are scarcely able to stand for more than a few minutes, from the heat and fatigue. They are all obliged to halt and rest frequently; at almost every stopping-place they fall, and many of them are asleep in an instant; yet no one complains, and they go on with great cheerfulness. At the camp, midway in the portage, Drewyer and Fields joined them; for, while Captain Lewis was looking for them at Medicine River, they returned to report the absence of Shannon, about whom they had been very uneasy. They had killed several buffalo at the bend of the Missouri above the falls, dried about eight hundred pounds of meat, and got one hundred pounds of tallow; they had also killed some deer, but had seen no elk."

Under this date, too, Captain Lewis, who was with another branch of the expedition, makes this note: "Such as were able to shake a foot amused themselves in dancing on the green to the music of the violin which Cruzatte plays extremely well."

The journal continues:—

"We were now occupied (at White Bear camp) in fitting up a boat of skins, the frame of which had been prepared for the purpose at Harper's Ferry in Virginia. It was made of iron, thirty-six feet long, four and one-half feet in the beam, and twenty-six inches wide in the bottom. Two men had been sent this morning for timber to complete it, but they could find scarcely any even tolerably straight sticks four and one-half feet long; and as the cottonwood is too soft and brittle, we were obliged to use willow and box-elder."

On the twenty-seventh, the main party, which was working on the upper part of the portage, joined that of Captain Clark at the lower camp, where a second cache, or place of deposit, had been formed, and where the boat-swivel was now hidden under the rocks. The journal says:—

"The party were employed in preparing timber for the boat, except two who were sent to hunt. About one in the afternoon a cloud arose from the southwest, and brought with it violent thunder, lightning, and hail. Soon after it passed, the hunters came in, from about four miles above us. They had killed nine elk and three bears. As they were hunting on the river they saw a low ground covered with thick brushwood, where from the tracks along shore they thought a bear had probably taken refuge. They therefore landed, without making a noise, and climbed a tree about twenty feet above the ground. Having fixed themselves securely, they raised a loud shout, and a bear instantly rushed toward them. These animals never climb, and therefore when he came to the tree and stopped to look at them, Drewyer shot him in the head. He proved to be the largest we had yet seen; his nose appeared to be like that of a common ox; his fore feet measured nine inches across; the hind feet were seven inches wide and eleven and three quarters long, exclusive of the talons. One of these animals came within thirty yards of the camp last night, and carried off some buffalo-meat which we had placed on a pole."

The party were very much annoyed here by the grizzlies which infested their camp at night. Their faithful dog always gave warning of the approach of one of these monsters; but the men were obliged to sleep with their guns by their side, ready to repel the enemy at a moment's notice.

Captain Clark finally broke up the camp on Portage Creek, June 28, having deposited in his cache whatever could be left behind without inconvenience. "On the following day," the journal says:—

"Finding it impossible to reach the upper end of the portage with the present load, in consequence of the state of the road after the rain, he sent back nearly all his party to bring on the articles which had been left yesterday. Having lost some notes and remarks which he had made on first ascending the river, he determined to go up to the Whitebear Islands along its banks, in order to supply the deficiency. He there left one man to guard the baggage, and went on to the falls, accompanied by his servant York, Chaboneau, and his wife with her young child.

"On his arrival there he observed a very dark cloud rising in the west, which threatened rain, and looked around for some shelter; but could find no place where the party would be secure from being blown into the river, if the wind should prove as violent as it sometimes does in the plains. At length, about a quarter of a mile above the falls, he found a deep ravine, where there were some shelving rocks, under which he took refuge. They were on the upper side of the ravine near the river, perfectly safe from the rain, and therefore laid down their guns, compass, and other articles which they carried with them. The shower was at first moderate; it then increased to a heavy rain, the effects of which they did not feel; but soon after, a torrent of rain and hail descended. The rain seemed to fall in a solid mass, and instantly, collecting in the ravine, came rolling down in a dreadful current, carrying the mud, rocks, and everything that opposed it. Captain Clark fortunately saw it a moment before it reached them, and springing up with his gun and shot-pouch in his left hand, with his right clambered up the steep bluff, pushing on the Indian woman with her child in her arms; her husband too had seized her hand and was pulling her tip the hill, but he was so terrified at the danger that he remained frequently motionless; and but for Captain Clark, himself and his wife and child would have been lost. So instantaneous was the rise of the water that, before Captain Clark had reached his gun and begun to ascend the bank, the water was up to his waist, and he could scarcely get up faster than it rose, till it reached the height of fifteen feet, with a furious current which, had they waited a moment longer, would have swept them into the river just above the Great Falls, down which they must inevitably have been precipitated. They reached the plain in safety and found York, who had separated from them just before the storm to hunt some buffalo, and was now returning to find his master. They had been obliged to escape so rapidly that Captain Clark lost his compass (that is, circumferentor) and umbrella, Chaboneau left his gun, with Captain Lewis' wiping-rod, shot-pouch, and tomahawk, and the Indian woman had just time to grasp her child, before the net in which it lay at her feet was carried down the current."

Such a storm is known in the West as a cloud-burst. Overland emigrants in the early rush to California often suffered loss from these sudden deluges. A party of men, with wagons and animals, have been known to be swept away and lost in a flood bursting in a narrow canyon in the mountains.

"Captain Clark now relinquished his intention of going up the river, and returned to the camp at Willow Run. Here he found that the party sent this morning for the baggage had all returned to camp in great confusion, leaving their loads in the plain. On account of the heat, they generally go nearly naked, and with no covering on their heads. The hail was so large, and driven so furiously against them by the high wind, that it knocked several of them down: one of them, particularly, was thrown on the ground three times, and most of them were bleeding freely, and complained of being much bruised. Willow Run had risen six feet since the rain; and, as the plains were so wet that they could not proceed, they passed the night at their camp.

"At the White Bear camp, also," (says Lewis), "we had not been insensible to the hailstorm, though less exposed. In the morning there had been a heavy shower of rain, after which it became fair. After assigning to the men their respective employments, Captain Lewis took one of them, and went to see the large fountain near the falls. . . . It is, perhaps, the largest in America, and is situated in a pleasant level plain, about twenty-five yards from the river, into which it falls over some steep, irregular rocks, with a sudden ascent of about six feet in one part of its course. The water boils up from among the rocks, and with such force near the centre that the surface seems higher there than the earth on the sides of the fountain, which is a handsome turf of fine green grass. The water is extremely pure, cold, and pleasant to the taste, not being impregnated with lime or any foreign substance. It is perfectly transparent, and continues its bluish cast for half a mile down the Missouri, notwithstanding the rapidity of the river. After examining it for some time, Captain Lewis returned to the camp. . . ."

"Two men were sent (June 30) to the falls to look for the articles lost yesterday; but they found nothing but the compass, covered with mud and sand, at the mouth of the ravine. The place at which Captain Clark had been caught by the storm was filled with large rocks. The men complain much of the bruises received yesterday from the hail. A more than usual number of buffalo appeared about the camp to-day, and furnished plenty of meat. Captain Clark thought that at one view he must have seen at least ten thousand."

Of the party at the upper camp, opposite White Bear Islands, the journal makes this observation:—

"The party continues to be occupied with the boat, the cross-bars for which are now finished, and there remain only the strips to complete the woodwork. The skins necessary to cover it have already been prepared; they amount to twenty-eight elk-skins and four buffalo-skins. Among our game were two beaver, which we have had occasion to observe are found wherever there is timber. We also killed a large bull-bat or goatsucker, of which there are many in this neighborhood, resembling in every respect those of the same species in the United States. We have not seen the leather-winged bat for some time, nor are there any of the small goatsucker in this part of the Missouri. We have not seen that species of goatsucker called the whippoorwill, which is commonly confounded in the United States with the large goatsucker which we observe here. This last prepares no nest, but lays its eggs on the open plains; they generally begin to sit on two eggs, and we believe raise only one brood in a season; at the present moment they are just hatching their young."

Dr. Coues says that we should bear in mind that this was written "when bats were birds and whales were fishes for most persons." The journal confounds bats, which are winged mammals, with goatsuckers, or whippoorwills, which are birds.

The second of July was an interesting date for the explorers. On that day we find the following entry in their journal:—

"A shower of rain fell very early this morning. We then despatched some men for the baggage left behind yesterday, and the rest were engaged in putting the boat together. This was accomplished in about three hours, and then we began to sew on the leather over the crossbars of iron on the inner side of the boat which form the ends of the sections. By two o'clock the last of the baggage arrived, to the great delight of the party, who were anxious to proceed. The mosquitoes we find very troublesome.

"Having completed our celestial observations, we went over to the large island to make an attack upon its inhabitants, the bears, which have annoyed us very much of late, and were prowling about our camp all last night. We found that the part of the island frequented by the bears forms an almost impenetrable thicket of the broad-leaved willow. Into this we forced our way in parties of three; but could see only one bear, which instantly attacked Drewyer. Fortunately, as he was rushing on, the hunter shot him through the heart within twenty paces and he fell, which enabled Drewyer to get out of his way. We then followed him one hundred yards, and found that the wound had been mortal.

"Not being able to discover any more of these animals, we returned to camp. Here, in turning over some of the baggage, we caught a rat somewhat larger than the common European rat, and of a lighter color; the body and outer parts of the legs and head of a light lead color; the inner side of the legs, as well as the belly, feet, and ears, white; the ears are not covered with hair, and are much larger than those of the common rat; the toes also are longer; the eyes are black and prominent, the whiskers very long and full; the tail is rather longer than the body, and covered with fine fur and hair of the same size with that on the back, which is very close, short, and silky in its texture. This was the first we had met, although its nests are very frequent in the cliffs of rocks and hollow trees, where we also found large quantities of the shells and seed of the prickly-pear."

The queer rat discovered by Lewis and Clark was then unknown to science. It is now known in the Far West as the pack-rat. It lives in holes and crevices of the rocks, and it subsists on the shells and seeds of the prickly pear, which is usually abundant in the hunting grounds of the little animal. The explorers were now constantly in full view of the Rocky Mountain, on which, however, their present title had not then been conferred. Under date of July 2, the journal says:—

"The mosquitoes are uncommonly troublesome. The wind was again high from the southwest. These winds are in fact always the coldest and most violent which we experience, and the hypothesis which we have formed on that subject is, that the air, coming in contact with the Snowy Mountains, immediately becomes chilled and condensed, and being thus rendered heavier than the air below, it descends into the rarefied air below, or into the vacuum formed by the constant action of the sun on the open unsheltered plains. The clouds rise suddenly near these mountains, and distribute their contents partially over the neighboring plains. The same cloud will discharge hail alone in one part, hail and rain in another, and rain only in a third, all within the space of a few miles; while at the same time there is snow falling on the mountains to the southeast of us. There is at present no snow on those mountains; that which covered them on our arrival, as well as that which has since fallen, having disappeared. The mountains to the north and northwest of us are still entirely covered with snow; indeed, there has been no perceptible diminution of it since we first saw them, which induces a belief either that the clouds prevailing at this season do not reach their summits or that they deposit their snow only. They glisten with great beauty when the sun shines on them in a particular direction, and most probably from this glittering appearance have derived the name of the Shining Mountains."

A mysterious noise, heard by the party, here engaged their attention, as it did years afterwards the attention of other explorers. The journal says:—

"Since our arrival at the falls we have repeatedly heard a strange noise coming from the mountains in a direction a little to the north of west. It is heard at different periods of the day and night (sometimes when the air is perfectly still and without a cloud), and consists of one stroke only, or of five or six discharges in quick succession. It is loud, and resembles precisely the sound of a six-pound piece of ordnance at the distance of three miles. The Minnetarees frequently mentioned this noise, like thunder, which they said the mountains made; but we had paid no attention to it, believing it to have been some superstition, or perhaps a falsehood. The watermen also of the party say that the Pawnees and Ricaras give the same account of a noise heard in the Black Mountains to the westward of them. The solution of the mystery given by the philosophy of the watermen is, that it is occasioned by the bursting of the rich mines of silver confined within the bosom of the mountains.''

Of these strange noises there are many explanations, the most plausible being that they are caused by the explosion of the species of stone known as the geode, fragments of which are frequently found among the mountains. The geode has a hollow cell within, lined with beautiful crystals of many colors.

Independence Day, 1805, was celebrated with becoming patriotism and cheerfulness by these far-wandering adventurers. Their record says:—

"An elk and a beaver are all that were killed to-day; the buffalo seem to have withdrawn from our neighborhood, though several of the men, who went to-day to visit the falls for the first time, mention that they are still abundant at that place. We contrived, however, to spread not a very sumptuous but a comfortable table in honor of the day, and in the evening gave the men a drink of spirits, which was the last of our stock. Some of them appeared sensible to the effects of even so small a quantity; and as is usual among them on all festivals, the fiddle was produced and a dance begun, which lasted till nine o'clock, when it was interrupted by a heavy shower of rain. They continued their merriment, however, till a late hour.''

Their bill-of-fare, according to Captain Lewis, was bacon, beans, suet dumplings, and buffalo meat, which, he says, "gave them no just cause to covet the sumptuous feasts of our countrymen on this day.'' More than a year passed before they again saw and tasted spirits.

Great expectations were entertained of the boat that was built here on the iron frame brought all the way from Harper's Ferry, Virginia. The frame was covered with dressed skins of buffalo and elk, the seams being coated with a composition of powdered charcoal and beeswax, in default of tar or pitch. This craft was well named the "Experiment,'' and a disappointing experiment it proved to be. Here is Captain Lewis' account of her failure:

"The boat having now become sufficiently dry, we gave her a coat of the composition, which after a proper interval was repeated, and the next morning, Tuesday, July 9th, she was launched into the water, and swam perfectly well. The seats were then fixed and the oars fitted; but after we had loaded her, as well as the canoes, and were on the point of setting out, a violent wind caused the waves to wet the baggage, so that we were forced to unload the boats. The wind continued high until evening, when to our great disappointment we discovered that nearly all the composition had separated from the skins and left the seams perfectly exposed; so that the boat now leaked very much. To repair this misfortune without pitch is impossible, and as none of that article is to be procured, we therefore, however reluctantly, are obliged to abandon her, after having had so much labor in the construction. We now saw that the section of the boat covered with buffalo-skins on which hair had been left answered better than the elk-skins, and leaked but little; while that part which was covered with hair about one-eighth of an inch retained the composition perfectly, and remained sound and dry. From this we perceived that had we employed buffalo instead of elk skins, not singed them so closely as we did, and carefully avoided cutting the leather in sewing, the boat would have been sufficient even with the present composition; or had we singed instead of shaving the elk-skins, we might have succeeded. But we discovered our error too late; the buffalo had deserted us, and the travelling season was so fast advancing that we had no time to spare for experiments; therefore, finding that she could be no longer useful, she was sunk in the water, so as to soften the skins, and enable us the more easily to take her to pieces.

"It now became necessary to provide other means for transporting the baggage which we had intended to stow in her. For this purpose we shall want two more canoes; but for many miles— from below the mouth of the Musselshell River to this place—we have not seen a single tree fit to be used in that way. The hunters, however, who have hitherto been sent after timber, mention that there is a low ground on the opposite side of the river, about eight miles above us by land, and more than twice that distance by water, in which we may probably find trees large enough for our purposes. Captain Clark determined, therefore, to set out by land for that place with ten of the best workmen, who would be occupied in building the canoes till the rest of the party, after taking the boat to pieces, and making the necessary deposits, should transport the baggage, and join them with the other six canoes.

"He accordingly passed over to the opposite side of the river with his party next day, and proceeded on eight miles by land, the distance by water being twenty-three and three quarter miles. Here he found two cottonwood trees; but, on cutting them down, one proved to be hollow, split at the top in falling, and both were much damaged at the bottom. He searched the neighborhood, but could find none which would suit better, and therefore was obliged to make use of those which he had felled, shortening them in order to avoid the cracks, and supplying the deficiency by making them as wide as possible. They were equally at a loss for wood of which they might make handles for their axes, the eyes of which not being round, they were obliged to split the timber in such a manner that thirteen of the handles broke in the course of the day, though made of the best wood they could find for the purpose, which was the chokecherry.

"The rest of the party took the frame of the boat to pieces, deposited it in a cache or hole, with a draught of the country from Fort Mandan to this place, and also some other papers and small articles of less importance."

High winds prevented the party from making rapid progress, and notwithstanding the winds they were greatly troubled with mosquitoes. Lest the reader should think the explorers too sensitive on the subject of these troublesome pests, it should be said that only western travellers can realize the numbers and venom of the mosquitoes of that region. Early emigrants across the continent were so afflicted by these insects that the air at times seemed full of gray clouds of them. It was the custom of the wayfarers to build a "smudge," as it was called, a low, smouldering fire of green boughs and brush, the dense smoke from which (almost as annoying as the mosquitoes) would drive off their persecutors as long, as the victims sat in the smoke. The sleeping tent was usually cleared in this way before "turning in" at night, every opening of the canvas being afterwards closed.

Captain Lewis, on the thirteenth of July, followed Captain Clark up the river; crossing the stream to the north bank, with his six canoes and all his baggage, he overtook the other party on the same day and found them all engaged in boat-building.

"On his way he passed a very large Indian lodge, which was probably designed as a great council-house; but it differed in its construction from all that we had seen, lower down the Missouri or elsewhere. The form of it was a circle two hundred and sixteen feet in circumference at the base; it was composed of sixteen large cottonwood poles about fifty feet long and at their thicker ends, which touched the ground, about the size of a man's body. They were distributed at equal distances, except that one was omitted to the cast, probably for the entrance. From the circumference of this circle the poles converged toward the centre, where they were united and secured by large withes of willow-brush. There was no covering over this fabric, in the centre of which were the remains of a large fire, and around it the marks of about eighty leathern lodges. He also saw a number of turtle-doves, and some pigeons, of which he shot one, differing in no respect from the wild pigeon of the United States. . . ."

"The buffalo have not yet quite gone, for the hunters brought in three, in very good order. It requires some diligence to supply us plentifully, for as we reserve our parched meal for the Rocky Mountains, where we do not expect to find much game, our principal article of food is meat, and the consumption of the whole thirty-two persons belonging to the party amounts to four deer, an elk and a deer, or one buffalo, every twenty-four hours. The mosquitoes and gnats persecute us as violently as below, so that we can get no sleep unless defended by biers (nets), with which we are all provided. We here found several plants hitherto unknown to us, of which we preserved specimens."

On the fourteenth of July, the boats were finally launched, and next day the journal records this important event:

"We rose early, embarked all our baggage on board the canoes, which, though eight in number, are heavily loaded, and at ten o'clock set out on our journey. . . . At the distance of seven and a half miles we came to the lower point of a woodland, at the entrance of a beautiful river, which, in honor of the Secretary of the Navy, we called Smith's River. This stream falls into a bend on the south side of the Missouri, and is eighty yards wide. As far as we could discern its course, it wound through a charming valley towards the southeast, in which many herds of buffalo were feeding, till, at the distance of twenty-five miles, it entered the Rocky Mountains and was lost from our view. . . .

"We find the prickly pear, one of the greatest beauties as well as greatest inconveniences of the plains, now in full bloom. The sunflower, too, a plant common on every part of the Missouri from its entrance to this place, is here very abundant, and in bloom. The lamb's-quarter, wild cucumber, sand-rush, and narrow dock, are also common."

The journal here records the fact that the great river had now become so crooked that it was expedient to note only its general course, leaving out all description of its turns and windings. The Missouri was now flowing due north, leaving its bends out of account, and the explorers, ascending the river, were therefore travelling south; and although the journal sets forth "the north bank" and "the south bank," it should be understood that west is meant by the one, and east by the other. Buffalo were observed in great numbers. Many obstacles to navigating the river were encountered. Under date of July 17, the journal says:

"The navigation is now very laborious. The river is deep, but with little current, and from seventy to one hundred yards wide; the low grounds are very narrow, with but little timber, and that chiefly the aspen tree. The cliffs are steep, and hang over the river so much that often we could not cross them, but were obliged to pass and repass from one side of the river to the other, in order to make our way. In some places the banks are formed of dark or black granite rising perpendicularly to a great height, through which the river seems, in the progress of time, to have worn its channel. On these mountains we see more pine than usual, but it is still in small quantities. Along the bottoms, which have a covering of high grass, we observed the sunflower blooming in great abundance. The Indians of the Missouri, more especially those who do not cultivate maize, make great use of the seed of this plant for bread, or in thickening their soup. They first parch and then pound it between two stones, until it is reduced to a fine meal. Sometimes they add a portion of water, and drink it thus diluted; at other times they add a sufficient proportion of marrow-grease to reduce it to the consistency of common dough, and eat it in that manner. This last composition we preferred to all the rest, and thought it at that time a very palatable dish."

They also feasted on a great variety of wild berries, purple, yellow, and black currants, which were delicious and more pleasant to the palate than those grown in their Virginia home-gardens; also service-berries, popularly known to later emigrants as "sarvice-berries." These grow on small bushes, two or three feet high; and the fruit is purple-skinned, with a white pulp, resembling a ripe gooseberry.

The journal, next day, has the following entry:—

"This morning early, before our departure, we saw a large herd of the big-horned animals, which were bounding among the rocks on the opposite cliff with great agility. These inaccessible spots secure them from all their enemies, and their only danger is in wandering among these precipices, where we would suppose it scarcely possible for any animal to stand; a single false step would precipitate them at least five hundred feet into the water.

"At one and one fourth miles we passed another single cliff on the left; at the same distance beyond which is the mouth of a large river emptying from the north. It is a handsome, bold, and clear stream, eighty yards wide—that is, nearly as broad as the Missouri—with a rapid current, over a bed of small smooth stones of various figures. The water is extremely transparent; the low grounds are narrow, but possess as much wood as those of the Missouri. The river has every appearance of being navigable, though to what distance we cannot ascertain, as the country which it waters is broken and mountainous. In honor of the Secretary of War we called it Dearborn's River."

General Henry Dearborn, who was then Secretary of War, in Jefferson's administration, gave his name, a few years later, to a collection of camps and log-cabins on Lake Michigan; and in due time Fort Dearborn became the great city of Chicago. Continuing, the journal says:

"Being now very anxious to meet with the Shoshonees or Snake Indians, for the purpose of obtaining the necessary information of our route, as well as to procure horses, it was thought best for one of us to go forward with a small party and endeavor to discover them, before the daily discharge of our guns, which is necessary for our subsistence, should give them notice of our approach. If by an accident they hear us, they will most probably retreat to the mountains, mistaking us for their enemies, who usually attack them on this side." . . . .

Captain Clark was now in the lead with a small party, and he came upon the remains of several Indian camps formed of willow-brush, Traces of Indians became more plentiful. The journal adds:—

"At the same time Captain Clark observed that the pine trees had been stripped of their bark about the same season, which our Indian woman says her countrymen do in order to obtain the sap and the soft parts of the wood and bark for food. About eleven o'clock he met a herd of elk and killed two of them; but such was the want of wood in the neighborhood that he was unable to procure enough to make a fire, and was therefore obliged to substitute the dung of the buffalo, with which he cooked his breakfast. They then resumed their course along an old Indian road. In the afternoon they reached a handsome valley, watered by a large creek, both of which extended a considerable distance into the mountain. This they crossed, and during the evening travelled over a mountainous country covered with sharp fragments of flint rock; these bruised and cut their feet very much, but were scarcely less troublesome than the prickly-pear of the open plains, which have now become so abundant that it is impossible to avoid them, and the thorns are so strong that they pierce a double sole of dressed deer-skin; the best resource against them is a sole of buffalo-hide in parchment (that is, hard dried). At night they reached the river much fatigued, having passed two mountains in the course of the day, and travelled thirty miles. Captain Clark's first employment, on lighting a fire, was to extract from his feet the thorns, which he found seventeen in number."

The dung of the buffalo, exposed for many years to the action of sun, wind, and rain, became as dry and firm as the finest compressed hay. As "buffalo chips," in these treeless regions, it was the overland emigrants' sole dependence for fuel.

The explorers now approached a wonderful pass in the Rocky Mountains which their journal thus describes:

"A mile and a half beyond this creek (Cottonwood Creek) the rocks approach the river on both sides, forming a most sublime and extraordinary spectacle. For five and three quarter miles these rocks rise perpendicularly from the water's edge to the height of nearly twelve hundred feet. They are composed of a black granite near their base, but from the lighter color above, and from the fragments, we suppose the upper part to be flint of a yellowish brown and cream color.

"Nothing can be imagined more tremendous than the frowning darkness of these rocks, which project over the river and menace us with destruction. The river, one hundred and fifty yards in width, seems to have forced its channel down this solid mass; but so reluctantly has it given way, that during the whole distance the water is very deep even at the edges, and for the first three miles there is not a spot, except one of a few yards, in which a man could stand between the water and the towering perpendicular of the mountain. The convulsion of the passage must have been terrible, since at its outlet there are vast columns of rock torn from the mountain, which are strewed on both sides of the river, the trophies, as it were, of its victory. Several fine springs burst out from the chasms of the rock, and contribute to increase the river, which has a strong current, but, very fortunately, we were able to overcome it with our oars, since it would have been impossible to use either the cord or the pole. We were obliged to go on some time after dark, not being able to find a spot large enough to encamp on; but at length, about two miles above a small island in the middle of the river, we met with a place on the left side, where we procured plenty of light wood and pitch pine. This extraordinary range of rocks we called the Gates of the Rocky Mountains."

Some of Captain Clark's men, engaged in hunting, gave the alarm to roving bands of Shoshonee Indians, hunting in that vicinity. The noise of their guns attracted the attention of the Indians, who, having set fire to the grass as a warning to their comrades, fled to the mountains. The whole country soon appeared to have taken fright, and great clouds of smoke were observed in all directions. Falling into an old Indian trail, Captain Clark waited, with his weary and footsore men, for the rest of the party to come up with them.

The explorers had now passed south, between the Big Belt range of mountains on the cast and the main chain of the Rocky Mountains on the west. Meagher County, Montana, now lies on the cast of their trail, and on the west side of that route is the county of Lewis and Clark. They were now—still travelling southward—approaching the ultimate sources of the great Missouri. The journal says:—

"We are delighted to find that the Indian woman recognizes the country; she tells us that to this creek her countrymen make excursions to procure white paint on its banks, and we therefore call it Whiteearth Creek. She says also that the Three Forks of the Missouri are at no great distance—a piece of intelligence which has cheered the spirits of us all, as we hope soon to reach the head of that river. This is the warmest day, except one, we have experienced this summer. In the shade the mercury stood at eighty degrees, which is the second time it has reached that height during this season. We camped on an island, after making nineteen and three quarters miles.

"In the course of the day we saw many geese, cranes, small birds common to the plains, and a few pheasants. We also observed a small plover or curlew of a brown color, about the size of a yellow-legged plover or jack-curlew, but of a different species. It first appeared near the mouth of Smith's River, but is so shy and vigilant that we were unable to shoot it. Both the broad and narrow-leaved willow continue, though the sweet willow has become very scarce. The rosebush, small honeysuckle, pulpy-leaved thorn, southernwood, sage, box-elder, narrow-leaved cottonwood, redwood, and a species of sumach, are all abundant. So, too, are the red and black gooseberries, service-berry, choke-cherry, and the black, yellow, red, and purple currants, which last seems to be a favorite food of the bear. Before camping we landed and took on board Captain Clark, with the meat he had collected during this day's hunt, which consisted of one deer and an elk; we had, ourselves, shot a deer and an antelope."

The party found quantities of wild onions of good flavor and size. They also observed wild flax, garlic, and other vegetable products of value. The journal adds:—

"We saw many otter and beaver to-day (July 24th). The latter seem to contribute very much to the number of islands, and the widening of the river. They begin by damming up the small channels of about twenty yards between the islands: this obliges the river to seek another outlet, and, as soon as this is effected, the channel stopped by the beaver becomes filled with mud and sand. The industrious animal is then driven to another channel, which soon shares the same fate, till the river spreads on all sides, and cuts the projecting points of the land into islands. We killed a deer, and saw great numbers of antelopes, cranes, some geese, and a few red-headed ducks. The small birds of the plains and the curlew are still abundant: we saw a large bear, but could not come within gunshot of him. There are numerous tracks of the elk, but none of the animals themselves; and, from the appearance of bones and old excrement, we suppose that buffalo sometimes stray into the valley, though we have as yet seen no recent sign of them. Along the water are a number of snakes, some of a uniform brown color, others black, and a third speckled on the abdomen, and striped with black and a brownish yellow on the back and sides. The first, which is the largest, is about four feet long; the second is of the kind mentioned yesterday; and the third resembles in size and appearance the garter-snake of the United States. On examining the teeth of all these several kinds, we found them free from poison: they are fond of the water, in which they take shelter on being pursued. The mosquitoes, gnats, and prickly pear, our three persecutors, still continue with us, and, joined with the labor of working the canoes, have fatigued us all excessively."

On Thursday, July 25, Captain Clark, who was in the lead, as usual, arrived at the famous Three Forks of the Missouri. The stream flowing in a generally northeastern direction was the true, or principal Missouri, and was named the Jefferson. The middle branch was named the Madison, in honor of James Madison, then Secretary of State, and the fork next to the eastward received the name of Albert Gallatin, then Secretary of the Treasury; and by these titles the streams are known to this day. The explorers had now passed down to their furthest southern limit, their trail being to the eastward of the modern cities of Helena and Butte, and separated only by a narrow divide (then unknown to them) from the sources of some of the streams that fall into the Pacific Ocean. Under the date of July 27, the journal says:—

"We are now very anxious to see the Snake Indians. After advancing for several hundred miles into this wild and mountainous country, we may soon expect that the game will abandon us. With no information of the route, we may be unable to find a passage across the mountains when we reach the head of the river—at least, such a pass as will lead us to the Columbia. Even are we so fortunate as to find a branch of that river, the timber which we have hitherto seen in these mountains does not promise us any fit to make canoes, so that our chief dependence is on meeting some tribe from whom we may procure horses. Our consolation is that this southwest branch can scarcely head with any other river than the Columbia; and that if any nation of Indians can live in the mountains we are able to endure as much as they can, and have even better means of procuring subsistence."

Chapter XII — At the Sources of the Missouri

The explorers were now (in the last days of July, 1805) at the head of the principal sources of the great Missouri River, in the fastnesses of the Rocky Mountains, at the base of the narrow divide that separates Idaho from Montana in its southern corner. Just across this divide are the springs that feed streams falling into the majestic Columbia and then to the Pacific Ocean. As has been already set forth, they named the Three Forks for President Jefferson and members of his cabinet. These names still survive, although Jefferson River is the true Missouri and not a fork of that stream. Upon the forks of the Jefferson Lewis bestowed the titles of Philosophy, Wisdom, and Philanthropy, each of these gifts and graces being, in his opinion, "an attribute of that illustrious personage, Thomas Jefferson," then President of the United States. But alas for the fleeting greatness of geographical honor! Philosophy River is now known as Willow Creek, and at its mouth, a busy little railroad town, is Willow City. The northwest fork is no longer Wisdom, but Big Hole River; deep valleys among the mountains are known as holes; and the stream called by that name, once Wisdom, is followed along its crooked course by a railroad that connects Dillon, Silver Bow, and Butte City, Montana. Vulgarity does its worst for Philanthropy; its modern name on the map is Stinking Water.

On the thirtieth of July, the party, having camped long enough to unpack and dry their goods, dress their deerskins and make them into leggings and moccasins, reloaded their canoes and began the toilsome ascent of the Jefferson. The journal makes this record:—

"Sacajawea, our Indian woman, informs us that we are encamped on the precise spot where her countrymen, the Snake Indians, had their huts five years ago, when the Minnetarees of Knife River first came in sight of them, and from whom they hastily retreated three miles up the Jefferson, and concealed themselves in the woods. The Minnetarees, however, pursued and attacked them, killed four men, as many women, and a number of boys; and made prisoners of four other boys and all the females, of whom Sacajawea was one. She does not, however, show any distress at these recollections, nor any joy at the prospect of being restored to her country; for she seems to possess the folly, or the philosophy, of not suffering her feelings to extend beyond the anxiety of having plenty to eat and a few trinkets to wear.

"This morning the hunters brought in some fat deer of the long-tailed red kind, which are quite as large as those of the United States, and are, indeed, the only kind we have found at this place. There are numbers of the sand-hill cranes feeding in the meadows: we caught a young one of the same color as the red deer, which, though it had nearly attained its full growth, could not fly; it is very fierce, and strikes a severe blow with its beak. . . .

"Captain Lewis proceeded after dinner through an extensive low ground of timber and meadow-land intermixed; but the bayous were so obstructed by beaver-dams that, in order to avoid them, he directed his course toward the high plain on the right. This he gained with some difficulty, after wading up to his waist through the mud and water of a number of beaver-dams. When he desired to rejoin the canoes he found the underbrush so thick, and the river so crooked, that this, joined to the difficulty of passing the beaver-dams, induced him to go on and endeavor to intercept the river at some point where it might be more collected into one channel, and approach nearer the high plain. He arrived at the bank about sunset, having gone only six miles in a direct course from the canoes; but he saw no traces of the men, nor did he receive any answer to his shouts and the firing of his gun. It was now nearly dark; a duck lighted near him, and he shot it. He then went on the head of a small island, where he found some driftwood, which enabled him to cook his duck for supper, and laid down to sleep on some willow-brush. The night was cool, but the driftwood gave him a good fire, and he suffered no inconvenience, except from the mosquitoes."

The easy indifference to discomfort with which these well-seasoned pioneers took their hardships must needs impress the reader. It was a common thing for men, or for a solitary man, to be caught out of camp by nightfall and compelled to bivouac, like Captain Lewis, in the underbrush, or the prairie-grass. As they pressed on, game began to fail them. Under date of July 31, they remark that the only game seen that day was one bighorn, a few antelopes, deer, and a brown bear, all of which escaped them. "Nothing was killed to-day," it is recorded, "nor have we had any fresh meat except one beaver for the last two days; so that we are now reduced to an unusual situation, for we have hitherto always had a great abundance of flesh." Indeed, one reason for this is found in Captain Lewis's remark: "When we have plenty of fresh meat, I find it impossible to make the men take any care of it, or use it with the least frugality, though I expect that necessity will shortly teach them this art." We shall see, later on, that the men, who were really as improvident of food as the Indians, had hard lessons from necessity.

Anxious to reach the Indians, who were believed to be somewhere ahead of them, Captain Lewis and three men went on up the Jefferson, Captain Clark and his party following with the canoes and luggage in a more leisurely manner. The advance party were so fortunate as to overtake a herd of elk, two of which they killed; what they did not eat they left secured for the other party with the canoes. Clark's men also had good luck in hunting, for they killed five deer and one bighorn. Neither party found fresh tracks of Indians, and they were greatly discouraged thereat. The journal speaks of a beautiful valley, from six to eight miles wide, where they saw ancient traces of buffalo occupation, but no buffalo. These animals had now completely disappeared; they were seldom seen in those mountains. The journal says of Lewis:—

"He saw an abundance of deer and antelope, and many tracks of elk and bear. Having killed two deer, they feasted sumptuously, with a dessert of currants of different colors—two species red, others yellow, deep purple, and black; to these were added black gooseberries and deep purple service-berries, somewhat larger than ours, from which they differ also in color, size, and the superior excellence of their flavor. In the low grounds of the river were many beaver-dams formed of willow-brush, mud, and gravel, so closely interwoven that they resist the water perfectly; some of them were five feet high, and caused the river to overflow several acres of land."

Meanwhile, the party with the canoes were having a fatiguing time as they toiled up the river. On the fourth of August, after they had made only fifteen miles, the journal has this entry:—

"The river is still rapid, and the water, though clear, is very much obstructed by shoals or ripples at every two hundred or three hundred yards. At all these places we are obliged to drag the canoes over the stones, as there is not a sufficient depth of water to float them, and in the other parts the current obliges us to have recourse to the cord. But as the brushwood on the banks will not permit us to walk on shore, we are under the necessity of wading through the river as we drag the boats. This soon makes our feet tender, and sometimes occasions severe falls over the slippery stones; and the men, by being constantly wet, are becoming more feeble. In the course of the day the hunters killed two deer, some geese and ducks, and the party saw some antelopes, cranes, beaver, and otter."

Captain Lewis had left a note for Captain Clark at the forks of the Jefferson and Wisdom rivers. Clark's journal says:—

"We arrived at the forks about four o'clock, but, unluckily, Captain Lewis's note had been attached to a green pole, which the beaver had cut down, and carried off with the note on it: an accident which deprived us of all information as to the character of the two branches of the river. Observing, therefore, that the northwest fork was most in our direction, we ascended it. We found it extremely rapid, and its waters were scattered in such a manner that for a quarter of a mile we were forced to cut a passage through the willow-brush that leaned over the little channels and united at the top. After going up it for a mile, we encamped on an island which had been overflowed, and was still so wet that we were compelled to make beds of brush to keep ourselves out of the mud. Our provision consisted of two deer which had been killed in the morning."

It should be borne in mind that this river, up which the party were making their way, was the Wisdom (now Big Hole), and was the northwest fork of the Jefferson, flowing from southeast to northwest; and near the point where it enters the Jefferson, it has a loop toward the northeast; that is to say, it comes from the southwest to a person looking up its mouth.

After going up the Wisdom River, Clark's party were overtaken by Drewyer, Lewis's hunter, who had been sent across between the forks to notify Clark that Lewis regarded the other fork—the main Jefferson—as the right course to take. The party, accordingly, turned about and began to descend the stream, in order to ascend the Jefferson. The journal says:—

"On going down, one of the canoes upset and two others filled with water, by which all the baggage was wet and several articles were irrecoverably lost. As one of them swung round in a rapid current, Whitehouse was thrown out of her; while down, the canoe passed over him, and had the water been two inches shallower would have crushed him to pieces; but he escaped with a severe bruise of his leg. In order to repair these misfortunes we hastened (down) to the forks, where we were joined by Captain Lewis. We then passed over to the left (east) side, opposite the entrance of the rapid fork, and camped on a large gravelly bar, near which there was plenty of wood. Here we opened, and exposed to dry, all the articles which had suffered from the water; none of them were completely spoiled except a small keg of powder; the rest of the powder, which was distributed in the different canoes, was quite safe, although it had been under the water for upward of an hour. The air is indeed so pure and dry that any wood-work immediately shrinks, unless it is kept filled with water; but we had placed our powder in small canisters of lead, each containing powder enough for the canister when melted into bullets, and secured with cork and wax, which answered our purpose perfectly. . . . ."

"In the evening we killed three deer and four elk, which furnished us once more with a plentiful supply of meat. Shannon, the same man who had been lost for fifteen days (August 28 to Sept. 11, 1804), was sent out this morning to hunt, up the northwest fork. When we decided on returning, Drewyer was directed to go in quest of him, but he returned with information that he had gone several miles up the (Wisdom) river without being able to find Shannon. We now had the trumpet sounded, and fired several guns; but he did not return, and we fear he is again lost."

This man, although an expert hunter, had an unlucky habit of losing himself in the wilderness, as many another good man has lost himself among the mountains or the great plains. This time, however, he came into camp again, after being lost three days.

On the eighth of August the party reached a point now known by its famous landmark, Beaver Head, a remarkable rocky formation which gives its name to Beaverhead County, Montana. The Indian woman, Sacajawea, recognized the so-called beaver-head, which, she said, was not far from the summer retreat of her countrymen, living on the other side of the mountains. The whole party were now together again, the men with the canoes having come up; and the journal says:—

"Persuaded of the absolute necessity of procuring horses to cross the mountains, it was determined that one of us should proceed in the morning to the head of the river, and penetrate the mountains till he found the Shoshonees or some other nation who can assist us in transporting our baggage, the greater part of which we shall be compelled to leave without the aid of horses.".
. .

Early the next day Captain Lewis took Drewyer, Shields, and M'Neal, and, slinging their knapsacks, they set out with a resolution to meet some nation of Indians before they returned, however long they might be separated from the party.

The party in the canoes continued to ascend the river, which was so crooked that they advanced but four miles in a direct line from their starting-place in a distance of eleven miles. In this manner, the party on foot leading those with the canoes, they repeatedly explored the various forks of the streams, which baffled them by their turnings and windings. Lewis was in the advance, and Clark brought up the rear with the main body. It was found necessary for the leading party to wade the streams, and occasionally they were compelled by the roughness of the way to leave the water-course and take to the hills, where great vigilance was required to keep them in sight of the general direction in which they must travel. On the 11th of August, 1805, Captain Lewis came in sight of the first Indian encountered since leaving the country of the Minnetarees, far back on the Missouri. The journal of that date says:

"On examining him with the glass Captain Lewis saw that he was of a different nation from any Indians we had hitherto met. He was armed with a bow and a quiver of arrows, and mounted on an elegant horse without a saddle; a small string attached to the under jaw answered as a bridle.

"Convinced that he was a Shoshonee, and knowing how much our success depended on the friendly offices of that nation, Captain Lewis was full of anxiety to approach without alarming him, and endeavor to convince him that he (Lewis) was a white man. He therefore proceeded toward the Indian at his usual pace. When they were within a mile of each other the Indian suddenly stopped. Captain Lewis immediately followed his example, took his blanket from his knapsack, and, holding it with both hands at the two corners, threw it above his head, and unfolded it as he brought it to the ground, as if in the act of spreading it. This signal, which originates in the practice of spreading a robe or skin as a seat for guests to whom they wish to show a distinguished kindness, is the universal sign of friendship among the Indians on the Missouri and the Rocky Mountains. As usual, Captain Lewis repeated this signal three times: still the Indian kept his position, and looked with an air of suspicion on Drewyer and Shields, who were now advancing on each side. Captain Lewis was afraid to make any signal for them to halt, lest he should increase the distrust of the Indian, who began to be uneasy, and they were too distant to hear his voice. He therefore took from his pack some beads, a looking-glass, and a few trinkets, which he had brought for the purpose, and, leaving his gun, advanced unarmed towards the Indian. He remained in the same position till Captain Lewis came within two hundred yards of him, when he turned his horse and began to move off slowly. Captain Lewis then called out to him in as loud a voice as he could, repeating the words tabba bone, which in the Shoshonee language mean white man. But, looking over his shoulder, the Indian kept his eyes on Drewyer and Shields, who were still advancing, without recollecting the impropriety of doing so at such a moment, till Captain Lewis made a signal to them to halt: this Drewyer obeyed, but Shields did not observe it, and still went forward. Seeing Drewyer halt, the Indian turned his horse about as if to wait for Captain Lewis, who now reached within one hundred and fifty paces, repeating the words tabba bone, and holding up the trinkets in his hand, at the same time stripping up the sleeve of his shirt to show the color of his skin. The Indian suffered him to advance within one hundred paces, then suddenly turned his horse, and, giving him the whip, leaped across the creek, and disappeared in an instant among the willow bushes: with him vanished all the hopes which the sight of him had inspired, of a friendly introduction to his countrymen."

Sadly disappointed by the clumsy imprudence of his men, Captain Lewis now endeavored to follow the track of the retreating Indian, hoping that this might lead them to an encampment, or village, of the Shoshonees. He also built a fire, the smoke of which might attract the attention of the Indians. At the same time, he placed on a pole near the fire a small assortment of beads, trinkets, awls, and paints, in order that the Indians, if they returned that way, might discover them and be thereby assured the strangers were white men and friends. Next morning, while trying to follow the trail of the lone Indian, they found traces of freshly turned earth where people had been digging for roots; and, later on, they came upon the fresh track of eight or ten horses. But these were soon scattered, and the explorers only found that the general direction of the trails was up into the mountains which define the boundary between Montana and Idaho. Skirting the base of these mountains (the Bitter Root), the party endeavored to find a plain trail, or Indian road, leading up to a practicable pass. Travelling in a southwesterly direction along the main stream, they entered a valley which led into the mountains. Here they ate their last bit of fresh meat, the remainder of a deer they had killed a day or two before; they reserved for their final resort, in case of famine, a small piece of salt pork. The journal says:—

"They then continued through the low bottom, along the main stream, near the foot of the mountains on their right. For the first five miles, the valley continues toward the southwest, being from two to three miles in width; then the main stream, which had received two small branches from the left in the valley, turned abruptly to the west through a narrow bottom between the mountains. The road was still plain, and, as it led them directly on toward the mountain, the stream gradually became smaller, till, after going two miles, it had so greatly diminished in width that one of the men, in a fit of enthusiasm, with one foot on each side of the river, thanked God that he had lived to bestride the Missouri. As they went along their hopes of soon seeing the Columbia (that is, the Pacific watershed) arose almost to painful anxiety, when after four miles from the last abrupt turn of the river (which turn had been to the west), they reached a small gap formed by the high mountains, which recede on each side, leaving room for the Indian road. From the foot of one of the lowest of these mountains, which rises with a gentle ascent of about half a mile, issues the remotest water of the Missouri.

"They had now reached the hidden sources of that river, which had never yet been seen by civilized man. As they quenched their thirst at the chaste and icy fountain—as they sat down by the brink of that little rivulet, which yielded its distant and modest tribute to the parent ocean— they felt themselves rewarded for all their labors and all their difficulties.

"They left reluctantly this interesting spot, and, pursuing the Indian road through the interval of the hills, arrived at the top of a ridge, from which they saw high mountains, partially covered with snow, still to the west of them.

"The ridge on which they stood formed the dividing line between the waters of the Atlantic and Pacific Oceans. They followed a descent much steeper than that on the eastern side, and at the distance of three-quarters of a mile reached a handsome, bold creek of cold, clear water running to the westward. They stopped to taste, for the first time, the waters of the Columbia; and, after a few minutes, followed the road across steep hills and low hollows, when they came to a spring on the side of a mountain. Here they found a sufficient quantity of dry willow-brush for fuel, and therefore halted for the night; and, having killed nothing in the course of the day, supped on their last piece of pork, and trusted to fortune for some other food to mix with a little flour and parched meal, which was all that now remained of their provisions."

Chapter XIII — From the Minnetarees to the Shoshonees

Travelling in a westerly direction, with a very gradual descent, Captain Lewis, on the thirteenth of August, came upon two Indian women, a man, and some dogs. The Indians sat down when the strangers first came in sight, as if to wait for their coming; but, soon taking alarm, they all fled, much to the chagrin of the white men. Now striking into a well-worn Indian road, they found themselves surely near a village. The journal says:—

"They had not gone along the road more than a mile, when on a sudden they saw three female Indians, from whom they had been concealed by the deep ravines which intersected the road, till they were now within thirty paces of each other. One of them, a young woman, immediately took to flight; the other two, an elderly woman and a little girl, seeing they were too near for them to escape, sat on the ground, and holding down their heads seemed as if reconciled to the death which they supposed awaited them. The same habit of holding down the head and inviting the enemy to strike, when all chance of escape is gone, is preserved in Egypt to this day.

"Captain Lewis instantly put down his rifle, and advancing toward them, took the woman by the hand, raised her up, and repeated the words 'tabba bone!' at the same time stripping up his shirt-sleeve to prove that he was a white man—for his hands and face had become by constant exposure quite as dark as their own. She appeared immediately relieved from her alarm; and Drewyer and Shields now coming up, Captain Lewis gave them some beads, a few awls, pewter mirrors, and a little paint, and told Drewyer to request the woman to recall her companion, who had escaped to some distance and, by alarming the Indians, might cause them to attack him without any time for explanation. She did as she was desired, and the young woman returned almost out of breath. Captain Lewis gave her an equal portion of trinkets, and painted the tawny checks of all three of them with vermilion,—a ceremony which among the Shoshonees is emblematic of peace.

"After they had become composed, he informed them by signs of his wishes to go to their camp, in order to see their chiefs and warriors; they readily obeyed, and conducted the party along the same road down the river. In this way they marched two miles, when they met a troop of nearly sixty warriors, mounted on excellent horses, riding at full speed toward them. As they advanced Captain Lewis put down his gun, and went with the flag about fifty paces in advance. The chief, who with two men was riding in front of the main body, spoke to the women, who now explained that the party was composed of white men, and showed exultingly the presents they had received. The three men immediately leaped from their horses, came up to Captain Lewis, and embraced him with great cordiality, putting their left arm over his right shoulder, and clasping his back, applying at the same time their left cheek to his, and frequently vociferating ah hi e! ah hi e! 'I am much pleased, I am much rejoiced.' The whole body of warriors now came forward, and our men received the caresses, and no small share of the grease and paint, of their new friends. After this fraternal embrace, of which the motive was much more agreeable than the manner, Captain Lewis lighted a pipe, and offered it to the Indians, who had now seated themselves in a circle around the party. But, before they would receive this mark of friendship, they pulled off their moccasins: a custom, as we afterward learned, which indicates the sacred sincerity of their professions when they smoke with a stranger, and which imprecates on themselves the misery of going barefoot forever if they prove faithless to their words—a penalty by no means light for those who rove over the thorny plains of this country. . . .

"After smoking a few pipes, some trifling presents were distributed among them, with which they seemed very much pleased, particularly with the blue beads and the vermilion. Captain Lewis then stated to the chief that the object of his visit was friendly, and should be explained as soon as he reached their camp; and that, as the sun was oppressive, and no water near, he wished to go there as soon as possible. They now put on their moccasins, and their chief, whose name was Cameahwait, made a short speech to the warriors. Captain Lewis then gave him the flag, which he informed him was among white men the emblem of peace; and, now that he had received it, was to be in future the bond of union between them. The chief then moved on; our party followed him; and the rest of the warriors, in a squadron, brought up the rear."

Arriving at the village, the ceremony of smoking the pipe of peace was solemnly observed; and the women and children of the tribe were permitted to gaze with wonder on the first white men they had ever seen. The Indians were not much better provided with food than were their half-famished visitors. But some cakes made of service-berries and choke-berries dried in the sun were presented to the white men "on which," says Captain Lewis, "we made a hearty meal." Later in the day, however, an Indian invited Captain Lewis into his wigwam and treated him to a small morsel of boiled antelope and a piece of fresh salmon roasted. This was the first salmon he had seen, and the captain was now assured that he was on the headwaters of the Columbia. This stream was what is now known as the Lemhi River. The water was clear and limpid, flowing down a bed of gravel; its general direction was a little north of west. The journal says:—

"The chief informed him that this stream discharged, at the distance of half a day's march, into another (Salmon River) of twice its size, coming from the southwest; but added, on further inquiry, that there was scarcely more timber below the junction of those rivers than in this neighborhood, and that the river was rocky, rapid, and so closely confined between high mountains that it was impossible to pass down it either by land or water to the great lake (Pacific Ocean), where, as he had understood, the white men lived.

"This information was far from being satisfactory, for there was no timber here that would answer the purpose of building canoes,—indeed not more than just sufficient for fuel; and even that consisted of the narrow-leaved cottonwood, the red and the narrow-leaved willow, chokecherry, service-berry, and a few currant bushes, such as are common on the Missouri. The prospect of going on by land is more pleasant, for there are great numbers of horses feeding in every direction round the camp, which will enable us to transport our stores, if necessary, over the mountains."

While Captain Lewis was thus engaged, his companions in the canoes were slowly and laboriously ascending the river on the other side of the divide. The character of the stream was much as it had been for several days, and the men were in the water three-fourths of the time, dragging the boats over the shoals. They had but little success in killing game, but caught, as they had done for some days before, numbers of fine trout.

"August 14. In order to give time for the boats to reach the forks of Jefferson River," proceeds the narrative, "Captain Lewis determined to remain where he was, and obtain all the information he could collect in regard to the country. Having nothing to eat but a little flour and parched meal, with the berries of the Indians, he sent out Drewyer and Shields, who borrowed horses from the natives, to hunt for a few hours. About the same time the young warriors set out for the same purpose. There are but few elk or black tailed deer in this neighborhood; and as the common red deer secrete themselves in the bushes when alarmed, they are soon safe from the arrows, which are but feeble weapons against any animals which the huntsmen cannot previously run down with their horses. The chief game of the Shoshonees, therefore, is the antelope, which, when pursued, retreats to the open plains, where the horses have full room for the chase. But such is its extraordinary fleetness and wind, that a single horse has no possible chance of outrunning it or tiring it down, and the hunters are therefore obliged to resort to stratagem.

"About twenty Indians, mounted on fine horses, and armed with bows and arrows, left the camp. In a short time they descried a herd of ten antelope: they immediately separated into little squads of two or three, and formed a scattered circle round the herd for five or six miles, keeping at a wary distance, so as not to alarm them till they were perfectly enclosed, and selecting, as far as possible, some commanding eminence as a stand. Having gained their positions, a small party rode towards the animals, and with wonderful dexterity the huntsmen preserved their seats, and the horses their footing, as they ran at full speed over the hills, down the steep ravines, and along the borders of the precipices. They were soon outstripped by the antelopes, which, on gaining the other extremity of the circle, were driven back and pursued by the fresh hunters. They turned and flew, rather than ran, in another direction; but there, too, they found new enemies. In this way they were alternately pursued backward and forward, till at length, notwithstanding the skill of the hunters, they all escaped and the party, after running for two hours, returned without having caught anything, and their horses foaming with sweat. This chase, the greater part of which was seen from the camp, formed a beautiful scene; but to the hunters it is exceedingly laborious, and so unproductive, even when they are able to worry the animal down and shoot him, that forty or fifty hunters will sometimes be engaged for half a day without obtaining more than two or three antelope.

"Soon after they returned, our two huntsmen came in with no better success. Captain Lewis therefore made a little paste with the flour, and the addition of some berries formed a very palatable repast. Having now secured the good will of Cameahwait, Captain Lewis informed him of his wish that he would speak to the warriors, and endeavor to engage them to accompany him to the forks of Jefferson River; where by this time another chief (Clark), with a large party of white men, was awaiting his (Lewis') return; that it would be necessary to take about thirty horses to transport the merchandise; that they should be well rewarded for their trouble; and that, when all the party should have reached the Shoshonee camp, they would remain some time among them to trade for horses, as well as concert plans for furnishing them in future with regular supplies of merchandise. He readily consented to do so, and after collecting the tribe together, he made a long harangue. In about an hour and a half he returned, and told Captain Lewis that they would be ready to accompany him in the morning."

But the Indians were suspicious and reluctant to take the word of the white man. Captain Lewis, almost at his wits' end, appealed to their courage. He said that if they were afraid of being led into a trap, he was sure that some among them were not afraid.

"To doubt the courage of an Indian is to touch the tenderest string of his mind, and the surest way to rouse him to any dangerous achievement. Cameahwait instantly replied that he was not afraid to die, and mounting his horse, for the third time harangued the warriors. He told them that he was resolved to go if he went alone, or if he were sure of perishing; that he hoped there were among those who heard him some who were not afraid to die, and who would prove it by mounting their horses and following him. This harangue produced an effect on six or eight only of the warriors, who now joined their chief. With these Captain Lewis smoked a pipe; and then, fearful of some change in their capricious temper, set out immediately."

The party now retraced the steps so lately taken by Captain Lewis and his men. On the second day out, one of the spies sent forward by the Indians came madly galloping back, much to the alarm of the white men. It proved, however, that the spy had returned to tell his comrades that one of the white hunters (Drewyer) had killed a deer. An Indian riding behind Captain Lewis, fearful that he should not get his share of the spoil, jumped off the horse and ran for a mile at full speed. The journal says:—

"Captain Lewis slackened his pace, and followed at a sufficient distance to observe them. When they reached the place where Drewyer had thrown out the intestines, they all dismounted in confusion and ran tumbling over each other like famished dogs. Each tore away whatever part he could, and instantly began to eat it. Some had the liver, some the kidneys—in short, no part on which we are accustomed to look with disgust escaped them. One of them, who had seized about nine feet of the entrails, was chewing at one end, while with his hand he was diligently clearing his way by discharging the contents at the other. It was indeed impossible to see these wretches ravenously feeding on the filth of animals, the blood streaming from their mouths, without deploring how nearly the condition of savages approaches that of the brute creation. Yet, though suffering with hunger, they did not attempt, as they might have done, to take by force the whole deer, but contented themselves with what had been thrown away by the hunter. Captain Lewis now had the deer skinned, and after reserving a quarter of it gave the rest of the animal to the chief, to be divided among the Indians, who immediately devoured nearly the whole of it without cooking. They now went toward the (Prairie) creek, where there was some brushwood to make a fire, and found Drewyer, who had killed a second deer. The same struggle for the entrails was renewed here, and on giving nearly the whole deer to the Indians, they devoured it even to the soft part of the hoofs. A fire being made, Captain Lewis had his breakfast, during which Drewyer brought in a third deer. This too, after reserving one-quarter, was given to the Indians, who now seemed completely satisfied and in good humor."

They now approached the forks of the Jefferson, where they had expected to meet Clark and his party with the canoes. Not seeing any signs of them, the Lewis party were placed in a critical position. The Indians were again alarmed and suspicious. Here Captain Clark's journal says:—

"As they went on towards the point, Captain Lewis, perceiving how critical his situation had become, resolved to attempt a stratagem, which his present difficulty seemed completely to justify. Recollecting the notes he had left at the point for us, he sent Drewyer for them with an Indian, who witnessed his taking them from the pole. When they were brought, Captain Lewis told Cameahwait that, on leaving his brother chief at the place where the river issues from the mountains, it was agreed that the boats should not be brought higher than the next forks we should meet; but that, if the rapid water prevented the boats from coming on as fast as they expected, his brother chief was to send a note to the first forks above him, to let him know where they were: that this note had been left this morning at the forks, and mentioned that the canoes were just below the mountains, and coming up slowly in consequence of the current. Captain

Lewis added that he would stay at the forks for his brother chief, but would send a man down the river; and that if Cameahwait doubted what he said, one of their young men could go with him, while he and the other two remained at the forks. This story satisfied the chief and the greater part of the Indians; but a few did not conceal their suspicions, observing that we told different stories, and complaining that their chief exposed them to danger by a mistaken confidence. Captain Lewis now wrote, by the light of some willow-brush, a note to Captain Clark, which he gave to Drewyer, with an order to use all possible expedition in descending the river, and engaged an Indian to accompany him by the promise of a knife and some beads.

"At bedtime the chief and five others slept round the fire of Captain Lewis, and the rest hid themselves in different parts of the willow-brush to avoid the enemy, who, they feared, would attack them in the night. Captain Lewis endeavored to assume a cheerfulness he did not feel, to prevent the despondency of the savages. After conversing gayly with them he retired to his mosquito-bier, by the side of which the chief now placed himself. He lay down, yet slept but little, being in fact scarcely less uneasy than his Indian companions. He was apprehensive that, finding the ascent of the river impracticable, Captain Clark might have stopped below Rattlesnake bluff, and the messenger would not meet him. The consequence of disappointing the Indians at this moment would most probably be that they would retire and secrete themselves in the mountains, so as to prevent our having an opportunity of recovering their confidence. They would also spread a panic through all the neighboring Indians, and cut us off from the supply of horses so useful and almost so essential to our success. He was at the same time consoled by remembering that his hopes of assistance rested on better foundations than their generosity—their avarice and their curiosity. He had promised liberal exchanges for their horses; but what was still more seductive, he had told them that one of their countrywomen, who had been taken with the Minnetarees, accompanied the party below; and one of the men had spread the report of our having with us a man (York) perfectly black, whose hair was short and curled. This last account had excited a great degree of curiosity, and they seemed more desirous of seeing this monster than of obtaining the most favorable barter for their horses."

On the following day, August 17, the two parties of explorers finally met. Under that date the journal has this interesting entry:—

"Captain Lewis rose very early and despatched Drewyer and the Indian down the river in quest of the boats. Shields was sent out at the same time to hunt, while M'Neal prepared a breakfast out of the remainder of the meat. Drewyer had been gone about two hours, and the Indians were all anxiously waiting for some news, when an Indian, who had straggled a short distance down the river, returned with a report that he had seen the white men, who were only a short distance below, and were coming on. The Indians were transported with joy, and the chief, in the warmth of his satisfaction, renewed his embrace to Captain Lewis, who was quite as much delighted as the Indians themselves. The report proved most agreeably true.

"On setting out at seven o'clock, Captain Clark, with Chaboneau and his wife, walked on shore; but they had not gone more than a mile before Captain Clark saw Sacajawea, who was with her husband one hundred yards ahead, begin to dance and show every mark of the most extravagant joy, turning round to him and pointing to several Indians, whom he now saw advancing on horseback, sucking her fingers at the same time, to indicate that they were of her native tribe. As they advanced, Captain Clark discovered among them Drewyer dressed like an Indian, from whom he learned the situation of the party. While the boats were performing the circuit, he went toward the forks with the Indians, who, as they went along, sang aloud with the greatest appearance of delight.

"We soon drew near the camp, and just as we approached it a woman made her way through the crowd toward Sacajawea; recognizing each other, they embraced with the most tender affection. The meeting of these two young women had in it something peculiarly touching, not only from the ardent manner in which their feelings were expressed, but also from the real interest of their situation. They had been companions in childhood; in the war with the Minnetarees they had both been taken prisoners in the same battle; they had shared and softened the rigors of their captivity till one of them had escaped from their enemies with scarce a hope of ever seeing her friend rescued from their hands.

"While Sacajawea was renewing among the women the friendships of former days, Captain Clark went on, and was received by Captain Lewis and the chief, who, after the first embraces and salutations were over, conducted him to a sort of circular tent or shade of willows. Here he was seated on a white robe; and the chief immediately tied in his hair six small shells resembling pearls, an ornament highly valued by these people, who procure them in the course of trade from the seacoast. The moccasins of the whole party were then taken off, and, after much ceremony, the smoking began. After this the conference was to be opened; and, glad of an opportunity of being able to converse more intelligibly, Sacajawea was sent for: she came into the tent, sat down, and was beginning to interpret, when in the person of Cameahwait she recognized her brother. She instantly jumped up, and ran and embraced him, throwing over him her blanket, and weeping profusely: the chief was himself moved, though not in the same degree. After some conversation between them she resumed her seat, and attempted to interpret for us; but her new situation seemed to overpower her, and she was frequently interrupted by her tears. After the council was finished, the unfortunate woman learned that all her family were dead except two brothers, one of whom was absent, and a son of her eldest sister, a small boy, who was immediately adopted by her."

The two parties, Indian and white, now went into a conference, the white chiefs explaining that it would be needful for their Indian friends to collect all their horses and help to transport the goods of the explorers over the Great Divide. The journal says:—

"The speech made a favorable impression. The chief, in reply, thanked us for our expressions of friendship toward himself and his nation, and declared their willingness to render us every service. He lamented that it would be so long before they should be supplied with firearms, but that till then they could subsist as they had heretofore done. He concluded by saying that there were not horses enough here to transport our goods, but that he would return to the village to-morrow, bring all his own horses, and encourage his people to come over with theirs. The conference being ended to our satisfaction, we now inquired of Cameahwait what chiefs were among the party, and he pointed out two of them. We then distributed our presents: to Cameahwait we gave a medal of small size, with the likeness of President Jefferson, and on the reverse a figure of hands clasped with a pipe and tomahawk; to this was added an uniform coat, a shirt, a pair of scarlet leggings, a carrot (or twist) of tobacco, and some small articles. Each of the other chiefs received a small medal struck during the presidency of General Washington, a shirt, handkerchief, leggings, knife, and some tobacco. Medals of the same sort were also presented to two young warriors, who, though not chiefs, were promising youths and very much respected in the tribe. These honorary gifts were followed by presents of paint, moccasins, awls, knives, beads, and looking-glasses. We also gave them all a plentiful meal of Indian corn, of which the hull is taken off by being boiled in lye; as this was the first they had ever tasted, they were very much pleased with it. They had, indeed, abundant sources of surprise in all they saw—the appearance of the men, their arms, their clothing, the canoes, the strange looks of the negro, and the sagacity of our dog, all in turn shared their admiration, which was raised to astonishment by a shot from the air-gun. This operation was instantly considered 'great medicine,' by which they, as well as the other Indians, mean something emanating directly from the Great Spirit, or produced by his invisible and incomprehensible agency. . . .

"After the council was over we consulted as to our future operations. The game did not promise to last here for many days; and this circumstance combined with many others to induce our going on as soon as possible. Our Indian information as to the state of the Columbia was of a very alarming kind; and our first object was, of course, to ascertain the practicability of descending it, of which the Indians discouraged our expectations. It was therefore agreed that Captain Clark should set off in the morning with eleven men, furnished, besides their arms, with tools for making canoes: that he should take Chaboneau and his wife to the camp of the Shoshonees, where he was to leave them, in order to hasten the collection of horses; that he should then lead his men down to the Columbia, and if he found it navigable, and the timber in sufficient quantity, begin to build canoes. As soon as he had decided as to the propriety of proceeding down the Columbia or across the mountains, he was to send back one of the men with information of it to Captain Lewis, who by that time would have brought up the whole party, and the rest of the baggage, as far as the Shoshonee village. Preparations were accordingly made at once to carry out the arrangement. . . ."

"In order to relieve the men of Captain Clark's party from the heavy weight of their arms, provisions, and tools, we exposed a few articles to barter for horses, and soon obtained three very good ones, in exchange for which we gave a uniform coat, a pair of leggings, a few handkerchiefs, three knives, and some other small articles, the whole of which did not, in the United States, cost more than twenty dollars; a fourth was purchased by the men for an old checkered shirt, a pair of old leggings, and a knife. The Indians seemed to be quite as well pleased as ourselves at the bargain they had made. We now found that the two inferior chiefs were somewhat displeased at not having received a present equal to that given to the great chief, who appeared in a dress so much finer than their own. To allay their discontent, we bestowed on them two old coats, and promised them if they were active in assisting us across the mountains they should have an additional present. This treatment completely reconciled them, and the whole Indian party, except two men and two women, set out in perfect good humor to return to their home with Captain Clark."

Chapter XIV — Across the Great Divide

Captain Clark had now left the water-shed of the Missouri behind him, and was pressing on, over a broken, hilly country, to the lands from which issue the tributaries of the Columbia. The Indian village which Captain Lewis had previously visited had been removed two miles up the stream on which it was situated, and was reached by Clark on August 20. The party was very ceremoniously received by Chief Cameahwait, and all hands began to explain to the white men the difficulties of the situation. How to transport the canoes and baggage over the mountains to some navigable stream leading into the Columbia was now the serious problem. The Indian chief and his old men dwelt on the obstacles in the way and argued that it was too late in the season to make the attempt. They even urged the white men to stay with them until another spring, when Indian guides would be furnished them to proceed on their journey westward.

On the twenty-first, Clark passed the junction of two streams, the Salmon and the Lemhi, which is now the site of Salmon City, Idaho. As Captain Lewis was the first white man who had seen these waters, Clark gave to the combined water-course the name of Lewis' River. The mountains here assumed a formidable aspect, and the stream was too narrow, rapid, and rock-bound to admit of navigation. The journal says of Captain Clark:—

"He soon began to perceive that the Indian accounts had not been exaggerated. At the distance of a mile he passed a small creek (on the right), and the points of four mountains, which were rocky, and so high that it seemed almost impossible to cross them with horses. The road lay over the sharp fragments of rocks which had fallen from the mountains, and were strewed in heaps for miles together; yet the horses, altogether unshod, travelled across them as fast as the men, without detaining them a moment. They passed two bold running streams, and reached the entrance of a small river, where a few Indian families resided, who had not been previously acquainted with the arrival of the whites; the guide was behind, and the woods were so thick that we came upon them unobserved, till at a very short distance. As soon as they saw us the women and children fled in great consternation; the men offered us everything they had—the fish on the scaffolds, the dried berries, and the collars of elks' tushes worn by the children. We took only a small quantity of the food, and gave them in return some small articles which conduced very much to pacify them. The guide now coming up, explained to them who we were and the object of our visit, which seemed to relieve their fears; still a number of the women and children did not recover from their fright, but cried during our stay, which lasted about an hour. The guide, whom we found a very intelligent, friendly old man, informed us that up this river there was a road which led over the mountains to the Missouri."

To add to their difficulties, game had almost entirely disappeared, and the abundant fish in the river could not be caught for lack of proper fishing-tackle. Timber from which canoes could be made, there was none, and the rapids in the rivers were sharp and violent. With his Indian guide and three men, Captain Clark now pressed on his route of survey, leaving the remainder of his men behind to hunt and fish. He went down the Salmon River about fifty-two miles, making his way as best he could along its banks. Finding the way absolutely blocked for their purposes, Captain Clark returned on the twenty-fifth of August and rejoined the party that he had left behind. These had not been able to kill anything, and for a time starvation stared them in the face. Under date of August 27, the journal says:—

"The men, who were engaged last night in mending their moccasins, all except one, went out hunting, but no game was to be procured. One of the men, however, killed a small salmon, and the Indians made a present of another, on which the whole party made a very slight breakfast. These Indians, to whom this life is familiar, seem contented, although they depend for subsistence on the scanty productions of the fishery. But our men, who are used to hardships, but have been accustomed to have the first wants of nature regularly supplied, feel very sensibly their wretched situation; their strength is wasting away; they begin to express their apprehensions of being without food in a country perfectly destitute of any means of supporting life, except a few fish. In the course of the day an Indian brought into the camp five salmon, two of which Captain Clark bought and made a supper for the party."

Two days later, Captain Clark and his men joined the main party, having met the only repulse that was suffered by the expedition from first to last. Eluding the vigilance of the Indians, caches, or hiding-places, for the baggage were constructed, filled, and concealed, the work being done after dark. The weather was now very cold, although August had not passed. Ink froze in the pen during the night, and the meadows were white with frost; but the days were warm, even hot.

In the absence of Captain Clark, his colleague and party had been visited by Cameahwait and about fifty of his band, with their women and children. Captain Lewis' journal says:—

"After they had camped near us and turned loose their horses, we called a council of all the chiefs and warriors, and addressed them in a speech. Additional presents were then distributed, particularly to the two second chiefs, who had, agreeably to their promises, exerted themselves in our favor. The council was then adjourned, and all the Indians were treated with an abundant meal of boiled Indian corn and beans. The poor wretches, who had no animal food and scarcely anything but a few fish, had been almost starved, and received this new luxury with great thankfulness. Out of compliment to the chief, we gave him a few dried squashes, which we had brought from the Mandans, and he declared it was the best food he had ever tasted except sugar, a small lump of which he had received from his sister Sacajawea. He now declared how happy they should all be to live in a country which produced so many good things; and we told him that it would not be long before the white men would put it in their power to live below the mountains, where they might themselves cultivate all these kinds of food, instead of wandering in the mountains. He appeared to be much pleased with this information, and the whole party being now in excellent temper after their repast, we began our purchase of horses. We soon obtained five very good ones, on very reasonable terms—that is, by giving for each horse merchandise which cost us originally about $6. We have again to admire the perfect decency and propriety of the Indians; for though so numerous, they do not attempt to crowd round our camp or take anything which they see lying about, and whenever they borrow knives or kettles or any other article from the men, they return them with great fidelity."

Captain Lewis anxiously wished to push on to meet Clark, who, as we have seen, was then far down on the Salmon River. Lewis was still at the forks of Jefferson River, it should be borne in mind; and their objective point was the upper Shoshonee village on the Lemhi River, across the divide. While on the way over the divide, Lewis was greatly troubled by the freaks of the Indians, who, regardless of their promises, would propose to return to the buffalo country on the eastern side of the mountains. Learning that Cameahwait and his chiefs had sent a messenger over to the Lemhi to notify the village to come and join an expedition of this sort, Captain Lewis was dismayed. His journal says:—

"Alarmed at this new caprice of the Indians, which, if not counteracted, threatened to leave ourselves and our baggage on the mountains, or even if we reached the waters of the Columbia, to prevent our obtaining horses to go on further, Captain Lewis immediately called the three chiefs together. After smoking a pipe he asked them if they were men of their word, and if we could rely on their promises. They readily answered in the affirmative. He then asked if they had not agreed to assist us in carrying our baggage over the mountains. To this they also answered yes. 'Why, then,' said he, 'have you requested your people to meet us to-morrow where it will be impossible for us to trade for horses, as you promised we should? If,' he continued, 'you had not promised to help us in transporting our goods over the mountains, we should not have attempted it, but have returned down the river; after which no white men would ever have come into your country. If you wish the whites to be your friends, to bring you arms, and to protect you from your enemies, you should never promise what you do not mean to perform. When I first met you, you doubted what I said, yet you afterward saw that I told you the truth. How, therefore, can you doubt what I now tell you? You see that I divide amongst you the meat which my hunters kill, and I promise to give all who assist us a share of whatever we have to eat. If, therefore, you intend to keep your promise, send one of the young men immediately, to order the people to remain at the village till we arrive.' The two inferior chiefs then said that they had wished to keep their word and to assist us; that they had not sent for the people, but on the contrary had disapproved of that measure, which was done wholly by the first chief. Cameahwait remained silent for some time; at last he said that he knew he had done wrong, but that, seeing his people all in want of provisions, he had wished to hasten their departure for the country where their wants might be supplied. He, however, now declared that, having passed his word, he would never violate it, and counter-orders were immediately sent to the village by a young man, to whom we gave a handkerchief in order to ensure despatch and fidelity. . . .

"This difficulty being now adjusted, our march was resumed with an unusual degree of alacrity on the part of the Indians. We passed a spot where, six years ago, the Shoshonees had suffered a very severe defeat from the Minnetarees; and late in the evening we reached the upper part of the cove, where the creek enters the mountains. The part of the cove on the northeast side of the creek has lately been burned, most probably as a signal on some occasion. Here we were joined by our hunters with a single deer, which Captain Lewis gave, as a proof of his sincerity, to the women and children, and remained supperless himself. As we came along we observed several large hares, some ducks, and many of the cock of the plains: in the low grounds of the cove were also considerable quantities of wild onions."

Arriving at the Shoshonee village on the Lemhi, Captain Lewis found a note from Captain Clark, sent back by a runner, informing him of the difficulty and impossibility of a water route to the Columbia. Cameahwait, being told that his white friends would now need twenty more horses, said that he would do what he could to help them. The journal here adds:—

"In order not to lose the present favorable moment, and to keep the Indians as cheerful as possible, the violins were brought out and our men danced, to the great diversion of the Indians. This mirth was the more welcome because our situation was not precisely that which would most dispose us to gayety; for we have only a little parched corn to eat, and our means of subsistence or of success depend on the wavering temper of the natives, who may change their minds to-morrow. . . .

"The Shoshonees are a small tribe of the nation called the Snake Indians, a vague appellation, which embraces at once the inhabitants of the southern parts of the Rocky Mountains and of the plains on either side. The Shoshonees with whom we now were amount to about one hundred warriors, and three times that number of women and children. Within their own recollection they formerly lived in the plains, but they have been driven into the mountains by the Pahkees, or the roving Indians of the Sascatchawan, and are now obliged to visit occasionally, and by stealth, the country of their ancestors. Their lives, indeed, are migratory. From the middle of May to the beginning of September they reside on the headwaters of the Columbia, where they consider themselves perfectly secure from the Pahkees, who have never yet found their way to that retreat. During this time they subsist chiefly on salmon, and, as that fish disappears on the approach of autumn, they are driven to seek subsistence elsewhere. They then cross the ridge to the waters of the Missouri, down which they proceed slowly and cautiously, till they are joined near the Three Forks by other bands, either of their own nation or of the Flatheads, with whom they associate against the common enemy. Being now strong in numbers, they venture to hunt the buffalo in the plains eastward of the mountains, near which they spend the winter, till the return of the salmon invites them to the Columbia. But such is their terror of the Pahkees, that, so long as they can obtain the scantiest subsistence, they do not leave the interior of the mountains; and, as soon as they have collected a large stock of dried meat, they again retreat, thus alternately obtaining their food at the hazard of their lives, and hiding themselves to consume it.

"In this loose and wandering life they suffer the extremes of want; for two thirds of the year they are forced to live in the mountains, passing whole weeks without meat, and with nothing to eat but a few fish and roots. Nor can anything be imagined more wretched than their condition at the present time, when the salmon is fast retiring, when roots are becoming scarce, and they have not yet acquired strength to hazard an encounter with their enemies. So insensible are they, however, to these calamities, that the Shoshonees are not only cheerful, but even gay; and their character, which is more interesting than that of any Indians we have seen, has in it much of the dignity of misfortune. In their intercourse with strangers they are frank and communicative; in their dealings they are perfectly fair; nor have we, during our stay with them, had any reason to suspect that the display of all our new and valuable wealth has tempted them into a single act of dishonesty. While they have generally shared with us the little they possess, they have always abstained from begging anything from us. With their liveliness of temper, they are fond of gaudy dresses and all sorts of amusements, particularly games of hazard; and, like most Indians, delight in boasting of their warlike exploits, either real or fictitious. In their conduct towards us they have been kind and obliging; and though on one occasion they seemed willing to neglect us, yet we scarcely knew how to blame the treatment by which we were to suffer, when we recollected how few civilized chiefs would have hazarded the comforts or the subsistence of their people for the sake of a few strangers. . . . .

"As war is the chief occupation, bravery is the first virtue among the Shoshonees. None can hope to be distinguished without having given proofs of it, nor can there be any preferment or influence among the nation, without some warlike achievement. Those important events which give reputation to a warrior, and entitle him to a new name, are: killing a white (or grizzly) bear, stealing individually the horses of the enemy, leading a party who happen to be successful either

83

in plundering horses or destroying the enemy, and lastly, scalping a warrior. These acts seem of nearly equal dignity, but the last, that of taking an enemy's scalp, is an honor quite independent of the act of vanquishing him. To kill your adversary is of no importance unless the scalp is brought from the field of battle; were a warrior to slay any number of his enemies in action, and others were to obtain the scalps or first touch the dead, they would have all the honors, since they have borne off the trophy. . . ."

"The names of these Indians vary in the course of their life. Originally given in childhood, from the mere necessity of distinguishing objects, or from some accidental resemblance to external objects, the young warrior is impatient to change it by some achievement of his own. Any important event—the stealing of horses, the scalping of an enemy, or the killing of a brown bear—entitles him at once to a new name, which he then selects for himself, and it is confirmed by the nation. Sometimes the two names subsist together; thus, the chief Cameahwait, which means 'One Who Never Walks,' has the war-name of Tooettecone, or 'Black Gun,' which he acquired when he first signalized himself. As each new action gives a warrior a right to change his name, many of them have several in the course of their lives. To give to a friend one's own name is an act of high courtesy, and a pledge, like that of pulling off the moccasin, of sincerity and hospitality. The chief in this way gave his name to Captain Clark when he first arrived, and he was afterward known among the Shoshonees by the name of Cameahwait."

On the thirtieth of August, the whole expedition being now reunited, and a sufficient number of horses having been purchased of the Shoshonees, the final start across the mountains was begun. The journal says:

"The greater part of the band, who had delayed their journey on our account, were also ready to depart. We took leave of the Shoshonees, who set out on their visit to the Missouri at the same time that we, accompanied by the old guide, his four sons, and another Indian, began the descent of the Lemhi River, along the same road which Captain Clark had previously pursued. After riding twelve miles we camped on the south bank of this river, and as the hunters had brought in three deer early in the morning, we did not feel the want of provisions."

Three days later, all the Indians, except the old guide, left them. They now passed up Fish Creek, and finding no track leading over the mountains they cut their way. Their journal says:—

"This we effected with much difficulty; the thickets of trees and brush through which we were obliged to cut our way required great labor; the road itself was over the steep and rocky sides of the hills, where the horses could not move without danger of slipping down, while their feet were bruised by the rocks and stumps of trees. Accustomed as these animals were to this kind of life, they suffered severely; several of them fell to some distance down the sides of the hills, some turned over with the baggage, one was crippled, and two gave out, exhausted with fatigue. After crossing the creek several times we at last made five miles, with great fatigue and labor, and camped on the left side of the creek in a small stony low ground. It was not, however, till after dark that the whole party was collected; and then, as it rained and we had killed nothing, we passed an uncomfortable night. The party had been too busily occupied with the horses to make any hunting excursion; and though, as we came along Fish Creek, we saw many beaver-dams, we saw none of the animals themselves."

The Indian guide appears here to have lost his way; but, not dismayed, he pushed on through a trackless wilderness, sometimes travelling on the snow that now covered the mountains. On the fourth of September, the party came upon a large encampment of Indians, who received them with much ceremony. The journal says:—

"September 5, we assembled the chiefs and warriors, and informed them who we were, and the purpose for which we had visited their country. All this was, however, conveyed to them through so many different languages, that it was not comprehended without difficulty. We therefore proceeded to the more intelligible language of presents, and made four chiefs by giving a medal and a small quantity of tobacco to each. We received in turn from the principal chief a present consisting of the skins of a blaireau (badger), an otter, and two antelopes, and were treated by the women to some dried roots and berries. We then began to traffic for horses, and succeeded in exchanging seven and purchasing eleven, for which we gave a few articles of merchandise.

"This encampment consists of thirty-three tents, in which were about four hundred souls, among whom eighty were men. They are called Ootlashoots, and represent themselves as one band of a nation called Tushepaws, a numerous people of four hundred and fifty tents, residing on the head-waters of the Missouri and Columbia rivers, and some of them lower down the latter river. In person these Indians are stout, and their complexion lighter than that common among Indians. The hair of the men is worn in queues of otter skin, falling in front over the shoulders. A shirt of dressed skin covers the body to the knee, and over this is worn occasionally a robe. To these are added leggings and moccasins. The women suffer their hair to fall in disorder over the face and shoulders, and their chief article of covering is a long shirt of skin, reaching down to the ankles, and tied round the waist. In other respects, as also in the few ornaments which they possess, their appearance is similar to that of the Shoshonees: there is, however, a difference between the languages of these two people, which is still farther increased by the very extraordinary pronunciation of the Ootlashoots. Their words have all a remarkably guttural sound, and there is nothing which seems to represent the tone of their speaking more exactly than the clucking of a fowl or the noise of a parrot. This peculiarity renders their voices scarcely audible, except at a short distance; and, when many of them are talking, forms a strange confusion of sounds. The common conversation that we overheard consisted of low, guttural sounds, occasionally broken by a low word or two, after which it would relapse, and could scarcely be distinguished. They seemed kind and friendly, and willingly shared with us berries and roots, which formed their sole stock of provisions. Their only wealth is their horses, which are very fine, and so numerous that this party had with them at least five hundred."

These Indians were on their way to join the other bands who were hunting buffalo on the Jefferson River, across the Great Divide. They set out the next morning, and the explorers resumed their toilsome journey, travelling generally in a northwesterly direction and looking for a pass across the Bitter Root Mountains. Very soon, all indications of game disappeared, and, September 14, they were forced to kill a colt, their stock of animal food being exhausted. They pressed on, however, through a savage wilderness, having frequent need to recur to horse-flesh. Here is an entry under date of September 18, in the journal: "We melted some snow, and supped on a little portable soup, a few canisters of which, with about twenty pounds' weight of bear's oil, are our only remaining means of subsistence. Our guns are scarcely of any service, for there is no living creature in these mountains, except a few small pheasants, a small species of gray squirrel, and a blue bird of the vulture kind, about the size of a turtle-dove, or jay. Even these are difficult to shoot."

"A bold running creek," up which Captain Clark passed on September 19, was appropriately named by him "Hungry Creek," as at that place they had nothing to eat. But, at about six miles' distance from the head of the stream, "he fortunately found a horse, on which he breakfasted, and hung the rest on a tree for the party in the rear." This was one of the wild horses, strayed from Indian bands, which they found in the wilderness, too wild to be caught and used, but not too wild to shoot and eat. Later, on the same day, this entry is made in the journal:

"The road along the creek is a narrow rocky path near the borders of very high precipices, from which a fall seems almost inevitable destruction. One of our horses slipped and rolled over with his load down the hillside, which was nearly perpendicular and strewed with large irregular rocks, nearly one hundred yards, and did not stop till he fell into the creek. We all expected he was killed, but to our astonishment, on taking off his load he rose, seemed but little injured, and in twenty minutes proceeded with his load. Having no other provision, we took some portable soup, our only refreshment during the day. This abstinence, joined with fatigue, has a visible effect on our health. The men are growing weak and losing their flesh very fast; several are afflicted with dysentery, and eruptions of the skin are very common."

Next day, the party descended the last of the Bitter Root range and reached level country. They were at last over the Great Divide. Three Indian boys were discovered hiding in the grass, in great alarm. Captain Clark at once dismounted from his horse, and, making signs of amity, went after the boys. He calmed their terrors, and, giving them some bits of ribbon, sent them home.

"Soon after the boys reached home, a man came out to meet the party, with great caution; but he conducted them to a large tent in the village, and all the inhabitants gathered round to view with a mixture of fear and pleasure these wonderful strangers. The conductor now informed Captain Clark, by signs, that the spacious tent was the residence of the great chief, who had set out three days ago with all the warriors to attack some of their enemies toward the southwest; that he would not return before fifteen or eighteen days, and that in the mean time there were only a few men left to guard the women and children. They now set before them a small piece of buffalo-meat, some dried salmon, berries, and several kinds of roots. Among these last is one which is round, much like an onion in appearance, and sweet to the taste. It is called quamash, and is eaten either in its natural state, or boiled into a kind of soup, or made into a cake, which is then called pasheco. After the long abstinence this was a sumptuous treat. They returned the kindness of the people by a few small presents, and then went on in company with one of the chiefs to a second village in the same plain, at the distance of two miles. Here the party were treated with great kindness, and passed the night. The hunters were sent out, but, though they saw some tracks of deer, were not able to procure anything."

The root which the Indians used in so many ways is now known as camas; it is still much sought for by the Nez Perces and other wandering tribes in the Northwest, and Camas Prairie, in that region, derives its name from the much-sought-for vegetable.

Captain Clark and his men stayed with these hospitable Indians several days. The free use of wholesome food, to which he had not lately been accustomed, made Clark very ill, and he contented himself with staying in the Indian villages, of which there were two. These Indians called themselves Chopunnish, or Pierced Noses; this latter name is now more commonly rendered *Nez Perces*, the French voyageurs having given it that translation into their own tongue.

But these people, so far as known, did not pierce their noses. After sending a man back on the trail to notify Captain Lewis of his progress, Captain Clark went on to the village of Chief Twisted-hair. Most of the women and children, though notified of the coming of the white man, were so scared by the appearance of the strangers that they fled to the woods. The men, however, received them without fear and gave them a plentiful supply of food. They were now on one of the upper branches of the Kooskooskee River, near what is the site of Pierce City, county seat of Shoshonee County, Idaho. The Indians endeavored, by means of signs, to explain to their visitors the geography of the country beyond.

"Among others, Twisted-hair drew a chart of the river on a white elk-skin. According to this, the Kooskooskee forks (confluence of its North fork) a few miles from this place; two days toward the south is another and larger fork (confluence of Snake River), on which the Shoshonee or Snake Indians fish; five days' journey further is a large river from the northwest (that is, the Columbia itself) into which Clark's River empties; from the mouth of that river (that is, confluence of the Snake with the Columbia) to the falls is five days' journey further; on all the forks as well as on the main river great numbers of Indians reside."

On the twenty-third of September, Captain Lewis and his party having come up, the white men assembled the Indians and explained to them where they came from and what was their errand across the continent. The Indians appeared to be entirely satisfied, and they sold their visitors as much provisions as their half-famished horses could carry. The journal here says:—

"All around the village the women are busily employed in gathering and dressing the pasheco-root, of which large quantities are heaped in piles over the plain. We now felt severely the consequence of eating heartily after our late privations. Captain Lewis and two of the men were taken very ill last evening; to-day he could hardly sit on his horse, while others were obliged to be put on horseback, and some, from extreme weakness and pain, were forced to lie down alongside of the road for some time. At sunset we reached the island where the hunters had been left on the 22d. They had been unsuccessful, having killed only two deer since that time, and two of them were very sick. A little below this island is a larger one on which we camped, and administered Rush's pills to the sick."

The illness of the party continued for several days, and not much progress was made down-stream. Having camped, on the twenty-seventh of September, in the Kooskooskee River, at a place where plenty of good timber was found, preparations for building five canoes were begun. From this time to the fifth of October, all the men capable of labor were employed in preparing the canoes. The health of the party gradually recruited, though they still suffered severely from want of food; and, as the hunters had but little success in procuring game, they were obliged on the second to kill one of their horses. Indians from different quarters frequently visited them, but all that could be obtained from them was a little fish and some dried roots. This diet was not only unnutritious, but in many cases it caused dysentery and nausea.

Chapter XV — Down the Pacific Slope

The early days of October were spent in making preparations for the descent of the river,—the Kooskooskee. Here they made their canoes, and they called their stopping-place Canoe Camp. This was at the junction of the north fork of the river with the main stream; and all below that point is called the Lower Kooskooskee, while that above is known as the upper river. The latitude of the camp, according to the journal of the explorers, was 46'0 34' 56" north. Here they buried in a cache their saddles, horse-gear, and a small supply of powder and musket balls for possible emergencies. The Kooskooskee, it should be borne in mind, is now better known as the Clearwater; it empties into the Snake River, and that into the Columbia. As far as the explorers knew the water-course down which they were to navigate, they called it Clark's River, in honor of Captain Clark. But modern geographers have displaced the name of that eminent explorer and map-maker and have divided the stream, or streams, with other nomenclature.

On the eighth of October the party set out on their long water journey in five canoes, one of which was a small craft intended to go on ahead and pilot the way (which, of course, was unknown) for the four larger ones, in which travelled the main party with their luggage. They met with disaster very soon after their start, one of the canoes having struck a rock, which made a hole in its side and caused the sinking of the craft. Fortunately, no lives were lost, but the voyage was interrupted. The party went ashore and did not resume their journey until their luggage was dried and the canoe repaired. On the ninth, says the journal:—

"The morning was as usual cool; but as the weather both yesterday and to-day was cloudy, our merchandise dried but slowly. The boat, though much injured, was repaired by ten o'clock so as to be perfectly fit for service; but we were obliged to remain during the day till the articles were sufficiently dry to be reloaded. The interval we employed in purchasing fish for the voyage, and conversing with the Indians. In the afternoon we were surprised at hearing that our old Shoshonee guide and his son had left us and had been seen running up the river several miles above. As he had never given any notice of his intention, nor had even received his pay for guiding us, we could not imagine the cause of his desertion; nor did he ever return to explain his conduct. We requested the chief to send a horseman after him to request that he would return and receive what we owed him. From this, however, he dissuaded us, and said very frankly that his nation, the Chopunnish, would take from the old man any presents that he might have on passing their camp. The Indians came about our camp at night, and were very gay and good-humored with the men. Among other exhibitions was that of a squaw who appeared to be crazy. She sang in a wild, incoherent manner, and offered to the spectators all the little articles she possessed, scarifying herself in a horrid manner if anyone refused her present. She seemed to be an object of pity among the Indians, who suffered her to do as she pleased without interruption."

The river was full of rapids and very dangerous rocks and reefs, and the voyagers were able to make only twenty miles a day for some distance along the stream. At the confluence of the Kooskooskee and the Snake River they camped for the night, near the present site of Lewiston, Idaho. This city, first settled in May, 1861, and incorporated in 1863, was named for Captain Lewis of our expedition. From this point the party crossed over into the present State of Washington. Of their experience at their camp here the journal says:—

"Our arrival soon attracted the attention of the Indians, who flocked in all directions to see us. In the evening the Indian from the falls, whom we had seen at Rugged rapid, joined us with his son in a small canoe, and insisted on accompanying us to the falls. Being again reduced to fish and roots, we made an experiment to vary our food by purchasing a few dogs, and after having been accustomed to horse-flesh, felt no disrelish for this new dish. The Chopunnish have great numbers of dogs, which they employ for domestic purposes, but never eat; and our using the flesh of that animal soon brought us into ridicule as dog-eaters."

When Fremont and his men crossed the continent to California, in 1842, they ate the flesh of that species of marmot which we know as the prairie-dog. Long afterwards, when Fremont was a candidate for the office of President of the United States, this fact was recalled to the minds of men, and the famous explorer was denounced as "a dog-eater."

The journal of the explorers gives this interesting account of the Indians among whom they now found themselves:—

"The Chopunnish or Pierced-nose nation, who reside on the Kooskooskee and Lewis' (Snake) rivers, are in person stout, portly, well-looking men; the women are small, with good features and generally handsome, though the complexion of both sexes is darker than that of the Tushepaws. In dress they resemble that nation, being fond of displaying their ornaments. The buffalo or elk-skin robe decorated with beads; sea-shells, chiefly mother-of-pearl, attached to an otter-skin collar and hung in the hair, which falls in front in two cues; feathers, paints of different kinds, principally white, green, and light blue, all of which they find in their own country; these are the chief ornaments they use. In the winter they wear a short skirt of dressed skins, long painted leggings and moccasins, and a plait of twisted grass round the neck. The dress of the women is more simple, consisting of a long shirt of argalia (argali) or ibex (bighorn) skin, reaching down to the ankles, without a girdle; to this are tied little pieces of brass, shells, and other small articles; but the head is not at all ornamented.

"The Chopunnish have very few amusements, for their life is painful and laborious; all their exertions are necessary to earn even their precarious subsistence. During the summer and autumn they are busily occupied in fishing for salmon and collecting their winter store of roots. In winter they hunt the deer on snow-shoes over the plains, and toward spring cross the mountains to the Missouri for the purpose of rafficking for buffalo-robe. The inconveniences of their comfortless life are increased by frequent encounters with their enemies from the west, who drive them over the mountains with the loss of their horses, and sometimes the lives of many of the nation."

After making a short stage on their journey, October 11, the party stopped to trade with the Indians, their stock of provisions being low. They were able to purchase a quantity of salmon and seven dogs. They saw here a novel kind of vapor bath which is thus described in the journal:—

"While this traffic was going on we observed a vapor bath or sweating-house, in a different form from that used on the frontier of the United States or in the Rocky Mountains. It was a hollow square six or eight feet deep, formed in the river bank by damming up with mud the other three sides and covering the whole completely, except an aperture about two feet wide at the top. The bathers descend by this hole, taking with them a number of heated stones and jugs of water; after being seated round the room they throw the water on the stones till the steam becomes of a temperature sufficiently high for their purposes. The baths of the Indians in the Rocky Mountains are of different sizes, the most common being made of mud and sticks like an oven, but the mode of raising the steam is exactly the same. Among both these nations it is very uncommon for a man to bathe alone; he is generally accompanied by one or sometimes several of his acquaintances; indeed, it is so essentially a social amusement, that to decline going in to bathe when invited by a friend is one of the highest indignities which can be offered to him. The Indians on the frontier generally use a bath which will accommodate only one person, formed of a wicker-work of willows about four feet high, arched at the top, and covered with skins. In this the patient sits, till by means of the heated stones and water he has perspired sufficiently. Almost universally these baths are in the neighborhood of running water, into which the Indians plunge immediately on coming out of the vapor bath, and sometimes return again and subject themselves to a second perspiration. This practice is, however, less frequent among our neighboring nations than those to the westward. This bath is employed either for pleasure or for health, and is used indiscriminately for all kinds of diseases."

The expedition was now on the Snake River, making all possible speed toward the Columbia, commonly known to the Indians as "The Great River." The stream was crowded with dangerous rapids, and sundry disasters were met with by the way; thus, on the fourteenth of October, a high wind blowing, one of the canoes was driven upon a rock sidewise and filled with water. The men on board got out and dragged the canoe upon the rock, where they held her above water. Another canoe, having been unloaded, was sent to the relief of the shipwrecked men, who, after being left on the rock for some time, were taken off without any other loss than the bedding of two of them. But accidents like this delayed the party, as they were forced to land and remain long enough to dry the goods that had been exposed to the water. Several such incidents are told in the journal of the explorers. Few Indians were to be seen along the banks of the river, but occasionally the party came to a pile of planks and timbers which were the materials from which were built the houses of such Indians as came here in the fishing season to catch a supply for the winter and for trading purposes. Occasionally, the complete scarcity of fuel compelled the explorers to depart from their general rule to avoid taking any Indian property without leave; and they used some of these house materials for firewood, with the intent to pay the rightful owners, if they should ever be found. On the sixteenth of October, they met with a party of Indians, of whom the journal gives this account:—

"After crossing by land we halted for dinner, and whilst we were eating were visited by five Indians, who came up the river on foot in great haste. We received them kindly, smoked with them, and gave them a piece of tobacco to smoke with their tribe. On receiving the present they set out to return, and continued running as fast as they could while they remained in sight. Their curiosity had been excited by the accounts of our two chiefs, who had gone on in order to apprise the tribes of our approach and of our friendly disposition toward them. After dinner we reloaded the canoes and proceeded. We soon passed a rapid opposite the upper point of a sandy island on the left, which has a smaller island near it. At three miles is a gravelly bar in the river; four miles beyond this the Kimooenim (Snake) empties into the Columbia, and at its mouth has an island just below a small rapid.

"We halted above the point of junction, on the Kimooenim, to confer with the Indians, who had collected in great numbers to receive us. On landing we were met by our two chiefs, to whose good offices we were indebted for this reception, and also the two Indians who had passed us a few days since on horseback; one of whom appeared to be a man of influence, and harangued the Indians on our arrival. After smoking with the Indians, we formed a camp at the point where the two rivers unite, near to which we found some driftwood, and were supplied by our two old chiefs with the stalks of willows and some small bushes for fuel.

"We had scarcely fixed the camp and got the fires prepared, when a chief came from the Indian camp about a quarter of a mile up the Columbia, at the head of nearly two hundred men. They formed a regular procession, keeping time to the music, or, rather, noise of their drums, which they accompanied with their voices; and as they advanced, they ranged themselves in a semicircle around us, and continued singing for some time. We then smoked with them all, and communicated, as well as we could by signs, our friendly intentions towards every nation, and our joy at finding ourselves surrounded by our children. After this we proceeded to distribute presents among them, giving the principal chief a large medal, a shirt, and a handkerchief; to the second chief, a medal of a smaller size; and to a third, who had come down from some of the upper villages, a small medal and a handkerchief. This ceremony being concluded, they left us; but in the course of the afternoon several of them returned, and remained with us till a late hour. After they had dispersed, we proceeded to purchase provisions, and were enabled to collect seven dogs, to which some of the Indians added small presents of fish, and one of them gave us twenty pounds of fat dried horse-flesh."

The explorers were still in the country which is now the State of Washington, at a point where the counties of Franklin, Yakima, and Walla Walla come together, at the junction of the Snake and the Columbia. We quote now from the journal:—

"From the point of junction the country is a continued plain, low near the water, from which it rises gradually, and the only elevation to be seen is a range of high country running from northeast to southwest, where it joins a range of mountains from the southwest, and is on the opposite side about two miles from the Columbia. There is on this plain no tree, and scarcely any shrubs, except a few willow-bushes; even of smaller plants there is not much more than the prickly-pear, which is in great abundance, and is even more thorny and troublesome than any we have yet seen. During this time the principal chief came down with several of his warriors, and smoked with us. We were also visited by several men and women, who offered dogs and fish for sale; but as the fish was out of season, and at present abundant in the river, we contented ourselves with purchasing all the dogs we could obtain.

"The nation among which we now are call themselves Sokulks; with them are united a few of another nation, who reside on a western branch which empties into the Columbia a few miles above the mouth of the latter river, and whose name is Chimnapum. The languages of these two nations, of each of which we obtained a vocabulary, differ but little from each other, or from that of the Chopunnish who inhabit the Kooskooskee and Lewis' rivers. In their dress and general appearance they also much resemble those nations; the men wearing a robe of deer- antelope-skin, under which a few of them have a short leathern shirt. The most striking difference is among the females, the Sokulk women being more inclined to corpulency than any we have yet seen. Their stature is low, their faces are broad, and their heads flattened in such a manner that the forehead is in a straight line from the nose to the crown of the head. Their eyes are of a dirty sable, their hair is coarse and black, and braided without ornament of any kind. Instead of wearing, as do the Chopunnish, long leathern shirts highly decorated with beads and shells, the Sokulk women have no other covering but a truss or piece of leather tied round the hips, and drawn tight between the legs. The ornaments usually worn by both sexes are large blue or white beads, either pendant from their ears, or round the neck, wrists, and arms; they have likewise bracelets of brass, copper, and horn, and some trinkets of shells, fishbones, and curious feathers.

"The houses of the Sokulks are made of large mats of rushes, and are generally of a square or oblong form, varying in length from fifteen to sixty feet, and supported in the inside by poles or forks about six feet high. The top is covered with mats, leaving a space of twelve or fifteen inches the whole length of the house, for the purpose of admitting the light and suffering the smoke to escape. The roof is nearly flat, which seems to indicate that rains are not common in this open country; and the house is not divided into apartments, the fire being in the middle of the enclosure, and immediately under the bole in the roof. The interior is ornamented with their nets, gigs, and other fishing-tackle, as well as the bow of each inmate, and a large quiver of arrows, which are headed with flint.

"The Sokulks seem to be of a mild and peaceable disposition, and live in a state of comparative happiness. The men, like those on the Kimooenim, are said to content themselves with a single wife, with whom the husband, we observe, shares the labors of procuring subsistence much more than is common among savages. What may be considered an unequivocal proof of their good disposition, is the great respect which is shown to old age. Among other marks of it, we noticed in one of the houses an old woman perfectly blind, and who, we were told, had lived more than a hundred winters. In this state of decrepitude, she occupied the best position in the house, seemed to be treated with great kindness, and whatever she said was listened to with much attention. They are by no means obtrusive; and as their fisheries supply them with a competent, if not an abundant subsistence, although they receive thankfully whatever we choose to give, they do not importune us by begging. Fish is, indeed, their chief food, except roots and casual supplies of antelope, which latter, to those who have only bows and arrows, must be very scanty. This diet may be the direct or the remote cause of the chief disorder which prevails among them, as well as among the Flatheads on the Kooskooskee and Lewis' rivers. With all these Indians a bad soreness of the eyes is a very common disorder, which is suffered to ripen by neglect, till many are deprived of one of their eyes, and some have totally lost the use of both. This dreadful calamity may reasonably, we think, be imputed to the constant reflection of the sun on the waters, where they are constantly fishing in the spring, summer, and fall, and during the rest of the year on the snows of a country which affords no object to relieve the sight.

"Among the Sokulks, indeed among all the tribes whose chief subsistence is fish, we have observed that bad teeth are very general; some have the teeth, particularly those of the upper jaw, worn down to the gums, and many of both sexes, even of middle age, have lost them almost entirely. This decay of the teeth is a circumstance very unusual among Indians, either of the mountains or the plains, and seems peculiar to the inhabitants of the Columbia. We cannot avoid regarding as one principal cause of it the manner in which they eat their food. The roots are swallowed as they are dug from the ground, frequently covered with a gritty sand; so little idea have they that this is offensive that all the roots they offer us for sale are in the same condition."

The explorers were now at the entrance of the mighty Columbia,—"The Great River" of which they had heard so much from the Indians. We might suppose that when they actually embarked upon the waters of the famous stream, variously known as "The River of the North" and "The Oregon," the explorers would be touched with a little of the enthusiasm with which they straddled the headwaters of the Missouri and gazed upon the snow-covered peaks of the

Rocky Mountains. But no such kindling of the imagination seems to have been noted in their journal. In this commonplace way, according to their own account, Captain Clark entered upon the mighty Columbia:—

"In the course of the day (October 17, 1805), Captain Clark, in a small canoe with two men, ascended the Columbia. At the distance of five miles he passed an island in the middle of the river, at the head of which was a small but not dangerous rapid. On the left bank, opposite to this island, was a fishing-place consisting of three mat houses. Here were great quantities of salmon drying on scaffolds; and, indeed, from the mouth of the river upward, he saw immense numbers of dead salmon strewed along the shore, or floating on the surface of the water, which is so clear that the fish may be seen swimming at the depth of fifteen or twenty feet. The Indians, who had collected on the banks to observe him, now joined him in eighteen canoes, and accompanied him up the river. A mile above the rapids he came to the lower point of an island, where the course of the stream, which had been from its mouth north eighty-three degrees west, now became due west. He proceeded in that direction, until, observing three house's of mats at a short distance, he landed to visit them. On entering one of these houses, he found it crowded with men, women, and children, who immediately provided a mat for him to sit on, and one of the party undertook to prepare something to eat. He began by bringing in a piece of pine wood that had drifted down the river, which he split into small pieces with a wedge made of elkhorn, by means of a mallet of stone curiously carved. The pieces of wood were then laid on the fire, and several round stones placed upon them. One of the squaws now brought a bucket of water, in which was a large salmon about half dried, and, as the stones became heated, they were put into the bucket till the salmon was sufficiently boiled for use. It was then taken out, put on a platter of rushes neatly made, and laid before Captain Clark, while another was boiled for each of his men. During these preparations he smoked with such about him as would accept of tobacco, but very few were desirous of smoking, a custom which is not general among them, and chiefly used as a matter of form in great ceremonies.

"After eating the fish, which was of an excellent flavor, Captain Clark set out and, at the distance of four miles from the last island, came to the lower point of another near the left shore, where he halted at two large mat-houses. Here, as at the three houses below, the inhabitants were occupied in splitting and drying salmon. The multitudes of this fish are almost inconceivable. The water is so clear that they can readily be seen at the depth of fifteen or twenty feet; but at this season they float in such quantities down the stream, and are drifted ashore, that the Indians have only to collect, split, and dry them on the scaffolds. Where they procure the timber of which these scaffolds are composed he could not learn; but as there is nothing but willow-bushes to be seen for a great distance from this place, it rendered very probable what the Indians assured him by signs, that they often used dried fish as fuel for the common occasions of cooking. From this island they showed him the entrance of the western branch of the Columbia, called the Tapteal, which, as far as could be seen, bears nearly west and empties about eight miles above into the Columbia, the general course of which is northwest."

The Tapteal, as the journal calls it, is now known as the Yakima, a stream which has its source in the Cascade range of mountains, Washington. The party tarried here long enough to secure from the Indians a tolerably correct description of the river upon which they were about to embark. One of the chiefs drew upon the skin-side of a buffalo robe a sketch of the Columbia. And this was transferred to paper and put into the journal. That volume adds here:—

"Having completed the purposes of our stay, we now began to lay in our stores. Fish being out of season, we purchased forty dogs, for which we gave small articles, such as bells, thimbles, knitting-needles, brass wire, and a few beads, an exchange with which they all seemed perfectly satisfied. These dogs, with six prairie-cocks killed this morning, formed a plentiful supply for the present. We here left our guide and the two young men who had accompanied him, two of the three being unwilling to go any further, and the third being of no use, as he was not acquainted with the river below. We therefore took no Indians but our two chiefs, and resumed our journey in the presence of many of the Sokulks, who came to witness our departure. The morning was cool and fair, and the wind from the southeast."

They now began again to meet Indians who had never before seen white men. On the nineteenth, says the journal:—

"The great chief, with two of his inferior chiefs and a third belonging to a band on the river below, made us a visit at a very early hour. The first of these was called Yelleppit,—a handsome, well-proportioned man, about five feet eight inches high, and thirty-five years of age, with a bold and dignified countenance; the rest were not distinguished in their appearance. We smoked with them, and after making a speech, gave a medal, a handkerchief, and a string of wampum to Yelleppit, but a string of wampum only to the inferior chiefs. He requested us to remain till the middle of the day, in order that all his nation might come and see us; but we excused ourselves by telling him that on our return we would spend two or three days with him. This conference detained us till nine o'clock, by which time great numbers of the Indians had come down to visit us. On leaving them we went on for eight miles, when we came to an island near the left shore, which continued six miles in length. At its lower extremity is a small island on which are five houses, at present vacant, though the scaffolds of fish are as usual abundant. A short distance below are two more islands, one of them near the middle of the river. On this there were seven houses, but as soon as the Indians, who were drying fish, saw us, they fled to their houses, and not one of them appeared till we had passed; when they came out in greater numbers than is usual for houses of that size, which induced us to think that the inhabitants of the five lodges had been alarmed at our approach and taken refuge with them. We were very desirous of landing in order to relieve their apprehensions, but as there was a bad rapid along the island all our care was necessary to prevent injury to the canoes. At the foot of this rapid is a rock on the left shore, which is fourteen miles from our camp of last night and resembles a hat in shape."

Later in the day, Captain Clark ascended a bluff on the river bank, where he saw "a very high mountain covered with snow." This was Mount St. Helen's, in Cowlitz County, Washington. The altitude of the peak is nine thousand seven hundred and fifty feet. "Having arrived at the lower ends of the rapids below the bluff before any of the rest of the party, he sat down on a rock to wait for them, and, seeing a crane fly across the river, shot it, and it fell near him. Several Indians had been before this passing on the opposite side towards the rapids, and some who were then nearly in front of him, being either alarmed at his appearance or the report of the gun, fled to their houses. Captain Clark was afraid that these people had not yet heard that the white men were coming, and therefore, in order to allay their uneasiness before the rest of the party should arrive, he got into the small canoe with three men, rowed over towards the houses, and, while crossing, shot a duck, which fell into the water. As he approached no person was to be seen except three men in the plains, and they, too, fled as he came near the shore. He landed in front of five houses close to each other, but no one appeared, and the doors, which were of mat, were closed. He went towards one of them with a pipe in his hand, and, pushing aside the mat, entered the lodge, where he found thirty-two persons, chiefly men and women, with a few children, all in the greatest consternation; some hanging down their heads, others crying and wringing their hands. He went up to them, and shook hands with each one in the most friendly manner; but their apprehensions, which had for a moment subsided, revived on his taking out a burning-glass, as there was no roof to the house, and lighting his pipe: he then offered it to several of the men, and distributed among the women and children some small trinkets which he had with him, and gradually restored a degree of tranquillity among them.

"Leaving this house, and directing each of his men to visit a house, he entered a second. Here he found the inmates more terrified than those in the first; but he succeeded in pacifying them, and afterward went into the other houses, where the men had been equally successful. Retiring from the houses, he seated himself on a rock, and beckoned to some of the men to come and smoke with him; but none of them ventured to join him till the canoes arrived with the two chiefs, who immediately explained our pacific intention towards them. Soon after the interpreter's wife (Sacajawea) landed, and her presence dissipated all doubts of our being well-disposed, since in this country no woman ever accompanies a war party: they therefore all came out, and seemed perfectly reconciled; nor could we, indeed, blame them for their terrors, which were perfectly natural. They told the two chiefs that they knew we were not men, for they had seen us fall from the clouds. In fact, unperceived by them, Captain Clark had shot the white crane, which they had seen fall just before he appeared to their eyes: the duck which he had killed also fell close by him; and as there were some clouds flying over at the moment, they connected the fall of the birds with his sudden appearance, and believed that he had himself actually dropped from the clouds; considering the noise of the rifle, which they had never heard before, the sound announcing so extraordinary an event. This belief was strengthened, when, on entering the room, he brought down fire from the heavens by means of his burning-glass. We soon convinced them, however, that we were merely mortals; and after one of our chiefs had explained our history and objects, we all smoked together in great harmony."

Chapter XVI — Down the Columbia to Tidewater

The voyagers were now drifting down the Columbia River, and they found the way impeded by many rapids, some of them very dangerous. But their skill in the handling of their canoes seems to have been equal to the occasion, although they were sometimes compelled to go around the more difficult rapids, making a short land portage. When they had travelled about forty miles down the river, they landed opposite an island on which were twenty-four houses of Indians; the people, known as the Pishquitpahs, were engaged in drying fish. No sooner had the white men landed than the Indians, to the number of one hundred, came across the stream bringing with them some firewood, a most welcome present in that treeless country. The visitors were entertained with presents and a long smoke at the pipe of peace. So pleased were they with the music of two violins played by Cruzatte and Gibson, of the exploring party, that they remained by the fire of the white men all night. The news of the arrival of the white strangers soon spread, and next morning about two hundred more of the Indians assembled to gaze on them. Later in the day, having gotten away from their numerous inquisitive visitors, the explorers passed downstream and landed on a small island to examine a curious vault, in which were placed the remains of the dead of the tribe. The journal says:—

"This place, in which the dead are deposited, is a building about sixty feet long and twelve feet wide, formed by placing in the ground poles or forks six feet high, across which a long pole is extended the whole length of the structure; against this ridge-pole are placed broad boards and pieces of canoes, in a slanting direction, so as to form a shed. It stands east and west, and neither of the extremities is closed. On entering the western end we observed a number of bodies wrapped carefully in leather robes, and arranged in rows on boards, which were then covered with a mat. This was the part destined for those who had recently died; a little further on, bones half decayed were scattered about, and in the centre of the building was a large pile of them heaped promiscuously on each other. At the eastern extremity was a mat, on which twenty-one skulls were placed in a circular form; the mode of interment being first to wrap the body in robes, then as it decays to throw the bones into the heap, and place the skulls together. From the different boards and pieces of canoes which form the vault were suspended, on the inside, fishing-nets, baskets, wooden bowls, robes, skins, trenchers, and trinkets of various kinds, obviously intended as offerings of affection to deceased relatives. On the outside of the vault were the skeletons of several horses, and great quantities of their bones were in the neighborhood, which induced us to believe that these animals were most probably sacrificed at the funeral rites of their masters."

Just below this stand the party met Indians who traded with tribes living near the great falls of the Columbia. That place they designated as "Tum-tum," a word that signifies the throbbing of the heart. One of these Indians had a sailor's jacket, and others had a blue blanket and a scarlet blanket. These articles had found their way up the river from white traders on the seashore.

On the twenty-first of October the explorers discovered a considerable stream which appeared to rise in the southeast and empty into the Columbia on the left. To this stream they gave the name of Lepage for Bastien Lepage, one of the voyageurs accompanying the party. The watercourse, however, is now known as John Day's River. John Day was a mighty hunter and backwoodsman from Kentucky who went across the continent, six years later, with a party bound for Astoria, on the Columbia. From the rapids below the John Day River the Lewis and Clark party caught their first sight of Mount Hood, a famous peak of the Cascade range of mountains, looming up in the southwest, eleven thousand two hundred and twenty-five feet high. Next day they passed the mouth of another river entering the Columbia from the south and called by the Indians the Towahnahiooks, but known to modern geography as the Des Chutes, one of the largest southern tributaries of the Columbia. Five miles below the mouth of this stream the party camped. Near them was a party of Indians engaged in drying and packing salmon. Their method of doing this is thus described:—

"The manner of doing this is by first opening the fish and exposing it to the sun on scaffolds. When it is sufficiently dried it is pounded between two stones till it is pulverized, and is then placed in a basket about two feet long and one in diameter, neatly made of grass and rushes, and lined with the skin of a salmon stretched and dried for the purpose. Here the fish are pressed down as hard as possible, and the top is covered with fish-skins, which are secured by cords through the holes of the basket. These baskets are then placed in some dry situation, the corded part upward, seven being usually placed as close as they can be put together, and five on the top of these. The whole is then wrapped up in mats, and made fast by cords, over which mats are again thrown. Twelve of these baskets, each of which contains from ninety to one hundred pounds, form a stack, which is left exposed till it is sent to market. The fish thus preserved keep sound and sweet for several years, and great quantities, they inform us, are sent to the Indians who live below the falls, whence it finds its way to the whites who visit the mouth of the Columbia. We observe, both near the lodges and on the rocks in the river, great numbers of stacks of these pounded fish. Besides fish, these people supplied us with filberts and berries, and we purchased a dog for supper; but it was with much difficulty that we were able to buy wood enough to cook it."

On the twenty-third the voyagers made the descent of the great falls which had so long been an object of dread to them. The whole height of the falls is thirty-seven feet, eight inches, in a distance of twelve hundred yards. A portage of four hundred and fifty yards was made around the first fall, which is twenty feet high, and perpendicular. By means of lines the canoes were let down the rapids below. At the season of high water the falls become mere rapids up which the salmon can pass. On this point the journal says:—

"From the marks everywhere perceivable at the falls, it is obvious that in high floods, which must be in the spring, the water below the falls rises nearly to a level with that above them. Of this rise, which is occasioned by some obstructions which we do not as yet know, the salmon must avail themselves to pass up the river in such multitudes that this fish is almost the only one caught in great abundance above the falls; but below that place we observe the salmon-trout, and the heads of a species of trout smaller than the salmon-trout, which is in great quantities, and which they are now burying, to be used as their winter food. A hole of any size being dug, the sides and bottom are lined with straw, over which skins are laid; on these the fish, after being well dried, are laid, covered with other skins, and the hole is closed with a layer of earth twelve or fifteen inches deep. . . .

"We saw no game except a sea-otter, which was shot in the narrow channel as we were coming down, but we could not get it. Having, therefore, scarcely any provisions, we purchased eight small fat dogs: a food to which we were compelled to have recourse, as the Indians were very unwilling to sell us any of their good fish, which they reserved for the market below. Fortunately, however, habit had completely overcome the repugnance which we felt at first at eating this animal, and the dog, if not a favorite dish, was always an acceptable one. The meridian altitude of to-day gave 45'0 42' 57.3" north as the latitude of our camp.

"On the beach, near the Indian huts, we observed two canoes of a different shape and size from any which we had hitherto seen. One of these we got by giving our smallest canoe a hatchet, and a few trinkets to the owner, who said he had obtained it from a white man below the falls in exchange for a horse. These canoes were very beautifully made: wide in the middle, and tapering towards each end, with curious figures carved on the bow. They were thin, but, being strengthened by crossbars about an inch in diameter, tied with strong pieces of bark through holes in the sides, were able to bear very heavy burdens, and seemed calculated to live in the roughest water."

At this point the officers of the expedition observed signs of uneasiness in the two friendly Indian chiefs who had thus far accompanied them. They also heard rumors that the warlike Indians below them were meditating an attack as the party went down. The journal says:—

"Being at all times ready for any attempt of that sort, we were not under greater apprehensions than usual at this intelligence. We therefore only re-examined our arms, and increased the ammunition to one hundred rounds. Our chiefs, who had not the same motives of confidence, were by no means so much at their ease, and when at night they saw the Indians leave us earlier than usual, their suspicions of an intended attack were confirmed, and they were very much alarmed.

"The Indians approached us with apparent caution, and behaved with more than usual reserve. Our two chiefs, by whom these circumstances were not observed, now told us that they wished to return home; that they could be no longer of any service to us; that they could not understand the language of the people below the falls; that those people formed a different nation from their own; that the two people had been at war with each other; and that as the Indians had expressed a resolution to attack us, they would certainly kill them. We endeavored to quiet their fears, and requested them to stay two nights longer, in which time we would see the Indians below, and make a peace between the two nations. They replied that they were anxious to return and see their horses. We however insisted on their remaining with us, not only in hopes of bringing about an accommodation between them and their enemies, but because they might be able to detect any hostile designs against us, and also assist us in passing the next falls, which are not far off, and represented as very difficult. They at length agreed to stay with us two nights longer."

The explorers now arrived at the next fall of the Columbia. Here was a quiet basin, on the margin of which were three Indian huts. The journal tells the rest of the story:—

"At the extremity of this basin stood a high black rock, which, rising perpendicularly from the right shore, seemed to run wholly across the river: so totally, indeed, did it appear to stop the passage, that we could not see where the water escaped, except that the current was seemingly drawn with more than usual velocity to the left of the rock, where was heard a great roaring. We landed at the huts of the Indians, who went with us to the top of the rock, from which we had a view of all the difficulties of the channel. We were now no longer at a loss to account for the rising of the river at the falls; for this tremendous rock was seen stretching across the river, to meet the high hills on the left shore, leaving a channel of only forty-five yards wide, through which the whole body of the Columbia pressed its way. The water, thus forced into so narrow a passage, was thrown into whirls, and swelled and boiled in every part with the wildest agitation. But the alternative of carrying the boats over this high rock was almost impossible in our present situation; and as the chief danger seemed to be, not from any obstructions in the channel, but from the great waves and whirlpools, we resolved to attempt the passage, in the hope of being able, by dexterous steering, to descend in safety. This we undertook, and with great care were able to get through, to the astonishment of the Indians in the huts we had just passed, who now collected to see us from the top of the rock. The channel continued thus confined for the space of about half a mile, when the rock ceased. We passed a single Indian hut at the foot of it, where the river again enlarges to the width of two hundred yards, and at the distance of a mile and a half stopped to view a very bad rapid; this is formed by two rocky islands which divide the channel, the lower and larger of which is in the middle of the river. The appearance of this place was so unpromising that we unloaded all the most valuable articles, such as guns, ammunition, our papers, etc., and sent them by land, with all the men that could not swim, to the extremity of these rapids. We then descended with the canoes, two at a time; though the canoes took in some water, we all went through safely; after which we made two miles, stopped in a deep bend of the river toward the right, and camped a little above a large village of twenty-one houses. Here we landed; and as it was late before all the canoes joined us, we were obliged to remain this evening, the difficulties of the navigation having permitted us to make only six miles."

They were then among the Echeloots, a tribe of the Upper Chinooks, now nearly extinct. The white men were much interested in the houses of these people, which, their journal set forth, were "the first wooden buildings seen since leaving the Illinois country." This is the manner of their construction:—

"A large hole, twenty feet wide and thirty in length, was dug to the depth of six feet; the sides of which were lined with split pieces of timber rising just above the surface of the ground, and smoothed to the same width by burning, or by being shaved with small iron axes. These timbers were secured in their erect position by a pole stretched along the side of the building near the eaves, and supported on a strong post fixed at each corner. The timbers at the gable ends rose gradually higher, the middle pieces being the broadest. At the top of these was a sort of semicircle, made to receive a ridge-pole the whole length of the house, propped by an additional post in the middle, and forming the top of the roof. From this ridge-pole to the eaves of the house were placed a number of small poles or rafters, secured at each end by fibres of the cedar. On these poles, which were connected by small transverse bars of wood, was laid a covering of white cedar, or arbor vitae, kept on by strands of cedar fibres; but a small space along the whole length of the ridge-pole was left uncovered, for the purpose of light, and of permitting the smoke to pass out. The roof, thus formed, had a descent about equal to that common among us, and near the eaves it was perforated with a number of small holes, made, most probably, for the discharge of arrows in case of an attack. The only entrance was by a small door at the gable end, cut out of the middle piece of timber, twenty-nine and a half inches high, fourteen inches broad, and reaching only eighteen inches above the earth. Before this hole is hung a mat; on pushing it aside and crawling through, the descent is by a small wooden ladder, made in the form of those used among us. One-half of the inside is used as a place of deposit for dried fish, of which large quantities are stored away, and with a few baskets of berries form the only family provisions; the other half, adjoining the door, remains for the accommodation of the family. On each side are arranged near the walls small beds of mats placed on little scaffolds or bedsteads, raised from eighteen inches to three feet from the ground; and in the middle of the vacant space is the fire, or sometimes two or three fires, when, as is usually the case, the house contains three families."

Houses very like these are built by the Ahts or Nootkas, a tribe of Indians inhabiting parts of Vancouver Island and the adjacent mainland. A Nootka calls his house an ourt.

The good offices of Lewis and Clark, who were always ready to make peace between hostile tribes, were again successful here. The Echeloots received the white men with much kindness, invited them to their houses, and returned their visits after the explorers had camped. Lewis and Clark told the Echeloot chiefs that the war was destroying them and their industries, bringing want and privation upon them. The Indians listened with attention to what was said, and after some talk they agreed to make peace with their ancient enemies. Impressed with the sincerity of this agreement, the captains of the expedition invested the principal chief with a medal and some small articles of clothing. The two faithful chiefs who had accompanied the white men from the headwaters of the streams now bade farewell to their friends and allies, the explorers. They bought horses of the Echeloots and returned to their distant homes by land.

Game here became more abundant, and on the twenty-sixth of October the journal records the fact that they received from the Indians a present of deer-meat, and on that day their hunters found plenty of tracks of elk and deer in the mountains, and they brought in five deer, four very large gray squirrels, and a grouse. Besides these delicacies, one of the men killed in the river a salmon-trout which was fried in bear's oil and, according to the journal, "furnished a dish of a very delightful flavor," doubtless a pleasing change from the diet of dog's flesh with which they had so recently been regaled.

Two of the Echeloot chiefs remained with the white men to guide them on their way down the river. These were joined by seven others of their tribe, to whom the explorers were kind and attentive. But the visitors could not resist the temptation to pilfer from the goods exposed to dry in the sun. Being checked in this sly business, they became ill-humored and returned, angry, down the river.

The explorers noticed here that the Indians flattened the heads of males as well as females. Higher up the river, only the women and female children had flat heads. The custom of artificially flattening the heads of both men and women, in infancy, was formerly practised by nearly all the tribes of the Chinook family along the Columbia River. Various means are used to accomplish this purpose, the most common and most cruel being to bind a flat board on the forehead of an infant in such a way that it presses on the skull and forces the forehead up on to the top of the head. As a man whose head has been flattened in infancy grows older, the deformity partly disappears; but the flatness of the head is always regarded as a tribal badge of great merit.

"On the morning of the twenty-eighth," says the journal, having dried our goods, we were about setting out, when three canoes came from above to visit us, and at the same time two others from below arrived for the same purpose. Among these last was an Indian who wore his hair in a que, and had on a round hat and a sailor's jacket, which he said he had obtained from the people below the great rapids, who bought them from the whites. This interview detained us till nine o'clock, when we proceeded down the river, which is now bordered with cliffs of loose dark colored rocks about ninety feet high, with a thin covering of pines and other small trees. At the distance of four miles we reached a small village of eight houses under some high rocks on the right with a small creek on the opposite side of the river.

"We landed and found the houses similar to those we had seen at the great narrows; on entering one of them we saw a British musket, a cutlass, and several brass tea-kettles, of which they seemed to be very fond. There were figures of men, birds, and different animals, which were cut and painted on the boards which form the sides of the room; though the workmanship of these uncouth figures was very rough, they were highly esteemed by the Indians as the finest frescos of more civilized people. This tribe is called the Chilluckittequaw; their language, though somewhat different from that of the Echeloots, has many of the same words, and is sufficiently intelligible to the neighboring Indians. We procured from them a vocabulary, and then, after buying five small dogs, some dried berries, and a white bread or cake made of roots, we left them. The wind, however, rose so high that we were obliged, after going one mile, to land on the left side, opposite a rocky island, and pass the day."

On the same day the white chiefs visited one of the most prominent of the native houses built along the river.

"This," says the journal, "was the residence of the principal chief of the Chilluckittequaw nation, who we found was the same between whom and our two chiefs we had made a peace at the Echeloot village. He received us, very kindly, and set before us pounded fish, filberts, nuts, the berries of the sacacommis, and white bread made of roots. We gave, in return, a bracelet of ribbon to each of the women of the house, with which they were very much pleased. The chief had several articles, such as scarlet and blue cloth, a sword, a jacket, and a hat, which must have been procured from the whites, and on one side of the room were two wide, split boards, placed together so as to make space for a rude figure of a man cut and painted on them. On pointing to this, and asking him what it meant, he said something, of which all that we understood was 'good,' and then stepped up to the painting, and took out his bow and quiver, which, with some other warlike instruments, were kept behind it.

"He then directed his wife to hand him his medicine-bag, from which he drew out fourteen forefingers, which he told us had belonged to the same number of his enemies, whom he had killed in fighting with the nations to the southeast, in which direction he pointed; alluding, no doubt, to the Snake Indians, the common enemy of the tribes on the Columbia. This bag is usually about two feet in length, and contains roots, pounded dirt, etc., which only the Indians know how to appreciate. It is suspended in the middle of the lodge; and it is considered as a species of sacrilege for any one but the owner to touch it. It is an object of religious fear; and, from its supposed sanctity, is the chief place for depositing their medals and more valuable articles. They have likewise small bags, which they preserve in their great medicine-bag, from whence they are taken, and worn around their waists and necks as amulets against any real or imaginary evils. This was the first time we had been apprised that the Indians ever carried from the field any other trophy than the scalp. These fingers were shown with great exultation; and, after an harangue, which we were left to presume was in praise of his exploits, the chief carefully replaced them among the valuable contents of his red medicine-bag. The inhabitants of this village being part of the same nation with those of the village we had passed above, the language of the two was the same, and their houses were of similar form and materials, and calculated to contain about thirty souls. They were unusually hospitable and good-humored, so that we gave to the place the name of the Friendly village. We breakfasted here; and after purchasing twelve dogs, four sacks of fish, and a few dried berries, proceeded on our journey. The hills as we passed were high, with steep, rocky sides, with pine and white oak, and an undergrowth of shrubs scattered over them."

Leaving the Friendly village, the party went on their way down the river. Four miles below they came to a small and rapid river which they called the Cataract River, but which is now known as the Klikitat. The rapids of the stream, according to the Indians, were so numerous that salmon could not ascend it, and the Indians who lived along its banks subsisted on what game they could kill with their bows and arrows and on the berries which, in certain seasons, were plentiful. Again we notice the purchase of dogs; this time only four were bought, and the party proceeded on their way. That night, having travelled thirty-two miles, they camped on the right bank of the river in what is now Skamania County, Washington. Three huts were inhabited by a considerable number of Indians, of whom the journal has this to say:—

"On our first arrival they seemed surprised, but not alarmed, and we soon became intimate by means of smoking and our favorite entertainment for the Indians, the violin. They gave us fruit, roots, and root-bread, and we purchased from them three dogs. The houses of these people are similar to those of the Indians above, and their language is the same; their dress also, consisting of robes or skins of wolves, deer, elk, and wildcat, is made nearly after the same model; their hair is worn in plaits down each shoulder, and round their neck is put a strip of some skin with the tail of the animal hanging down over the breast; like the Indians above, they are fond of otter-skins, and give a great price for them. We here saw the skin of a mountain sheep, which they say lives among the rocks in the mountains; the skin was covered with white hair; the wool was long, thick, and coarse, with long coarse hair on the top of the neck and on the back, resembling somewhat the bristles of a goat. Immediately behind the village is a pond, in which were great numbers of small swan."

The "mountain sheep" mentioned here are not the bighorn of which we have heard something in the earlier part of this narrative, but a species of wild goat found among the Cascade Mountains. The "wildcat" above referred to is probably that variety of lynx known in Canada and most of the Northern States and the Pacific as the *loup-cervier*, or vulgarly, the "lucifee."

On the last day of October, the next of the more difficult rapids being near, Captain Clark went ahead to examine the "shoot," as the explorers called the place which we know as the chute. In the thick wood that bordered the river he found an ancient burial-place which he thus describes:—

"It consists of eight vaults made of pine or cedar boards closely connected, about eight feet square and six in height; the top covered with wide boards sloping a little, so as to convey off the rain. The direction of all of these vaults is east and west, the door being on the eastern side, partially stopped with wide boards decorated with rude pictures of men and other animals. On entering he found in some of them four dead bodies, carefully wrapped in skins, tied with cords of grass and bark, lying on a mat, in a direction east and west. The other vaults contained only bones, which were in some of them piled to the height of four feet. On the tops of the vaults, and on poles attached to them, bung brass kettles and frying-pans with holes in their bottoms, baskets, bowls, sea-shells, skins, pieces of cloth, hair, bags of trinkets and small bones—the offerings of friendship or affection, which have been saved by a pious veneration from the ferocity of war, or the more dangerous temptations of individual gain. The whole of the walls as well as the door were decorated with strange figures cut and painted on them; and besides were several wooden images of men, some so old and decayed as to have almost lost their shape, which were all placed against the sides of the vaults. These images, as well as those in the houses we have lately seen, do not appear to be at all the objects of adoration; in this place they were most probably intended as resemblances of those whose decease they indicate; when we observe them in houses, they occupy the most conspicuous part, but are treated more like ornaments than objects of worship."

The white men were visited at their camp by many Indians from the villages farther up the stream. The journal says:—

"We had an opportunity of seeing to-day the hardihood of the Indians of the neighboring village. One of the men shot a goose, which fell into the river and was floating rapidly toward the great shoot, when an Indian observing it plunged in after it. The whole mass of the waters of the Columbia, just preparing to descend its narrow channel, carried the animal down with great rapidity. The Indian followed it fearlessly to within one hundred and fifty feet of the rocks, where he would inevitably have been dashed to pieces; but seizing his prey he turned round and swam ashore with great composure. We very willingly relinquished our right to the bird in favor of the Indian who had thus saved it at the imminent hazard of his life; he immediately set to work and picked off about half the feathers, and then, without opening it, ran a stick through it and carried it off to roast."

With many hair's-breadth escapes, the expedition now passed through the rapids or "great shoot." The river here is one hundred and fifty yards wide and the rapids are confined to an area four hundred yards long, crowded with islands and rocky ledges. They found the Indians living along the banks of the stream to be kindly disposed; but they had learned, by their intercourse with tribes living below, to set a high value on their wares. They asked high prices for anything they had for sale. The journal says:—

"We cannot learn precisely the nature of the trade carried on by the Indians with the inhabitants below. But as their knowledge of the whites seems to be very imperfect, and as the only articles which they carry to market, such as pounded fish, bear-grass, and roots, cannot be an object of much foreign traffic, their intercourse appears to be an intermediate trade with the natives near the mouth of the Columbia. From them these people obtain, in exchange for their fish, roots, and bear-grass, blue and white beads, copper tea-kettles, brass armbands, some scarlet and blue robes, and a few articles of old European clothing. But their great object is to obtain beads, an article which holds the first place in their ideas of relative value, and to procure which they will sacrifice their last article of clothing or last mouthful of food. Independently of their fondness for them as an ornament, these beads are the medium of trade, by which they obtain from the Indians still higher up the river, robes, skins, chappelel bread, bear-grass, etc. Those Indians in turn employ them to procure from the Indians in the Rocky Mountains, bear-grass, pachico-roots, robes, etc.

"These Indians are rather below the common size, with high cheek-bones; their noses are pierced, and in full dress ornamented with a tapering piece of white shell or wampum about two inches long. Their eyes are exceedingly sore and weak; many of them have only a single eye, and some are perfectly blind. Their teeth prematurely decay, and in frequent instances are altogether worn away. Their general health, however, seems to be good, the only disorder we have remarked being tumors in different parts of the body."

The more difficult rapid was passed on the second day of November, the luggage being sent down by land and the empty canoes taken down with great care. The journal of that date says:—

"The rapid we have just passed is the last of all the descents of the Columbia. At this place the first tidewater commences, and the river in consequence widens immediately below the rapid. As we descended we reached, at the distance of one mile from the rapid, a creek under a bluff on the left; at three miles is the lower point of Strawberry Island. To this immediately succeed three small islands covered with wood. In the meadow to the right, at some distance from the hills, stands a perpendicular rock about eight hundred feet high and four hundred yards around the base. This we called Beacon Rock. Just below is an Indian village of nine houses, situated between two small creeks. At this village the river widens to nearly a mile in extent; the low grounds become wider, and they as well as the mountains on each side are covered with pine, spruce-pine, cottonwood, a species of ash, and some alder. After being so long accustomed to the dreary nakedness of the country above, the change is as grateful to the eye as it is useful in supplying us with fuel. Four miles from the village is a point of land on the right, where the hills become lower, but are still thickly timbered. The river is now about two miles wide, the current smooth and gentle, and the effect of the tide has been sensible since leaving the rapid. Six miles lower is a rock rising from the middle of the river to the height of one hundred feet, and about eighty yards at its base. We continued six miles further, and halted for the night under a high projecting rock on the left side of the river, opposite the point of a large meadow.

"The mountains, which, from the great shoot to this place, are high, rugged, and thickly covered with timber, chiefly of the pine species, here leave the river on each side; the river becomes two and one-half miles in width; the low grounds are extensive and well supplied with wood. The Indians whom we left at the portage passed us on their way down the river, and seven others, who were descending in a canoe for the purpose of trading below, camped with us. We had made from the foot of the great shoot twenty-nine miles to-day. The ebb tide rose at our camp about nine inches; the flood must rise much higher. We saw great numbers of water-fowl, such as swan, geese, ducks of various kinds, gulls, plovers, and the white and gray brant, of which last we killed eighteen."

Chapter XVII — From Tidewater to the Sea

Near the mouth of the river which the explorers named Quicksand River (now Sandy), they met a party of fifteen Indians who had lately been down to the mouth of the Columbia. These people told the white men that they had seen three vessels at anchor below, and, as these must needs be American, or European, the far-voyaging explorers were naturally pleased. When they had camped that night, they received other visitors of whom the journal makes mention:—

"A canoe soon after arrived from the village at the foot of the last rapid, with an Indian and his family, consisting of a wife, three children, and a woman who had been taken prisoner from the Snake Indians, living on a river from the south, which we afterward found to be the Multnomah. Sacajawea was immediately introduced to her, in hopes that, being a Snake Indian, they might understand each other; but their language was not sufficiently intelligible to permit them to converse together. The Indian had a gun with a brass barrel and cock, which he appeared to value highly."

The party had missed the Multnomah River in their way down, although this is one of the three largest tributaries of the Columbia, John Day's River and the Des Chutes being the other two. A group of islands near the mouth of the Multnomah hides it from the view of the passing voyager. The stream is now more generally known as the Willamette, or Wallamet. The large city of Portland, Oregon, is built on the river, about twelve miles from its junction with the Columbia. The Indian tribes along the banks of the Multnomah, or Willamette, subsisted largely on the wappatoo, an eatable root, about the size of a hen's egg and closely resembling a potato. This root is much sought after by the Indians and is eagerly bought by tribes living in regions where it is not to be found. The party made great use of the wappatoo after they had learned how well it served in place of bread. They bought here all that the Indians could spare and then made their way down the river to an open prairie where they camped for dinner and found many signs of elk and deer. The journal says:—

"When we landed for dinner, a number of Indians from the last village came down for the purpose, as we supposed, of paying us a friendly visit, as they had put on their favorite dresses. In addition to their usual covering they had scarlet and blue blankets, sailors' jackets and trousers, shirts and hats. They had all of them either war-axes, spears, and bows and arrows, or muskets and pistols, with tin powder-flasks. We smoked with them and endeavored to show them every attention, but we soon found them very assuming and disagreeable companions. While we were eating, they stole the pipe with which they were smoking, and the greatcoat of one of the men. We immediately searched them all, and discovered the coat stuffed under the root of a tree near where they were sitting; but the pipe we could not recover. Finding us determined not to suffer any imposition, and discontented with them, they showed their displeasure in the only way which they dared, by returning in an ill-humor to their village.

"We then proceeded and soon met two canoes, with twelve men of the same Skilloot nation, who were on their way from below. The larger of the canoes was ornamented with the figure of a bear in the bow and a man in the stern, both nearly as large as life, both made of painted wood and very neatly fixed to the boat. In the same canoe were two Indians, finely dressed and with round hats. This circumstance induced us to give the name of Image-canoe to the large island, the lower end of which we now passed at the distance of nine miles from its head."

Here they had their first full view of Mt. St. Helen's, sometimes called Mt. Ranier. The peak is in Washington and is 9,750 feet high. It has a sugar-loaf, or conical, shape and is usually covered with snow. The narrative of the expedition continues as follows:—

"The Skilloots that we passed to-day speak a language somewhat different from that of the Echeloots or Chilluckittequaws near the long narrows. Their dress, however, is similar, except that the Skilloots possess more articles procured from the white traders; and there is this farther difference between them, that the Skilloots, both males and females, have the head flattened. Their principal food is fish, wappatoo roots, and some elk and deer, in killing which with arrows they seem to be very expert; for during the short time we remained at the village, three deer were brought in. We also observed there a tame blaireau, (badger)."

The journal, November 5, says:—

"Our choice of a camp had been very unfortunate; for on a sand-island opposite us were immense numbers of geese, swan, ducks, and other wild fowl, which during the whole night serenaded us with a confusion of noises which completely prevented our sleeping. During the latter part of the night it rained, and we therefore willingly left camp at an early hour. We passed at three miles a small prairie, where the river is only three-quarters of a mile in width, and soon after two houses on the left, half a mile distant from each other; from one of which three men came in a canoe merely to look at us, and having done so returned home. At eight miles we came to the lower point of an island, separated from the right side by a narrow channel, on which, a short distance above the end of the island, is situated a large village. It is built more compactly than the generality of the Indian villages, and the front has fourteen houses, which are ranged for a quarter of a mile along the channel. As soon as we were discovered seven canoes came out to see us, and after some traffic, during which they seemed well disposed and orderly, accompanied us a short distance below."

The explorers now met Indians of a different nation from those whom they had seen before. The journal says:—

"These people seem to be of a different nation from those we have just passed; they are low in stature, ill shaped, and all have their heads flattened. They call themselves Wahkiacum, and their language differs from that of the tribes above, with whom they trade for wappatoo-roots. The houses are built in a different style, being raised entirely above ground, with the caves about five feet high and the door at the corner. Near the end, opposite this door, is a single fireplace, round which are the beds, raised four feet from the floor of earth; over the fire are hung the fresh fish, which, when dried, are stowed away with the wappatoo-roots under the beds. The dress of the men is like that of the people above, but the women are clad in a peculiar manner, the robe not reaching lower than the hip, and the body being covered in cold weather by a sort of corset of fur, curiously plaited and reaching from the arms to the hip; added to this is a sort of petticoat, or rather tissue of white cedar bark, bruised or broken into small strands, and woven into a girdle by several cords of the same material. Being tied round the middle, these strands hang down as low as the knee in front, and to the mid-leg behind; they are of sufficient thickness to answer the purpose of concealment whilst the female stands in an erect position, but in any other attitude form but a very ineffectual defence. Sometimes the tissue is strings of silk-grass, twisted and

107

knotted at the end. After remaining with them about an hour, we proceeded down the channel with an Indian dressed in a sailor's jacket for our pilot, and on reaching the main channel were visited by some Indians who have a temporary residence on a marshy island in the middle of the river, where is a great abundance of water-fowl."

The tribe of Indians known as the Wahkiacums has entirely disappeared; but the name survives as that of one of the counties of Washington bordering on the Columbia. Wahkiacum is the county lying next west of Cowlitz. When the explorers passed down the river under the piloting of their Indian friend wearing a sailor's jacket, they were in a thick fog. This cleared away and a sight greeted their joyful vision. Their story says:—

"At a distance of twenty miles from our camp, we halted at a village of Wahkiacums, consisting of seven ill-looking houses, built in the same form with those above, and situated at the foot of the high hills on the right, behind two small marshy islands. We merely stopped to purchase some food and two beaver skins, and then proceeded. Opposite to these islands the hills on the left retire, and the river widens into a kind of bay, crowded with low islands, subject to be overflowed occasionally by the tide. We had not gone far from this village when, the fog suddenly clearing away, we were at last presented with the glorious sight of the ocean—that ocean, the object of all our labors, the reward of all our anxieties. This animating sight exhilarated the spirits of all the party, who were still more delighted on hearing the distant roar of the breakers. We went on with great cheerfulness along the high, mountainous country which bordered the right bank: the shore, however, was so bold and rocky, that we could not, until at a distance of fourteen miles from the last village, find any spot fit for an encampment. Having made during the day thirty-four miles, we now spread our mats on the ground, and passed the night in the rain. Here we were joined by our small canoe, which had been separated from us during the fog this morning. Two Indians from the last village also accompanied us to the camp; but, having detected them in stealing a knife, they were sent off."

It is not very easy for us, who have lived comfortably at home, or who have travelled only in luxurious railway-cars and handsomely equipped steamers, to realize the joy and rapture with which these far-wandering explorers hailed the sight of the sea,—the sea to which they had so long been journeying, through deserts, mountain-passes, and tangled wildernesses. In his diary Captain Clark thus sets down some indication of his joy on that memorable day, November 8, 1805: "Great joy in camp. We are in view of the Ocean, this great Pacific Ocean which we have been so long anxious to see, and the roaring or noise made by the waves breaking on the rocky shores (as I suppose) may be heard distinctly." Later, same day, he says, "Ocean in view! O! the joy!" Fortunately, the hardships to be undergone on the shores of the ocean were then unknown and undreamed of; the travellers were thankful to see the sea, the goal of all their hopes, the end of their long pilgrimage across the continent.

That night they camped near the mouth of the river in what is now known as Gray's Bay, on the north side of the river, in the southwest corner of Wahkiacum County. Before they could reach their camping-place, the water was so rough that some of the men had an unusual experience,—seasickness. They passed a disagreeable night on a narrow, rocky bench of land. Next day they say:

"Fortunately for us, the tide did not rise as high as our camp during the night; but being accompanied by high winds from the south, the canoes, which we could not place beyond its reach, were filled with water, and were saved with much difficulty. Our position was very uncomfortable, but as it was impossible to move from it, we waited for a change of weather. It rained, however, during the whole day, and at two o'clock in the afternoon the flood tide set in, accompanied by a high wind from the south, which, about four o'clock, shifted to the southwest and blew almost a gale directly from the sea. The immense waves now broke over the place where we were camped; the large trees, some of them five or six feet thick, which had lodged at the point, were drifted over our camp, and the utmost vigilance of every man could scarcely save our canoes from being crushed to pieces. We remained in the water, and drenched with rain, during the rest of the day, our only food being some dried fish and some rain-water which we caught. Yet, though wet and cold, and some of them sick from using salt water, the men were cheerful, and full of anxiety to see more of the ocean. The rain continued all night."

This was the beginning of troubles. Next day, the wind having lulled, the party set forth again, only to be beaten back and compelled to take to the shore again. This was their experience for several days. For example, under date of the eleventh the journal says:—

"The wind was still high from the southwest, and drove the waves against the shore with great fury; the rain too fell in torrents, and not only drenched us to the skin, but loosened the stones on the hillsides, which then came rolling down upon us. In this comfortless situation we remained all day, wet, cold, with nothing but dried fish to satisfy our hunger; the canoes in one place at the mercy of the waves, the baggage in another, and all the men scattered on floating logs, or sheltering themselves in the crevices of the rocks and hillsides. A hunter was despatched in hopes of finding some fresh meat; but the hills were so steep, and so covered with undergrowth and fallen timber, that he could not penetrate them, and he was forced to return."

And this is the record for the next day:—

"About three o'clock a tremendous gale of wind arose accompanied with lightning, thunder, and hail: at six it lightened up for a short time, but a violent rain soon began, and lasted through the day. During the storm, one of our boats, secured by being sunk with great quantities of stone, got loose, but, drifting against a rock, was recovered without having received much injury. Our situation now became much more dangerous, for the waves were driven with fury against the rocks and trees, which till now had afforded us refuge: we therefore took advantage of the low tide, and moved about half a mile round a point to a small brook, which we had not observed before on account of the thick bushes and driftwood which concealed its mouth. Here we were more safe, but still cold and wet; our clothes and bedding rotten as well as wet, our baggage at a distance, and the canoes, our only means of escape from this place, at the mercy of the waves. Still, we continued to enjoy good health, and even had the luxury of feasting on some salmon and three salmon trout which we caught in the brook. Three of the men attempted to go round a point in our small Indian canoe, but the high waves rendered her quite unmanageable, these boats requiring the seamanship of the natives to make them live in so rough a sea."

It should be borne in mind that the canoes of the explorers were poor dug-outs, unfit to navigate the turbulent waters of the bay, and the men were not so expert in that sort of seamanship as were the Indians whom they, with envy, saw breasting the waves and making short voyages in the midst of the storms. It continued to rain without any intermission, and the waves dashed up among the floating logs of the camp in a very distracting manner. The party now had nothing but dried fish to eat, and it was with great difficulty that a fire could be built.

On the fifteenth of the month, Captain Lewis having found a better camping-place near a sandy beach, they started to move their luggage thither; but before they could get under way, a high wind from the southwest sprung up and they were forced to remain. But the sun came out and they were enabled to dry their stuff, much of which had been spoiled by the rain which had prevailed for the past ten days. Their fish also was no longer fit to eat, and they were indeed in poor case. Captain Lewis was out on a prospecting trip, and the party set out and found a beach through which a pleasant brook flowed to the river, making a very good camping-place. At the mouth of this stream was an ancient Chinook village, which, says the journal, "has at present no inhabitants but fleas." The adventurers were compelled to steer wide of all old Indian villages, they were so infested with fleas. At times, so great was the pest, the men were forced to take off all their clothing and soak themselves and their garments in the river before they could be rid of the insects. The site of their new camp was at the southeast end of Baker's Bay, sometimes called Haley's Bay, a mile above a very high point of rocks. On arriving at this place, the voyagers met with an unpleasant experience of which the journal gives this account:—

"Here we met Shannon, who had been sent back to meet us by Captain Lewis. The day Shannon left us in the canoe, he and Willard proceeded till they met a party of twenty Indians, who, having never heard of us, did not know where they (our men) came from; they, however, behaved with so much civility, and seemed so anxious that the men should go with them toward the sea, that their suspicions were excited, and they declined going on. The Indians, however, would not leave them; the men being confirmed in their suspicions, and fearful that if they went into the woods to sleep they would be cut to pieces in the night, thought it best to pass the night in the midst of the Indians. They therefore made a fire, and after talking with them to a late hour, laid down with their rifles under their heads. As they awoke that morning they found that the Indians had stolen and concealed their guns. Having demanded them in vain, Shannon seized a club, and was about assaulting one of the Indians, whom he suspected as a thief, when another Indian began to load a fowling-piece with the intention of shooting him. He therefore stopped, and explained by signs that if they did not give up the guns a large party would come down the river before the sun rose to such a height, and put every one of them to death. Fortunately, Captain Lewis and his party appeared at this time. The terrified Indians immediately brought the guns, and five of them came on with Shannon. To these men we declared that if ever any one of their nation stole anything from us, he should be instantly shot. They reside to the north of this place, and speak a language different from that of the people higher up the river.

"It was now apparent that the sea was at all times too rough for us to proceed further down the bay by water. We therefore landed, and having chosen the best spot we could select, made our camp of boards from the old (Chinook) village. We were now situated comfortably, and being visited by four Wahkiacums with wappatoo-roots, were enabled to make an agreeable addition to our food."

On the seventeenth Captain Lewis with a small party of his men coasted the bay as far out as Cape Disappointment and some distance to the north along the seacoast. Game was now plenty, and the camp was supplied with ducks, geese, and venison. Bad weather again set in. The journal under date of November 22 says:—

"It rained during the whole night, and about daylight a tremendous gale of wind rose from the S.S.E., and continued through the day with great violence. The sea ran so high that the water came into our camp, which the rain prevents us from leaving. We purchased from the old squaw, for armbands and rings, a few wappatoo-roots, on which we subsisted. They are nearly equal in flavor to the Irish potato, and afford a very good substitute for bread. The bad weather drove several Indians to our camp, but they were still under the terrors of the threat which we made on first seeing them, and behaved with the greatest decency.

"The rain continued through the night, November 23, and the morning was calm and cloudy. The hunters were sent out, and killed three deer, four brant, and three ducks. Towards evening seven Clatsops came over in a canoe, with two skins of the sea-otter. To this article they attached an extravagant value; and their demands for it were so high, that we were fearful it would too much reduce our small stock of merchandise, on which we had to depend for subsistence on our return, to venture on purchasing it. To ascertain, however, their ideas as to the value of different objects, we offered for one of these skins a watch, a handkerchief, an American dollar, and a bunch of red beads; but neither the curious mechanism of the watch, nor even the red beads, could tempt the owner: he refused the offer, but asked for tiacomoshack, or chief beads, the most common sort of coarse blue-colored beads, the article beyond all price in their estimation. Of these blue beads we had but few, and therefore reserved them for more necessitous circumstances."

The officers of the expedition had hoped and expected to find here some of the trading ships that were occasionally sent along the coast to barter with the natives; but none were to be found. They were soon to prepare for winter-quarters, and they still hoped that a trader might appear in the spring before they set out on their homeward journey across the continent. Very much they needed trinkets to deal with the natives in exchange for, the needful articles of food on the route. But (we may as well say here) no such relief ever appeared. It is strange that President Jefferson, in the midst of his very minute orders and preparations for the benefit of the explorers, did not think of sending a relief ship to meet the party at the mouth of the Columbia. They would have been saved a world of care, worry, and discomfort. But at that time the European nations who held possessions on the Pacific coast were very suspicious of the Americans, and possibly President Jefferson did not like to risk rousing their animosity.

The rain that now deluged the unhappy campers was so incessant that they might well have thought that people should be web-footed to live in such a watery region. In these later days, Oregon is sometimes known as "The Web-foot State." Captain Clark, in his diary, November 28, makes this entry: "O! how disagreeable is our situation dureing this dreadfull weather!" The gallant captain's spelling was sometimes queer. Under that date he adds:—

"We remained during the day in a situation the most cheerless and uncomfortable. On this little neck of land we are exposed, with a miserable covering which does not deserve the name of a shelter, to the violence of the winds; all our bedding and stores, as well as our bodies, are completely wet; our clothes are rotting with constant exposure, and we have no food except the dried fish brought from the falls, to which we are again reduced. The hunters all returned hungry and drenched with rain, having seen neither deer nor elk, and the swan and brant were too shy to be approached. At noon the wind shifted to the northwest, and blew with such tremendous fury that many trees were blown down near us. This gale lasted with short intervals during the whole night."

Of course, in the midst of such violent storms, it was impossible to get game, and the men were obliged to resort once more to a diet of dried fish, This food caused much sickness in the

111

camp, and it became imperatively necessary that efforts should again be made to find game. On the second of December, to their great joy an elk was killed, and next day they had a feast. The journal says;

"The wind was from the east and the morning fair; but, as if one whole day of fine weather were not permitted, toward night it began to rain. Even this transient glimpse of sunshine revived the spirits of the party, who were still more pleased when the elk killed yesterday was brought into camp. This was the first elk we had killed on the west side of the Rocky Mountains, and condemned as we have been to the dried fish, it formed a most nourishing food. After eating the marrow of the shank-bones, the squaw chopped them fine, and by boiling extracted a pint of grease, superior to the tallow itself of the animal. A canoe of eight Indians, who were carrying down wappatoo-roots to trade with the Clatsops, stopped at our camp; we bought a few roots for small fish-hooks, and they then left us. Accustomed as we were to the sight, we could not but view with admiration the wonderful dexterity with which they guide their canoes over the most boisterous seas; for though the waves were so high that before they had gone half a mile the canoe was several times out of sight, they proceeded with the greatest calmness and security. Two of the hunters who set out yesterday had lost their way, and did not return till this evening. They had seen in their ramble great signs of elk and had killed six, which they had butchered and left at a great distance. A party was sent in the morning."

On the third of December Captain Clark carved on the trunk of a great pine tree this inscription:—

"WM. CLARK DECEMBER 3D 1805 BY LAND FROM THE U. STATES IN 1804 & 5."

A few days later, Captain Lewis took with him a small party and set out to find a suitable spot on which to build their winter camp. He did not return as soon as he was expected, and considerable uneasiness was felt in camp on that account. But he came in safely. He brought good news; they had discovered a river on the south side of the Columbia, not far from their present encampment, where there were an abundance of elk and a favorable place for a winter camp. Bad weather detained them until the seventh of December, when a favorable change enabled them to proceed. They made their way slowly and very cautiously down-stream, the tide being against them. The narrative proceeds:—

"We at length turned a point, and found ourselves in a deep bay: here we landed for breakfast, and were joined by the party sent out three days ago to look for the six elk, killed by the Lewis party. They had lost their way for a day and a half, and when they at last reached the place, found the elk so much spoiled that they brought away nothing but the skins of four of them. After breakfast we coasted round the bay, which is about four miles across, and receives, besides several small creeks, two rivers, called by the Indians, the one Kilhowanakel, the other Netul. We named it Meriwether's Bay, from the Christian name of Captain Lewis, who was, no doubt, the first white man who had surveyed it. The wind was high from the northeast, and in the middle of the day it rained for two hours, and then cleared off. On reaching the south side of the bay we ascended the Netul three miles, to the first point of high land on its western bank, and formed our camp in a thick grove of lofty pines, about two hundred yards from the water, and thirty feet above the level of the high tides."

Chapter XVIII — Camping by the Pacific

Next in importance to the building of a winter camp was the fixing of a place where salt could be made. Salt is absolutely necessary for the comfort of man, and the supply brought out from the United States by the explorers was now nearly all gone. They were provided with kettles in which sea-water could be boiled down and salt be made. It would be needful to go to work at once, for the process of salt-making by boiling in ordinary kettles is slow and tedious; not only must enough for present uses be found, but a supply to last the party home again was necessary. Accordingly, on the eighth of December the journal has this entry to show what was to be done:—

"In order, therefore, to find a place for making salt, and to examine the country further, Captain Clark set out with five men, and pursuing a course S. 60'0 W., over a dividing ridge through thick pine timber, much of which bad fallen, passed the beads of two small brooks. In the neighborhood of these the land was swampy and overflowed, and they waded knee-deep till they came to an open ridgy prairie, covered with the plant known on our frontier by the name of sacacommis (bearberry). Here is a creek about sixty yards wide and running toward Point Adams; they passed it on a small raft. At this place they discovered a large herd of elk, and after pursuing them for three miles over bad swamps and small ponds, killed one of them. The agility with which the elk crossed the swamps and bogs seems almost incredible; as we followed their track the ground for a whole acre would shake at our tread and sometimes we sunk to our hips without finding any bottom. Over the surface of these bogs is a species of moss, among which are great numbers of cranberries; and occasionally there rise from the swamp small steep knobs of earth, thickly covered with pine and laurel. On one of these we halted at night, but it was scarcely large enough to suffer us to lie clear of the water, and had very little dry wood. We succeeded, however, in collecting enough to make a fire; and having stretched the elk-skin to keep off the rain, which still continued, slept till morning."

Next day the party were met by three Indians who had been fishing for salmon, of which they had a goodly supply, and were now on their way home to their village on the seacoast. They, invited Captain Clark and his men to accompany them; and the white men accepted the invitation. These were Clatsops. Their village consisted of twelve families living in houses of split pine boards, the lower half of the house being underground. By a small ladder in the middle of the house-front, the visitors reached the floor, which was about four feet below the surface. Two fires were burning in the middle of the room upon the earthen floor. The beds were ranged around the room next to the wall, with spaces beneath them for bags, baskets, and household articles.

Captain Clark was received with much attention, clean mats were spread for him, and a repast of fish, roots, and berries was set before him. He noticed that the Clatsops were well dressed and clean, and that they frequently washed their faces and hands, a ceremony, he remarked, that is by no means frequent among other Indians. A high wind now prevailed, and as the evening was stormy, Captain Clark resolved to stay all night with his hospitable Clatsops. The narrative proceeds:—

"The men of the village now collected and began to gamble. The most common game was one in which one of the company was banker, and played against all the rest. He had a piece of bone, about the size of a large bean, and having agreed with any individual as to the value of the stake, would pass the bone from one hand to the other with great dexterity, singing at the same time to divert the attention of his adversary; then holding it in his hands, his antagonist was challenged to guess in which of them the bone was, and lost or won as he pointed to the right or wrong hand. To this game of hazard they abandoned themselves with great ardor; sometimes everything they possess is sacrificed to it; and this evening several of the Indians lost all the beads which they had with them. This lasted for three hours; when, Captain Clark appearing disposed to sleep, the man who had been most attentive, and whose name was Cuskalah, spread two new mats near the fire, ordered his wife to retire to her own bed, and the rest of the company dispersed at the same time. Captain Clark then lay down, but the violence with which the fleas attacked him did not leave his rest unbroken."

Next morning, Captain Clark walked along the seashore, and he observed that the Indians were walking up and down, examining the shore and the margin of a creek that emptied here. The narrative says:—

"He was at a loss to understand their object till one of them came to him, and explained that they were in search of any fish which might have been thrown on shore and left by the tide, adding in English, 'sturgeon is very good.' There is, indeed, every reason to believe that these Clatsops depend for their subsistence, during the winter, chiefly on the fish thus casually thrown on the coast. After amusing himself for some time on the beach, he returned towards the village, and shot on his way two brant. As he came near the village, one of the Indians asked him to shoot a duck about thirty steps distant: he did so, and, having accidentally shot off its head, the bird was brought to the village, when all the Indians came round in astonishment. They examined the duck, the musket, and the very small bullets, which were a hundred to the pound, and then exclaimed, Clouch musque, waket, commatax musquet: Good musket; do not understand this kind of musket. They now placed before him their best roots, fish, and syrup, after which he attempted to purchase a sea-otter skin with some red beads which he happened to have about him; but they declined trading, as they valued none except blue or white beads. He therefore bought nothing but a little berry-bread and a few roots, in exchange for fish-hooks, and then set out to return by the same route he had come. He was accompanied by Cuskalah and his brother as far as the third creek, and then proceeded to the camp through a heavy rain. The whole party had been occupied during his absence in cutting down trees to make huts, and in hunting."

This was the occupation of all hands for several days, notwithstanding the discomfort of the continual downpour. Many of the men were ill from the effects of sleeping and living so constantly in water. Under date of December 12, the journal has this entry:—

"We continued to work in the rain at our houses. In the evening there arrived two canoes of Clatsops, among whom was a principal chief, called Comowol. We gave him a medal and treated his companions with great attention; after which we began to bargain for a small sea-otter skin, some wappatoo-roots, and another species of root called shanataque. We readily perceived that they were close dealers, stickled much for trifles, and never closed the bargain until they thought they had the advantage. The wappatoo is dear, as they themselves are obliged to give a high price for it to the Indians above. Blue beads are the articles most in request; the white occupy the next place in their estimation; but they do not value much those of any other color. We succeeded at last in purchasing their whole cargo for a few fish-hooks and a small sack of Indian tobacco, which we had received from the Shoshonees.''

The winter camp was made up of seven huts, and, although it was not so carefully fortified as was the fort in the Mandan country (during the previous winter), it was so arranged that intruders could be kept out when necessary. For the roofs of these shelters they were provided with "shakes" split out from a species of pine which they called "balsam pine," and which gave them boards, or puncheons, or shakes, ten feet long and two feet wide, and not more than an inch and a half thick. By the sixteenth of December their meat-house was finished, and their meat, so much of which had been spoiled for lack of proper care, was cut up in small pieces and hung under cover. They had been told by the Indians that very little snow ever fell in that region, and the weather, although very, very wet, was mild and usually free from frost. They did have severe hailstorms and a few flurries of snow in December but the rain was a continual cause of discomfort. Of the trading habits of the Clatsops the journal has this to say:—

"Three Indians came in a canoe with mats, roots, and the berries of the sacacommis. These people proceed with a dexterity and finesse in their bargains which, if they have not learned it from their foreign visitors, may show how nearly allied is the cunning of savages to the little arts of traffic. They begin by asking double or treble the value of what they have to sell, and lower their demand in proportion to the greater or less degree of ardor or knowledge of the purchaser, who, with all his management, is not able to procure the article for less than its real value, which the Indians perfectly understand. Our chief medium of trade consists of blue and white beads, files,—with which they sharpen their tools,—fish-hooks, and tobacco; but of all these articles blue beads and tobacco are the most esteemed.''

But, although their surroundings were not of a sort to make one very jolly, when Christmas came they observed the day as well as they could. Here is what the journal says of the holiday:—

"We were awaked at daylight by a discharge of firearms, which was followed by a song from the men, as a compliment to us on the return of Christmas, which we have always been accustomed to observe as a day of rejoicing. After breakfast we divided our remaining stock of tobacco, which amounted to twelve carrots (hands), into two parts; one of which we distributed among such of the party as make use of it, making a present of a handkerchief to the others. The remainder of the day was passed in good spirits, though there was nothing in our situation to excite much gayety. The rain confined us to the house, and our only luxuries in honor of the season were some poor elk, so much spoiled that we ate it through sheer necessity, a few roots, and some spoiled pounded fish.

"The next day brought a continuation of rain, accompanied with thunder, and a high wind from the southeast. We were therefore obliged to still remain in our huts, and endeavored to dry our wet articles before the fire. The fleas, which annoyed us near the portage of the Great Falls, have taken such possession of our clothes that we are obliged to have a regular search every day through our blankets as a necessary preliminary to sleeping at night. These animals, indeed, are so numerous that they are almost a calamity to the Indians of this country. When they have once obtained the mastery of any house it is impossible to expel them, and the Indians have frequently different houses, to which they resort occasionally when the fleas have rendered their permanent residence intolerable; yet, in spite of these precautions, every Indian is constantly attended by multitudes of them, and no one comes into our house without leaving behind him swarms of these tormenting insects."

Although the condition of the exploring party was low, the men did not require very much to put them in good spirits. The important and happy event of finishing their fort and the noting of good weather are thus set forth in the journal under date of December 30:—

"Toward evening the hunters brought in four elk (which Drewyer had killed), and after a long course of abstinence and miserable diet, we had a most sumptuous supper of elk's tongues and marrow. Besides this agreeable repast, the state of the weather was quite exhilarating. It had rained during the night, but in the morning, though the high wind continued, we enjoyed the fairest and most pleasant weather since our arrival; the sun having shone at intervals, and there being only three showers in the course of the day. By sunset we had completed the fortification, and now announced to the Indians that every day at that hour the gates would be closed, and they must leave the fort and not enter it till sunrise. The Wahkiacums who remained with us, and who were very forward in their deportment, complied very reluctantly with this order; but, being excluded from our houses, formed a camp near us. . . .

"January 1, 1806. We were awaked at an early hour by the discharge of a volley of small arms, to salute the new year. This was the only mode of commemorating the day which our situation permitted; for, though we had reason to be gayer than we were at Christmas, our only dainties were boiled elk and wappatoo, enlivened by draughts of pure water. We were visited by a few Clatsops, who came by water, bringing roots and berries for sale. Among this nation we observed a man about twenty-five years old, of a much lighter complexion than the Indians generally: his face was even freckled, and his hair long, and of a colour inclining to red. He was in habits and manners perfectly Indian; but, though he did not speak a word of English, he seemed to understand more than the others of his party; and, as we could obtain no account of his origin, we concluded that one of his parents, at least, must have been white."

A novel addition to their bill of fare was fresh blubber, or fat, from a stranded whale. Under date of January 3 the journal says:—

"At eleven o'clock we were visited by our neighbor, the Tia or chief, Comowool, who is also called Coone, and six Clatsops. Besides roots and berries, they brought for sale three dogs, and some fresh blubber. Having been so long accustomed to live on the flesh of dogs, the greater part of us have acquired a fondness for it, and our original aversion for it is overcome, by reflecting that while we subsisted on that food we were fatter, stronger, and in general enjoyed better health than at any period since leaving the buffalo country, eastward of the mountains. The blubber, which is esteemed by the Indians an excellent food, has been obtained, they tell us, from their neighbors, the Killamucks, a nation who live on the seacoast to the southeast, near one of whose villages a whale had recently been thrown and foundered."

Five men had been sent out to form a camp on the seashore and go into the manufacture of salt as expeditiously as possible. On the fifth of January, two of them came into the fort bringing a gallon of salt, which was decided to be "white, fine and very good," and a very agreeable addition to their food, which had been eaten perfectly fresh for some weeks past. Captain Clark, however, said it was a "mere matter of indifference" to him whether he had salt or not, but he hankered for bread. Captain Lewis, on the other hand, said the lack of salt was a great inconvenience; "the want of bread I consider trivial," was his dictum. It was estimated that the

116

salt-makers could turn out three or four quarts a day, and there was good prospect of an abundant supply for present needs and for the homeward journey. An expedition to the seashore was now planned, and the journal goes on to tell how they set out:—

"The appearance of the whale seemed to be a matter of importance to all the neighboring Indians, and as we might be able to procure some of it for ourselves, or at least purchase blubber from the Indians, a small parcel of merchandise was prepared, and a party of the men held in readiness to set out in the morning. As soon as this resolution was known, Chaboneau and his wife requested that they might be permitted to accompany us. The poor woman stated very earnestly that she had travelled a great way with us to see the great water, yet she had never been down to the coast, and now that this monstrous fish was also to be seen, it seemed hard that she should be permitted to see neither the ocean nor the whale. So reasonable a request could not be denied; they were therefore suffered to accompany Captain Clark, who, January 6th, after an early breakfast, set out with twelve men in two canoes."

After a long and tedious trip, the camp of the saltmakers was reached, and Captain Clark and his men went on to the remains of the whale, only the skeleton being left by the rapacious and hungry Indians. The whale had been stranded between two shore villages tenanted by the Killamucks, as Captain Clark called them. They are now known as the Tillamook Indians, and their name is preserved in Tillamook County, Oregon. The white men found it difficult to secure much of the blubber, or the oil. Although the Indians had large quantities of both, they sold it with much reluctance. In Clark's private diary is found this entry: "Small as this stock (of oil and lubber) is I prize it highly; and thank Providence for directing the whale to us; and think him more kind to us than he was to Jonah, having sent this monster to be swallowed by us instead of swallowing us as Jonah's did." While here, the party had a startling experience, as the journal says:—

"Whilst smoking with the Indians, Captain Clark was surprised, about ten o'clock, by a loud, shrill outcry from the opposite village, on hearing which all the Indians immediately started up to cross the creek, and the guide informed him that someone had been killed. On examination one of the men (M'Neal) was discovered to be absent, and a guard (Sergeant Pryor and four men) despatched, who met him crossing the creek in great haste. An Indian belonging to another band, who happened to be with the Killamucks that evening, had treated him with much kindness, and walked arm in arm with him to a tent where our man found a Chinnook squaw, who was an old acquaintance. From the conversation and manner of the stranger, this woman discovered that his object was to murder the white man for the sake of the few articles on his person; when he rose and pressed our man to go to another tent where they would find something better to eat, she held M'Neal by the blanket; not knowing her object, he freed himself from her, and was going on with his pretended friend, when she ran out and gave the shriek which brought the men of the village over, and the stranger ran off before M'Neal knew what had occasioned the alarm."

The "mighty hunter" of the Lewis and Clark expedition was Drewyer, whose name has frequently been mentioned in these pages. Under date of January 12, the journal has this just tribute to the man:—

"Our meat is now becoming scarce; we therefore determined to jerk it, and issue it in small quantities, instead of dividing it among the four messes, and leaving to each the care of its own provisions; a plan by which much is lost, in consequence of the improvidence of the men. Two hunters had been despatched in the morning, and one of them, Drewyer, had before evening killed seven elk. We should scarcely be able to subsist, were it not for the exertions of this most excellent hunter. The game is scarce, and nothing is now to be seen except elk, which for almost all the men are very difficult to be procured; but Drewyer, who is the offspring of a Canadian Frenchman and an Indian woman, has passed his life in the woods, and unites, in a wonderful degree, the dexterous aim of the frontier huntsman with the intuitive sagacity of the Indian, in pursuing the faintest tracks through the forest. All our men, however, have indeed become so expert with the rifle that we are never under apprehensions as to food; since, whenever there is game of any kind, we are almost certain of procuring it."

The narrative of the explorers gives this account of the Chinooks:—

"The men are low in stature, rather ugly, and ill made; their legs being small and crooked, their feet large, and their heads, like those of the women, flattened in a most disgusting manner. These deformities are in part concealed by robes made of sea-otter, deer, elk, beaver or fox skins. They also employ in their dress robes of the skin of a cat peculiar to this country, and of another animal of the same size, which is light and durable, and sold at a high price by the Indians who bring it from above. In addition to these are worn blankets, wrappers of red, blue, or spotted cloth, and some old sailors' clothes, which are very highly prized. The greater part of the men have guns, with powder and ball.

"The women have in general handsome faces, but are low and disproportioned, with small feet and large legs, occasioned, probably, by strands of beads, or various strings, drawn so tight above the ankles as to prevent the circulation of the blood. Their dress, like that of the Wahkiacums, consists of a short robe and a tissue of cedar bark. Their hair hangs loosely down the shoulders and back; and their ears, neck, and wrists are ornamented with blue beads. Another decoration, which is very highly prized, consists of figures made by puncturing the arms or legs; and on the arms of one of the squaws we observed the name of J. Bowman, executed in the same way. In language, habits, and in almost every other particular, they resemble the Clatsops, Cathlamahs, and, indeed, all the people near the mouth of the Columbia, though they appeared to be inferior to their neighbors in honesty as well as spirit. No ill treatment or indignity on our part seemed to excite any feeling except fear; nor, although better provided than their neighbors with arms, have they enterprise enough either to use them advantageously against the animals of the forest, or offensively against the tribes near them, who owe their safety more to the timidity than the forbearance of the Chinooks. We had heard instances of pilfering while we were among them, and therefore gave a general order excluding them from our encampment, so that whenever an Indian wished to visit us, he began by calling out 'No Chinook.' It is not improbable that this first impression may have left a prejudice against them, since, when we were among the Clatsops and other tribes at the mouth of the Columbia, they had less opportunity of stealing, if they were so disposed."

The weeks remaining before the party set out on their return were passed without notable incident. The journal is chiefly occupied with comments on the weather, which was variable, and some account of the manners and customs of the Indian tribes along the Columbia River. At that time, so few traders had penetrated the wilds of the Lower Columbia that the Indians were not supplied with firearms to any great extent. Their main reliance was the bow and arrow. A few shotguns were seen among them, but no rifles, and great was the admiration and wonder with which the Indians saw the white men slay birds and animals at a long distance. Pitfalls for elk were constructed by the side of fallen trees over which the animals might leap. Concerning the manufactures of the Clatsops, they reported as follows:—

"Their hats are made of cedar-bark and bear-grass, interwoven together in the form of a European hat, with a small brim of about two inches, and a high crown widening upward. They are light, ornamented with various colors and figures, and being nearly water-proof, are much more durable than either chip or straw hats. These hats form a small article of traffic with the whites, and their manufacture is one of the best exertions of Indian industry. They are, however, very dexterous in making a variety of domestic utensils, among which are bowls, spoons, scewers (skewers), spits, and baskets. The bowl or trough is of different shapes—round, semicircular, in the form of a canoe, or cubic, and generally dug out of a single piece of wood; the larger vessels have holes in the sides by way of handles, and all are executed with great neatness. In these vessels they boil their food, by throwing hot stones into the water, and extract oil from different animals in the same way. Spoons are not very abundant, nor is there anything remarkable in their shape, except that they are large and the bowl broad. Meat is roasted on one end of a sharp skewer, placed erect before the fire, with the other end fixed in the ground.

"But the most curious workmanship is that of the basket. It is formed of cedar-bark and bear-grass, so closely interwoven that it is water-tight, without the aid of either gum or resin. The form is generally conic, or rather the segment (frustum) of a cone, of which the smaller end is the bottom of the basket; and being made of all sizes, from that of the smallest cup to the capacity of five or six gallons, they answer the double purpose of a covering for the head or to contain water. Some of them are highly ornamented with strands of bear-grass, woven into figures of various colors, which require great labor; yet they are made very expeditiously and sold for a trifle. It is for the construction of these baskets that the bear-grass forms an article of considerable traffic. It grows only near the snowy region of the high mountains; the blade, which is two feet long and about three-eighths of an inch wide, is smooth, strong, and pliant; the young blades particularly, from their not being exposed to the sun and air, have an appearance of great neatness, and are generally preferred. Other bags and baskets, not waterproof, are made of cedar-bark, silk-grass, rushes, flags, and common coarse sedge, for the use of families. In these manufactures, as in the ordinary work of the house, the instrument most in use is a knife, or rather a dagger. The handle of it is small, and has a strong loop of twine for the thumb, to prevent its being wrested from the band. On each side is a blade, double-edged and pointed; the longer from nine to ten inches, the shorter from four to five. This knife is carried habitually in the hand, sometimes exposed, but mostly, when in company with strangers, is put under the robe."

Naturally, all of the Columbia River Indians were found to be expert in the building and handling of canoes. Here their greatest skill was employed. And, it may be added, the Indians of the North Pacific coast to-day are equally adept and skilful. The canoes of the present race of red men do not essentially differ from those of the tribes described by Lewis and Clark, and who are now extinct. The Indians then living above tide-water built canoes of smaller size than those employed by the nations farther down the river. The canoes of the Tillamooks and other tribes living on the seacoast were upwards of fifty feet long, and would carry eight or ten thousand pounds' weight, or twenty-five or thirty persons. These were constructed from the trunk of a single tree, usually white cedar. The bow and stern rose much higher than the gunwale, and were adorned by grotesque figures excellently well carved and fitted to pedestals cut in the solid wood of the canoe. The same method of adornment may be seen among the aborigines of Alaska and other regions of the North Pacific, to-day. The figures are made of small pieces of wood neatly fitted together by inlaying and mortising, without any spike of any kind. When one reflects that the Indians seen by Lewis and Clark constructed their large canoes with very poor tools, it is impossible to withhold one's admiration of their industry and patience. The journal says:—

"Our admiration of their skill in these curious constructions was increased by observing the very inadequate implements which they use. These Indians possess very few axes, and the only tool they employ, from felling the tree to the delicate workmanship of the images, is a chisel made of an old file, about an inch or an inch and a half in width. Even of this, too, they have not learned the proper management; for the chisel is sometimes fixed in a large block of wood, and, being held in the right hand, the block is pushed with the left, without the aid of a mallet. But under all these disadvantages, their canoes, which one would suppose to be the work of years, are made in a few weeks. A canoe, however, is very highly prized, being in traffic an article of the greatest value except a wife, and of equal value with her; so that a lover generally gives a canoe to the father in exchange for his daughter. . . .

"The harmony of their private life is secured by their ignorance of spirituous liquors, the earliest and most dreadful present which civilization has given to the other natives of the continent. Although they have had so much intercourse with whites, they do not appear to possess any knowledge of those dangerous luxuries; at least they have never inquired after them, which they probably would have done if once liquors bad been introduced among them. Indeed, we have not observed any liquor of intoxicating quality among these or any Indians west of the Rocky Mountains, the universal beverage being pure water. They, however, sometimes almost intoxicate themselves by smoking tobacco, of which they are excessively fond, and the pleasures of which they prolong as much as possible, by retaining vast quantities at a time, till after circulating through the lungs and stomach it issues in volumes from the mouth and nostrils."

A long period of quiet prevailed in camp after the first of February, before the final preparations for departure were made. Parties were sent out every day to hunt, and the campers were able to command a few days' supply of provision in advance. The flesh of the deer was now very lean and poor, but that of the elk was growing better and better. It was estimated by one of the party that they killed, between December 1, 1805, and March 20, 1806, elk to the number of one hundred and thirty-one, and twenty deer. Some of this meat they smoked for its better preservation, but most of it was eaten fresh. No record was kept of the amount of fish consumed by the party; but they were obliged at times to make fish their sole article of diet. Late in February they were visited by Comowool, the principal Clatsop chief, who brought them a sturgeon and quantities of a small fish which had just begun to make its appearance in the Columbia. This was known as the anchovy, but oftener as the candle-fish; it is so fat that it may be burned like a torch, or candle. The journal speaks of Comowool as "by far the most friendly and decent savage we have seen in this neighborhood."

Chapter XIX — With Faces turned Homeward

The officers of the expedition had decided to begin their homeward march on the first of April; but a natural impatience induced them to start a little earlier, and, as a matter of record, it may be said that they evacuated Fort Clatsop on the 23d of March, 1806. An examination of their stock of ammunition showed that they had on hand a supply of powder amply sufficient for their needs when travelling the three thousand miles of wilderness in which their sole reliance for food must be the game to be killed. The powder was kept in leaden canisters, and these, when empty, were used for making balls for muskets and rifles. Three bushels of salt were collected for their use on the homeward journey.

What they needed now most of all was an assortment of small wares and trinkets with which to trade with the Indians among whom they must spend so many months before reaching civilization again. They had ample letters of credit from the Government at Washington, and if they had met with white traders on the seacoast, they could have bought anything that money would buy. They had spent nearly all their stock in coming across the continent. This is Captain Lewis's summary of the goods on hand just before leaving Fort Clatsop:—

"All the small merchandise we possess might be tied up in a couple of handkerchiefs. The rest of our stock in trade consists of six blue robes, one scarlet ditto, five robes which we made out of our large United States flag, a few old clothes trimmed with ribbons, and one artillerist's uniform coat and hat, which probably Captain Clark will never wear again. We have to depend entirely upon this meagre outfit for the purchase of such horses and provisions as it will be in our power to obtain—a scant dependence, indeed, for such a journey as is before us."

One of their last acts was to draw up a full list of the members of the party, and, making several copies of it, to leave these among the friendly Indians with instructions to give a paper to the first white men who should arrive in the country. On the back of the paper was traced the track by which the explorers had come and that by which they expected to return. This is a copy of one of these important documents:—

"The object of this list is, that through the medium of some civilized person who may see the same, it may be made known to the informed world, that the party consisting of the persons whose names are hereunto annexed, and who were sent out by the government of the U'States in May, 1804, to explore the interior of the Continent of North America, did penetrate the same by way of the Missouri and Columbia Rivers, to the discharge of the latter into the Pacific Ocean, where they arrived on the 14th of November, 1805, and from whence they departed the 23d day of March, 1806, on their return to the United States by the same rout they had come out."

Curiously enough, one of these papers did finally reach the United States. During the summer of 1806, the brig "Lydia," Captain Hill, entered the Columbia for the purpose of trading with the natives. From one of these Captain Hill secured the paper, which he took to Canton, China, in January, 1807. Thence it was sent to a gentleman in Philadelphia, having travelled nearly all the way round the world.

Fort Clatsop, as they called the rude collection of huts in which they had burrowed all winter, with its rude furniture and shelters, was formally given to Comowool, the Clatsop chief who had been so kind to the party. Doubtless the crafty savage had had his eye on this establishment, knowing that it was to be abandoned in the spring.

The voyagers left Fort Clatsop about one o'clock in the day, and, after making sixteen miles up the river, camped for the night. Next day, they reached an Indian village where they purchased "some wappatoo and a dog for the invalids." They still had several men on the sick list in consequence of the hard fare of the winter. The weather was cold and wet, and wood for fuel was difficult to obtain. In a few days they found themselves among their old friends, the Skilloots, who had lately been at war with the Chinooks. There was no direct intercourse between the two nations as yet, but the Chinooks traded with the Clatsops and Wahkiacums, and these in turn traded with the Skilloots, and in this way the two hostile tribes exchanged the articles which they had for those which they desired. The journal has this to say about the game of an island on which the explorers tarried for a day or two, in order to dry their goods and mend their canoes:—

"This island, which has received from the Indians the appropriate name of Elalah (Elallah), or Deer Island, is surrounded on the water-side by an abundant growth of cottonwood, ash, and willow, while the interior consists chiefly of prairies interspersed with ponds. These afford refuge to great numbers of geese, ducks, large swan, sandhill cranes, a few canvas-backed ducks, and particularly the duckinmallard, the most abundant of all. There are also great numbers of snakes resembling our garter-snakes in appearance, and like them not poisonous. Our hunters brought in three deer, a goose, some ducks, an eagle, and a tiger-cat. Such is the extreme voracity of the vultures, that they had devoured in the space of a few hours four of the deer killed this morning; and one of our men declared that they had besides dragged a large buck about thirty yards, skinned it, and broken the backbone."

The vulture here referred to is better known as the California condor, a great bird of prey which is now so nearly extinct that few specimens are ever seen, and the eggs command a great price from those who make collections of such objects. A condor killed by one of the hunters of the Lewis and Clark expedition measured nine feet and six inches from tip to tip of its wings, three feet and ten inches from the point of the bill to the end of the tail, and six inches and a half from the back of the head to the tip of the beak. Very few of the condors of the Andes are much larger than this, though one measuring eleven feet from tip to tip has been reported.

While camped at Quicksand, or Sandy River, the party learned that food supplies up the Columbia were scarce. The journal says that the Indians met here were descending the river in search of food. It adds:—

"They told us, that they lived at the Great Rapids; but that the scarcity of provisions there had induced them to come down, in the hopes of finding subsistence in the more fertile valley. All the people living at the Rapids, as well as the nations above them, were in much distress for want of food, having consumed their winter store of dried fish, and not expecting the return of the salmon before the next full moon, which would be on the second of May: this information was not a little embarrassing. From the Falls to the Chopunnish nation, the plains afforded neither deer, elk, nor antelope for our subsistence. The horses were very poor at this season, and the dogs must be in the same condition, if their food, the dried fish, had failed. Still, it was obviously inexpedient for us to wait for the return of the salmon, since in that case we might not reach the Missouri before the ice would prevent our navigating it. We might, besides, hazard the loss of our horses, as the Chopunnish, with whom we had left them, would cross the mountains as early as possible, or about the beginning of May, and take our horses with them, or suffer them to disperse, in either of which cases the passage of the mountains will be almost impracticable. We therefore, after much deliberation, decided to remain where we were till we could collect meat enough to last us till we should reach the Chopunnish nation, and to obtain canoes from the natives as we ascended, either in exchange for our pirogues, or by purchasing them with skins and merchandise. These canoes, again, we might exchange for horses with the natives of the plains, till we should obtain enough to travel altogether by land. On reaching the southeast branch of the Columbia, four or five men could be sent on to the Chopunnish to have our horses in readiness; and thus we should have a stock of horses sufficient both to transport our baggage and supply us with food, as we now perceived that they would form our only certain dependance for subsistence."

On the third of April this entry is made:—

"A considerable number of Indians crowded about us to-day, many of whom came from the upper part of the river. These poor wretches confirm the reports of scarcity among the nations above; which, indeed, their appearance sufficiently proved, for they seemed almost starved, and greedily picked the bones and refuse meat thrown away by us.

"In the evening Captain Clark returned from an excursion. On setting out yesterday at half-past eleven o'clock, he directed his course along the south side of the (Columbia) river, where, at the distance of eight miles, he passed a village of the Nechacohee tribe, belonging to the Eloot nation. The village itself is small, and being situated behind Diamond Island, was concealed from our view as we passed both times along the northern shore. He continued till three o'clock, when he landed at the single house already mentioned as the only remains of a village of twenty-four straw huts. Along the shore were great numbers of small canoes for gathering wappatoo, which were left by the Shahalas, who visit the place annually. The present inhabitants of the house are part of the Neerchokioo tribe of the same (Shahala) nation. On entering one of the apartments of the house, Captain Clark offered several articles to the Indians in exchange for wappatoo; but they appeared sullen and ill-humored, and refused to give him any. He therefore sat down by the fire opposite the men, and taking a port-fire match from his pocket, threw a small piece of it into the flame; at the same time he took his pocket-compass, and by means of a magnet, which happened to be in his inkhorn, made the needle turn round very briskly. The match now took fire and burned violently, on which the Indians, terrified at this strange exhibition, immediately brought a quantity of wappatoo and laid it at his feet, begging him to put out the bad fire, while an old woman continued to speak with great vehemence, as if praying and imploring protection. Having received the roots, Captain Clark put up the compass, and as the match went out of itself tranquillity was restored, though the women and children still took refuge in their beds and behind the men. He now paid them for what he had used, and after lighting his pipe and smoking with them, continued down the river."

The excursion from which Captain Clark had returned, as noted in this extract, was up the Multnomah River. As we have already seen, the explorers missed that stream when they came down the Columbia; and they had now passed it again unnoticed, owing to the number of straggling islands that hide its junction with the Columbia. Convinced that a considerable river must drain the region to the south, Captain Clark went back alone and penetrating the intricate channels among the islands, found the mouth of the Multnomah, now better known as the

Willamette. He was surprised to find that the depth of water in the river was so great that large vessels might enter it. He would have been much more surprised if he had been told that a large city, the largest in Oregon, would some day be built on the site of the Indian huts which he saw. Here Captain Clark found a house occupied by several families of the Neechecolee nation. Their mansion was two hundred and twenty-six feet long and was divided into apartments thirty feet square.

The most important point in this region of the Columbia was named Wappatoo Island by the explorers. This is a large extent of country lying between the Willamette and an arm of the Columbia which they called Wappatoo Inlet, but which is now known as Willamette Slough. It is twenty miles long and from five to ten miles wide. Here is an interesting description of the manner of gathering the roots of the wappatoo, of which we have heard so much in this region of country:—

"The chief wealth of this island consists of the numerous ponds in the interior, abounding with the common arrowhead (sagittaria sagittifolia) to the root of which is attached a bulb growing beneath it in the mud. This bulb, to which the Indians give the name of wappatoo,(1) is the great article of food, and almost the staple article of commerce on the Columbia. It is never out of season; so that at all times of the year the valley is frequented by the neighboring Indians who come to gather it. It is collected chiefly by the women, who employ for the purpose canoes from ten to fourteen feet in length, about two feet wide and nine inches deep, and tapering from the middle, where they are about twenty inches wide. They are sufficient to contain a single person and several bushels of roots, yet so very light that a woman can carry them with ease. She takes one of these canoes into a pond where the water is as high as the breast, and by means of her toes separates from the root this bulb, which on being freed from the mud rises immediately to the surface of the water, and is thrown into the canoe. In this manner these patient females remain in the water for several hours, even in the depth of winter. This plant is found through the whole extent of the valley in which we now are, but does not grow on the Columbia farther eastward."

(1) In the Chinook jargon "Wappatoo" stands for potato.

The natives of this inland region, the explorers found, were larger and better-shaped than those of the sea-coast, but they were nearly all afflicted with sore eyes. The loss of one eye was common, and not infrequently total blindness was observed in men of mature years, while blindness was almost universal among the old people. The white men made good use of the eye-water which was among their supplies; it was gratefully received by the natives and won them friends among the people they met. On the fifth of April the journal has this entry:—

"In the course of his chase yesterday, one of our men (Collins), who had killed a bear, found the den of another with three cubs in it. He returned to-day in hopes of finding her, but brought only the cubs, without being able to see the dam; and on this occasion Drewyer, our most experienced huntsman, assured us that he had never known a single instance where a female bear, which had once been disturbed by a hunter and obliged to leave her young, returned to them again. The young bears were sold for wappatoo to some of the many Indians who visited us in parties during the day and behaved very well."

And on the ninth is this entry:—

"The wind having moderated, we reloaded the canoes and set out by seven o'clock. We stopped to take up the two hunters who left us yesterday, but were unsuccessful in the chase, and then proceeded to the Wahclellah village, situated on the north side of the river, about a mile below Beacon Rock. During the whole of the route from camp we passed along under high, steep, and rocky sides of the mountains, which now close on each side of the river, forming stupendous precipices, covered with fir and white cedar. Down these heights frequently descend the most beautiful cascades, one of which, a large creek, throws itself over a perpendicular rock three hundred feet above the water, while other smaller streams precipitate themselves from a still greater elevation, and evaporating in a mist, collect again and form a second cascade before they reach the bottom of the rocks. We stopped to breakfast at this village. We here found the tomahawk which had been stolen from us on the fourth of last November. They assured us they had bought it of the Indians below; but as the latter had already informed us that the Wahclellahs had such an article, which they had stolen, we made no difficulty about retaking our property."

The Columbia along the region through which the expedition was now passing is a very wild and picturesque stream. The banks are high and rocky, and some of the precipices to which the journal refers are of a vast perpendicular height. On the Oregon side of the river are five cascades such as those which the journal mentions. The most famous and beautiful of these is known as Multnomah Falls. This cataract has a total fall of more than six hundred feet, divided into two sections. The other cascades are the Bridal Veil, the Horsetail, the Latourelle, and the Oneonta, and all are within a few miles of each other.

On the ninth of April the voyagers reached the point at which they were to leave tidewater, fifty-six miles above the mouth of the Multnomah, or Willamette. They were now at the entrance of the great rapids which are known as the Cascades of the Columbia, and which occupy a space on the river about equal to four miles and a half. They were still navigating the stream with their canoes, camping sometimes on the north side and sometimes on the south side of the river. This time they camped on the north side, and during the night lost one of their boats, which got loose and drifted down to the next village of the Wahclellahs, some of whom brought it back to the white men's camp and were rewarded for their honesty by a present of two knives. It was found necessary to make a portage here, but a long and severe rainstorm set in, and the tents and the skins used for protecting the baggage were soaked. The journal goes on with the narrative thus:—

We determined to take the canoes first over the portage, in hopes that by the afternoon the rain would cease, and we might carry our baggage across without injury. This was immediately begun by almost the whole party, who in the course of the day dragged four of the canoes to the head of the rapids, with great difficulty and labor. A guard, consisting of one sick man and three who had been lamed by accidents, remained with Captain Lewis (and a cook) to guard the baggage. This precaution was absolutely necessary to protect it from the Wahclellahs, whom we discovered to be great thieves, notwithstanding their apparent honesty in restoring our boat; indeed, so arrogant and intrusive have they become that nothing but our numbers, we are convinced, saves us from attack. They crowded about us while we were taking up the boats, and one of them had the insolence to throw stones down the bank at two of our men.

"We now found it necessary to depart from our mild and pacific course of conduct. On returning to the head of the portage, many of them met our men and seemed very ill-disposed. Shields had stopped to purchase a dog, and being separated from the rest of the party, two Indians pushed him out of the road, and attempted to take the dog from him. He had no weapon but a long knife, with which he immediately attacked them both, hoping to put them to death before they had time to draw their arrows; but as soon as they saw his design they fled into the woods. Soon afterward we were told by an Indian who spoke Clatsop, which we had ourselves learned during the winter, that the Wahclellahs had carried off Captain Lewis' dog to their village below. Three men well armed were instantly despatched in pursuit of them, with orders to fire if there was the slightest resistance or hesitation. At the distance of two miles they came within sight of the thieves, who, finding themselves pursued, left the dog and made off. We now ordered all the Indians out of our camp, and explained to them that whoever stole any of our baggage, or insulted our men, should be instantly shot; a resolution which we were determined to enforce, as it was now our only means of safety.

"We were visited during the day by a chief of the Clahclellahs, who seemed mortified at the behavior of the Indians, and told us that the persons at the head of their outrages were two very bad men who belonged to the Wahclellah tribe, but that the nation did not by any means wish to displease us. This chief seemed very well-disposed, and we had every reason to believe was much respected by the neighboring Indians. We therefore gave him a small medal and showed him all the attention in our power, with which he appeared very much gratified."

The portage of these rapids was very difficult and tiresome. The total distance of the first stage was twenty-eight hundred yards along a narrow way rough with rocks and now slippery with rain. One of the canoes was lost here by being driven out into the strong current, where the force of the water was so great that it could not be held by the men; the frail skiff drifted down the rapids and disappeared. They now had two canoes and two periogues left, and the loads were divided among these craft. This increased the difficulties of navigation, and Captain Lewis crossed over to the south side of the river in search of canoes to be purchased from the Indians, who lived in a village on that side of the stream. The narrative continues:

"The village now consisted of eleven houses, crowded with inhabitants, and about sixty fighting men. They were very well disposed, and we found no difficulty in procuring two small canoes, in exchange for two robes and four elk-skins. He also purchased with deer-skins three dogs,—an animal which has now become a favorite food, for it is found to be a strong, healthy diet, preferable to lean deer or elk, and much superior to horseflesh in any state. With these he proceeded along the south side of the river, and joined us in the evening."

Above the rapids the party encountered two tribes of Indians from whom they endeavored to buy horses, for they were now approaching a point when they must leave the river and travel altogether by land. One of these tribes was known as the Weocksockwillacurns, and the other was the Chilluckittequaws. These jaw-breaking names are commended to those who think that the Indian names of northern Maine are difficult to handle. Trees were now growing scarcer, and the wide lowlands spread out before the explorers stretched to the base of the Bitter Root Mountains without trees, but covered with luxuriant grass and herbage. After being confined so long to the thick forests and mountains of the seacoast, the party found this prospect very exhilarating, notwithstanding the absence of forests and thickets. The climate, too, was much more agreeable than that to which they had lately been accustomed, being dry and pure.

Chapter XX — The Last Stage of the Columbia

On the thirteenth of April the party reached the series of falls and rapids which they called the Long Narrows. At the point reached the river is confined, for a space of about fourteen miles, to narrow channels and rocky falls. The Long Narrows are now known as the Dalles. The word "dalles" is French, and signifies flagstones, such as are used for sidewalks. Many of the rocks in these narrows are nearly flat on top, and even the precipitous banks look like walls of rock. At the upper end of the rapids, or dalles, is Celilo City, and at the lower end is Dalles City, sometimes known as "The Dalles." Both of these places are in Oregon; the total fall of the water from Celilo to the Dalles is over eighty feet. Navigation of these rapids is impossible. As the explorers had no further use for their pirogues, they broke them up for fuel. The merchandise was laboriously carried around on the river bank. They were able to buy four horses from the Skilloots for which they paid well in goods. It was now nearly time for the salmon to begin to run, and under date of April 19 the journal has this entry:—

"The whole village was filled with rejoicing to-day at having caught a single salmon, which was considered as the harbinger of vast quantities in four or five days. In order to hasten their arrival the Indians, according to custom, dressed the fish and cut it into small pieces, one of which was given to each child in the village. In the good humor excited by this occurrence they parted, though reluctantly, with four other horses, for which we gave them two kettles, reserving only a single small one for a mess of eight men. Unluckily, however, we lost one of the horses by the negligence of the person to whose charge he was committed. The rest were, therefore, hobbled and tied; but as the nations here do not understand gelding, all the horses but one were stallions; this being the season when they are most vicious, we had great difficulty in managing them, and were obliged to keep watch over them all night. . . .

"As it was obviously our interest to preserve the goodwill of these people, we passed over several small thefts which they committed, but this morning we learnt that six tomahawks and a knife had been stolen during the night. We addressed ourselves to the chief, who seemed angry with his people, and made a harangue to them; but we did not recover the articles, and soon afterward two of our spoons were missing. We therefore ordered them all from our camp, threatening to beat severely any one detected in purloining. This harshness irritated them so much that they left us in an ill-humor, and we therefore kept on our guard against any insult. Besides this knavery, the faithlessness of the people is intolerable; frequently, after receiving goods in exchange for a horse, they return in a few hours and insist on revoking the bargain or receiving some additional value. We discovered, too, that the horse which was missing yesterday had been gambled away by the fellow from whom we had purchased him, to a man of a different nation, who had carried him off. We succeeded in buying two more horses, two dogs, and some chappelell, and also exchanged a couple of elk-skins for a gun belonging to the chief. . . . One of the canoes, for which the Indians would give us very little, was cut up for fuel; two others, together with some elk-skins and pieces of old iron, we bartered for beads, and the remaining two small ones were despatched early next morning, with all the baggage which could not be carried on horseback. We had intended setting out at the same time, but one of our horses broke loose during the night, and we were under the necessity of sending several men in search of him.

127

In the mean time, the Indians, who were always on the alert, stole a tomahawk, which we could not recover, though several of them were searched; and another fellow was detected in carrying off a piece of iron, and kicked out of camp; upon which Captain Lewis, addressing them, told them he was not afraid to fight them, for, if he chose, he could easily put them all to death, and burn their village, but that he did not wish to treat them ill if they kept from stealing; and that, although, if he could discover who had the tomahawks, he would take away their horses, yet he would rather lose the property altogether than take the horse of an innocent man. The chiefs were present at this harangue, hung their heads, and made no reply.

"At ten o'clock the men returned with the horse, and soon after an Indian, who had promised to go with us as far as the Chopunnish, came with two horses, one of which he politely offered to assist in carrying our baggage. We therefore loaded nine horses, and, giving the tenth to Bratton, who was still too sick to walk, at about ten o'clock left the village of these disagreeable people."

At an Indian village which they reached soon after leaving that of the disagreeable Skilloots, they found the fellow who had gambled away the horse that he had sold. Being faced with punishment, he agreed to replace the animal he had stolen with another, and a very good horse was brought to satisfy the white men, who were now determined to pursue a rigid course with the thievish Indians among whom they found themselves. These people, the Eneeshurs, were stingy, inhospitable, and overbearing in their ways. Nothing but the formidable numbers of the white men saved them from insult, pillage, and even murder. While they were here, one of the horses belonging to the party broke loose and ran towards the Indian village. A buffalo robe attached to him fell off and was gathered in by one of the Eneeshurs. Captain Lewis, whose patience was now exhausted, set out, determined to burn the village unless the Indians restored the robe. Fortunately, however, one of his men found the missing article hidden in a hut, and so any act of violent reprisal was not necessary.

So scarce had now become fuel, the party were obliged to buy what little wood they required for their single cooking-fire. They could not afford a fire to keep them warm, and, as the nights were cold and they lay without any shelter, they were most uncomfortable, although the days were warm. They were now travelling along the Columbia River, using their horses for a part of their luggage, and towing the canoes with the remainder of the stuff. On the twenty-third of April they arrived at the mouth of Rock Creek, on the Columbia, a considerable stream which they missed as they passed this point on their way down, October 21. Here they met a company of Indians called the Wahhowpum, with whom they traded pewter buttons, strips of tin and twisted wire for roots, dogs, and fuel. These people were waiting for the arrival of the salmon. The journal says:—

"After arranging the camp we assembled all the warriors, and having smoked with them, the violins were produced, and some of the men danced. This civility was returned by the Indians in a style of dancing, such as we had not yet seen. The spectators formed a circle round the dancers, who, with their robes drawn tightly round the shoulders, and divided into parties of five or six men, perform by crossing in a line from one side of the circle to the other. All the parties, performers as well as spectators, sing, and after proceeding in this way for some time, the spectators join, and the whole concludes by a promiscuous dance and song. Having finished, the natives retired at our request, after promising to barter horses with us in the morning."

They bought three horses of these Indians and hired three more from a Chopunnish who was to accompany them. The journal adds:—

"The natives also had promised to take our canoes in exchange for horses; but when they found that we were resolved on travelling by land they refused giving us anything, in hopes that we would be forced to leave them. Disgusted at this conduct, we determined rather to cut them to pieces than suffer these people to enjoy them, and actually began to split them, on which they gave us several strands of beads for each canoe. We had now a sufficient number of horses to carry our baggage, and therefore proceeded wholly by land."

Next day the party camped near a tribe of Indians known as the Pishquitpah. These people had never seen white men before, and they flocked in great numbers around the strangers, but were very civil and hospitable, although their curiosity was rather embarrassing. These people were famous hunters, and both men and women were excellent riders. They were now travelling on the south side of the river, in Oregon, and, after leaving the Pishquitpahs, they encountered the "Wollawollahs," as they called them. These Indians are now known as the Walla Walla tribe, and their name is given to a river, a town, and a fort of the United States. In several of the Indian dialects walla means "running water," and when the word is repeated, it diminishes the size of the object; so that Walla Walla means "little running water." Near here the explorers passed the mouth of a river which they called the Youmalolam; it is a curious example of the difficulty of rendering Indian names into English. The stream is now known as the Umatilla. Here they found some old acquaintances of whom the journal has this account:—

"Soon after we were joined by seven Wollawollahs, among whom we recognized a chief by the name of Yellept, who had visited us on the nineteenth of October, when we gave him a medal with the promise of a larger one on our return. He appeared very much pleased at seeing us again, and invited us to remain at his village three or four days, during which he would supply us with the only food they had, and furnish us with horses for our journey. After the cold, inhospitable treatment we have lately received, this kind offer was peculiarly acceptable; and after a hasty meal we accompanied him to his village, six miles above, situated on the edge of the low country, about twelve miles below the mouth of Lewis' River.

"Immediately on our arrival Yellept, who proved to be a man of much influence, not only in his own but in the neighboring nations, collected the inhabitants, and having made a harangue, the purport of which was to induce the nations to treat us hospitably, he set them an example by bringing himself an armful of wood, and a platter containing three roasted mullets. They immediately assented to one part, at least, of the recommendation, by furnishing us with an abundance of the only sort of fuel they employ, the stems of shrubs growing in the plains. We then purchased four dogs, on which we supped heartily, having been on short allowance for two days past. When we were disposed to sleep, the Indians retired immediately on our request, and indeed, uniformly conducted themselves with great propriety. These people live on roots, which are very abundant in the plains, and catch a few salmon-trout; but at present they seem to subsist chiefly on a species of mullet, weighing from one to three pounds. They informed us that opposite the village there was a route which led to the mouth of the Kooskooskee, on the south side of Lewis' River; that the road itself was good, and passed over a level country well supplied with water and grass; and that we should meet with plenty of deer and antelope. We knew that a road in that direction would shorten the distance at least eighty miles; and as the report of our guide was confirmed by Yellept and other Indians, we did not hesitate to adopt this route: they added, however, that there were no houses, nor permanent Indian residences on the road and that it would therefore be prudent not to trust wholly to our guns, but to lay in a stock of provisions.

"Taking their advice, therefore, we next day purchased ten dogs. While the trade for these was being conducted by our men, Yellept brought a fine white horse, and presented him to Captain Clark, expressing at the same time a wish to have a kettle; but, on being informed that we had already disposed of the last kettle we could spare, he said he would be content with any present we chose to make him in return. Captain Clark thereupon gave him his sword, for which the chief had before expressed a desire, adding one hundred balls, some powder, and other small articles, with which he appeared perfectly satisfied. We were now anxious to depart, and requested Yellept to lend us canoes for the purpose of crossing the river; but he would not listen to any proposal of the kind. He wished us to remain for two or three days; but, at all events, would not consent to our going to-day, for he had already sent to invite his neighbors, the Chimnapoos, to come down this evening and join his people in a dance for our amusement. We urged in vain that, by setting out sooner, we would the earlier return with the articles they desired; for a day, he observed, would make but little difference. We at length mentioned that, as there was no wind it was now the best time to cross the river, and we would merely take the horses over and return to sleep at their village. To this he assented; we then crossed with our horses, and having hobbled them, returned to their camp.

"Fortunately, there was among these Wollwaollahs a prisoner belonging to a tribe of Shoshonee or Snake Indians, residing to the south of the Multnomah and visiting occasionally the heads of Wollawollah Creek. Our Shoshonee woman, Sacajawea, though she belonged to a tribe near the Missouri, spoke the same language as this prisoner; by their means we were able to explain ourselves to the Indians, and answer all their inquiries with respect to ourselves and the object of our journey. Our conversation inspired them with much confidence, and they soon brought several sick persons, for whom they requested our assistance. We splintered (splinted) the broken arm of one, gave some relief to another, whose knee was contracted by rheumatism, and administered what we thought beneficial for ulcers and eruptions of the skin on various parts of the body which are very common disorders among them. But our most valuable medicine was eye-water, which we distributed, and which, indeed, they required very much.

"A little before sunset the Chimnapoos, amounting to one hundred men and a few women, came to the village, and, joining the Wollawollahs, who were about the same number of men, formed themselves in a circle round our camp, and waited very patiently till our men were disposed to dance, which they did for about an hour, to the music of the violin. They then requested the Indians to dance. With this they readily complied; and the whole assemblage, amounting, with the women and children of the village, to several hundred, stood up, and sang and danced at the same time. The exercise was not, indeed, very violent nor very graceful; for the greater part of them were formed into a solid column, round a kind of hollow square, stood on the same place, and merely jumped up at intervals, to keep time to the music. Some, however, of the more active warriors entered the square and danced round it sideways, and some of our men joined in with them, to the great satisfaction of the Indians. The dance continued till ten o'clock."

By the thirtieth of April the expedition was equipped with twenty-three horses, most of which were young and excellent animals; but many of them were afflicted with sore backs. All Indians are cruel masters and hard riders, and their saddles are so rudely made that it is almost impossible for an Indian's horse to be free from scars; yet they continue to ride after the animal's back is scarified in the most horrible manner.

The expedition was now in what we know as Walla Walla County, Washington, and they were travelling along the river Walla Walla, leaving the Columbia, which has here a general direction of northerly. The course of the party was northeast, their objective point being that where Waitesburg is now built, near the junction of Coppie Creek and the Touchet River. They were in a region of wood in plenty, and for the first time since leaving the Long Narrows, or Dalles, they had as much fuel as they needed. On the Touchet, accordingly, they camped for the sake of having a comfortable night; the nights were cold, and a good fire by which to sleep was an attraction not easily resisted. The journal, April 30, has this entry:—

"We were soon supplied by Drewyer with a beaver and an otter, of which we took only a part of the beaver, and gave the rest to the Indians. The otter is a favorite food, though much inferior, at least in our estimation, to the dog, which they will not eat. The horse is seldom eaten, and never except when absolute necessity compels them, as the only alternative to dying of hunger. This fastidiousness does not, however, seem to proceed so much from any dislike to the food, as from attachment to the animal itself; for many of them eat very heartily of the horse-beef which we give them."

On the first day of May, having travelled forty miles from their camp near the mouth of the Walla Walla, they camped between two points at which are now situated the two towns of Prescott, on the south, and Waitesburg, on the north. Their journal says:—

"We had scarcely encamped when three young men came up from the Wollawollah village, with a steel-trap which had inadvertently been left behind, and which they had come a whole day's journey in order to restore. This act of integrity was the more pleasing, because, though very rare among Indians, it corresponded perfectly with the general behavior of the Wollawollahs, among whom we had lost carelessly several knives, which were always returned as soon as found. We may, indeed, justly affirm, that of all the Indians whom we had met since leaving the United States, the Wollawollahs were the most hospitable, honest, and sincere."

Chapter XXI — Overland east of the Columbia

It was now early in May, and the expedition, travelling eastward along Touchet Creek, were in the country of their friends, the Chopunnish. On the third, they were agreeably surprised to meet Weahkootnut, whom they had named Bighorn from the fact that he wore a horn of that animal suspended from his left arm. This man was the first chief of a large band of Chopunnish, and when the expedition passed that way, on their path to the Pacific, the last autumn, he was very obliging and useful to them, guiding them down the Snake, or Lewis River. He had now heard that the white men were on their return, and he had come over across the hills to meet them. As we may suppose, the meeting was very cordial, and Weahkootnut turned back with his white friends and accompanied them to the mouth of the Kooskooskee, a stream of which our readers have heard before; it is now known as the Clearwater.

Captain Lewis told Weahkootnut that his people were hungry, their slender stock of provisions being about exhausted. The chief told them that they would soon come to a Chopunnish house where they could get food. But the journal has this entry:—

"We found the house which Weahkootnut had mentioned, where we halted for breakfast. It contained six families, so miserably poor that all we could obtain from them were two lean dogs and a few large cakes of half-cured bread, made of a root resembling the sweet potato, of all which we contrived to form a kind of soup. The soil of the plain is good, but it has no timber. The range of southwest mountains is about fifteen miles above us, but continues to lower, and is still covered with snow to its base. After giving passage to Lewis' (Snake) River, near their northeastern extremity, they terminate in a high level plain between that river and the Kooskooskee. The salmon not having yet called them to the rivers, the greater part of the Chopunnish are now dispersed in villages through this plain, for the purpose of collecting quamash and cows, which here grow in great abundance, the soil being extremely fertile, in many places covered with long-leaved pine, larch, and balsam-fir, which contribute to render it less thirsty than the open, unsheltered plains."

By the word "cows," in this sentence, we must understand that the story-teller meant cowas, a root eaten by the Indians and white explorers in that distant region. It is a knobbed, irregular root, and when cooked resembles the ginseng. At this place the party met some of the Indians whom Captain Clark had treated for slight diseases, when they passed that way, the previous autumn. They bad sounded the praises of the white men and their medicine, and others were now waiting to be treated in the same manner. The Indians were glad to pay for their treatment, and the white men were not sorry to find this easy method of adding to their stock of food, which was very scanty at this time. The journal sagely adds, "We cautiously abstain from giving them any but harmless medicines; and as we cannot possibly do harm, our prescriptions, though unsanctioned by the faculty, may be useful, and are entitled to some remuneration." Very famous and accomplished doctors might say the same thing of their practice. But the explorers did not meet with pleasant acquaintances only; in the very next entry is recorded this disagreeable incident:

"Four miles beyond this house we came to another large one, containing ten families, where we halted and made our dinner on two dogs and a small quantity of roots, which we did not procure without much difficulty. Whilst we were eating, an Indian standing by, looking with great derision at our eating dogs, threw a poor half-starved puppy almost into Captain Lewis' plate, laughing heartily at the humor of it. Captain Lewis took up the animal and flung it with great force into the fellow's face; and seizing his tomahawk, threatened to cut him down if he dared to repeat such insolence. He immediately withdrew, apparently much mortified, and we continued our repast of dog very quietly. Here we met our old Chopunnish guide, with his family; and soon afterward one of our horses, which had been separated from the rest in charge of Twisted-hair, and had been in this neighborhood for several weeks, was caught and restored to us."

Later in that day the party came to a Chopunnish house which was one hundred and fifty-six feet long and fifteen feet wide. Thirty families were living in this big house, each family having its fire by itself burning on the earthen floor, along through the middle of the great structure. The journal says:—

"We arrived very hungry and weary, but could not purchase any provisions, except a small quantity of the roots and bread of the cows. They had, however, heard of our medical skill, and made many applications for assistance, but we refused to do anything unless they gave us either dogs or horses to eat. We soon had nearly fifty patients. A chief brought his wife with an abscess on her back, and promised to furnish us with a horse to-morrow if we would relieve her. Captain Clark, therefore, opened the abscess, introduced a tent, and dressed it with basilicon. We also prepared and distributed some doses of flour of sulphur and cream of tartar, with directions for its use. For these we obtained several dogs, but too poor for use, and therefore postponed our medical operations till the morning. In the mean time a number of Indians, besides the residents of the village, gathered about us or camped in the woody bottom of the creek."

It will be recollected that when the expedition was in this region (on the Kooskooskee), during the previous September, on their way westward, they left their horses with Chief Twisted-hair, travelling overland from that point. They were now looking for that chief, and the journal says:—

"About two o'clock we collected our horses and set out, accompanied by Weahkoonut, with ten or twelve men and a man who said he was the brother of Twisted-hair. At four miles we came to a single house of three families, but could not procure provisions of any kind; and five miles further we halted for the night near another house, built like the rest, of sticks, mats, and dried hay, and containing six families. It was now so difficult to procure anything to eat that our chief dependence was on the horse which we received yesterday for medicine; but to our great disappointment he broke the rope by which he was confined, made his escape, and left us supperless in the rain."

Next day they met an Indian who brought them two canisters of powder, which they at once knew to be some of that which they had buried last autumn. The Indian said that his dog had dug it up in the meadow by the river, and he had restored it to its rightful owners. As a reward for his honesty, the captains gave him a flint and steel for striking fire; and they regretted that their own poverty prevented them from being more liberal to the man.

They observed that the Rocky Mountains, now in full sight, were still covered with snow, and the prospect of crossing them was not very rosy. Their Chopunnish guide told them that it would be impossible to cross the mountains before the next full moon, which would be about the first of

June. The journal adds: "To us, who are desirous of reaching the plains of the Missouri—if for no other reason, for the purpose of enjoying a good meal—this intelligence was by no means welcome, and gave no relish to the remainder of the horse killed at Colter's Creek, which formed our supper, as part of which had already been our dinner." Next day, accordingly, the hunters turned out early in the morning, and before noon returned with four deer and a duck, which, with the remains of horse-beef on hand, gave them a much more plentiful stock of provisions than had lately fallen to their lot. During the previous winter, they were told, the Indians suffered very much for lack of food, game of all sorts being scarce. They were forced to boil and eat the moss growing on the trees, and they cut down the pine-trees for the sake of the small nut to be found in the pine-cones. Here they were met by an old friend, Neeshnepahkeeook and the Shoshonee, who had acted as interpreter for them. The journal says:—

"We gave Neeshnepahkeeook and his people some of our game and horse-beef, besides the entrails of the deer, and four fawns which we found inside of two of them. They did not eat any of them perfectly raw, but the entrails had very little cooking; the fawns were boiled whole, and the hide, hair, and entrails all consumed. The Shoshonee was offended at not having as much venison as he wished, and refused to interpret; but as we took no notice of him, he became very officious in the course of a few hours, and made many efforts to reinstate himself in our favor. The brother of Twisted-hair, and Neeshnepahkeeook, now drew a sketch, which we preserved, of all the waters west of the Rocky Mountains."

They now met Twisted-hair, in whose care they had left their horses and saddles the previous fall, and this was the result of their inquiries:—

"Between three and four o'clock in the afternoon we set out, in company with Neeshuepahkeeook and other Indians, the brother of Twisted-hair having left us. Our route was up a high steep hill to a level plain with little wood, through which we passed in a direction parallel to the (Kooskooskee) River for four miles, when we met Twisted-hair and six of his people. To this chief we had confided our horses and a part of our saddles last autumn, and we therefore formed very unfavorable conjectures on finding that he received us with great coldness. Shortly afterward he began to speak in a very loud, angry manner, and was answered by Neeshnepahkeeook. We now discovered that a violent quarrel had arisen between these chiefs, on the subject, as we afterward understood, of our horses. But as we could not learn the cause, and were desirous of terminating the dispute, we interposed, and told them we should go on to the first water and camp. We therefore set out, followed by all the Indians, and having reached, at two miles' distance, a small stream running to the right, we camped with the two chiefs and their little bands, forming separate camps at a distance from each other. They all appeared to be in an ill humor; and as we had already heard reports that the Indians had discovered and carried off our saddles, and that the horses were very much scattered, we began to be uneasy, lest there should be too much foundation for the report. We were therefore anxious to reconcile the two chiefs as soon as possible, and desired the Shoshonee to interpret for us while we attempted a mediation, but be peremptorily refused to speak a word. He observed that it was a quarrel between the two chiefs, and he had therefore no right to interfere; nor could all our representations, that by merely repeating what we said he could not possibly be considered as meddling between the chiefs, induce him to take any part in it.

"Soon afterward Drewyer returned from hunting, and was sent to invite Twisted-hair to come and smoke with us. He accepted the invitation, and as we were smoking the pipe over our fire he informed us that according to his promise on leaving us at the falls of the Columbia, he had collected our horses and taken charge of them as soon as he reached home. But about this time Neeshnepahkeeook and Turmachemootoolt (Broken-arm), who, as we passed, were on a war-party against the Shoshonees on the south branch of Lewis' River, returned; and becoming jealous of him, because the horses had been confided to his care, were constantly quarrelling with him. At length, being an old man and unwilling to live in perpetual dispute with these two chiefs, he had given up the care of the horses, which had consequently become very much scattered. The greater part of them were, however, still in the neighborhood; some in the forks between the Chopunnish and Kooskooskee, and three or four at the village of Broken Arm, about half a day's march higher up the river. He added, that on the rise of the river in the spring, the earth had fallen from the door of the cache, and exposed the saddles, some of which had probably been lost; but that, as soon as he was acquainted with the situation of them, he had them buried in another deposit, where they now were. He promised that, if we would stay the next day at his house, a few miles distant, he would collect such of the horses as were in the neighborhood, and send his young men for those in the forks, over the Kooskooskee. He moreover advised us to visit Broken Arm, who was a chief of great eminence, and he would himself guide us to his dwelling.

"We told him that we would follow his advice in every respect; that we had confided our horses to his care, and expected he would deliver them to us, on which we should cheerfully give him the two guns and the ammunition we had promised him. With this he seemed very much pleased, and declared he would use every exertion to restore the horses. We now sent for Neesbnepahkeeook, or Cut Nose, and, after smoking for some time, began by expressing to the two chiefs our regret at seeing a misunderstanding between them. Neeshnepahkeeook replied that Twisted Hair was a bad old man, and wore two faces; for, instead of taking care of our horses, he had suffered his young men to hunt with them, so that they had been very much injured, and it was for this reason that Broken Arm and himself had forbidden him to use them. Twisted Hair made no reply to this speech, and we then told Neeshnepahkeeook of our arrangement for the next day. He appeared to be very well satisfied, and said he would himself go with us to Broken Arm, who expected to see us, and had TWO BAD HORSES FOR US; by which expression we understood that Broken Arm intended to make us a present of two horses."

Next day, the party reached the house of Twisted-hair, and began to look for their horses and saddles. The journal gives this account of the search:—

"Late in the afternoon, Twisted-hair returned with about half the saddles we had left in the autumn, and some powder and lead which were buried at the same place. Soon after, the Indians brought us twenty-one of our horses, the greater part of which were in excellent order, though some had not yet recovered from hard usage, and three had sore backs. We were, however, very glad to procure them in any condition. Several Indians came down from the village of Tunnachemootoolt and passed the night with us. Cut-nose and Twisted-hair seem now perfectly reconciled, for they both slept in the house of the latter. The man who had imposed himself upon us as a brother of Twisted-hair also came and renewed his advances, but we now found that he was an impertinent, proud fellow, of no respectability in the nation, and we therefore felt no inclination to cultivate his intimacy. Our camp was in an open plain, and soon became very uncomfortable, for the wind was high and cold, and the rain and hail, which began about seven o'clock, changed in two hours to a heavy fall of snow, which continued till after six o'clock

135

(May 10th), the next morning, when it ceased, after covering the ground eight inches deep and leaving the air keen and cold. We soon collected our horses, and after a scanty breakfast of roots set out on a course S. 35'0 E."

They were now following the general course of the Kooskooskee, or Clearwater, as the stream is called, and their route lay in what is now Nez Perce County, Idaho. They have passed the site of the present city of Lewiston, named for Captain Lewis. They have arrived in a region inhabited by the friendly Chopunnish, or Nez Perce, several villages of which nation were scattered around the camp of the white men. The narrative says:

"We soon collected the men of consideration, and after smoking, explained how destitute we were of provisions. The chief spoke to the people, who immediately brought two bushels of dried quamash-roots, some cakes of the roots of cows, and a dried salmon-trout; we thanked them for this supply, but observed that, not being accustomed to live on roots alone, we feared that such diet might make our men sick, and therefore proposed to exchange one of our good horses, which was rather poor, for one that was fatter, and which we might kill. The hospitality of the chief was offended at the idea of an exchange; he observed that his people had an abundance of young horses, and that if we were disposed to use that food we might have as many as we wanted. Accordingly, they soon gave us two fat young horses, without asking anything in return, an act of liberal hospitality much greater than any we have witnessed since crossing the Rocky Mountains, if it be not in fact the only really hospitable treatment we have received in this part of the world. We killed one of the horses, and then telling the natives that we were fatigued and hungry, and that as soon as we were refreshed we would communicate freely with them, began to prepare our repast.

"During this time a principal chief, called Hohastillpilp, came from his village, about six miles distant, with a party of fifty men, for the purpose of visiting us. We invited him into our circle, and he alighted and smoked with us, while his retinue, with five elegant horses, continued mounted at a short distance. While this was going on, the chief had a large leathern tent spread for us, and desired that we would make it our home so long as we remained at his village. We removed there, and having made a fire, and cooked our supper of horseflesh and roots, collected all the distinguished men present, and spent the evening in making known who we were, what were the objects of our journey, and in answering their inquiries. To each of the chiefs Tunnachemootoolt and Hohastillpilp we gave a small medal, explaining their use and importance as honorary distinctions both among the whites and the red men. Our men were well pleased at once more having made a hearty meal. They had generally been in the habit of crowding into the houses of the Indians, to purchase provisions on the best terms they could; for the inhospitality of the country was such, that often, in the extreme of hunger, they were obliged to treat the natives with but little ceremony; but this Twisted Hair had told us was very disagreeable. Finding that these people are so kind and liberal, we ordered our men to treat them with the greatest respect, and not to throng round their fires, so that they now agree perfectly well together. After the council the Indians felt no disposition to retire, and our tent was filled with them all night."

As the expedition was here in a populous country, among many bands of Indians, it was thought wise to have a powwow with the head men and explain to them what were the intentions of the United States Government. But, owing to the crooked course which their talk must needs take, it was very difficult to learn if the Indians finally understood what was said. Here is the journal's account of the way in which the powwow was conducted:—

"We collected the chiefs and warriors, and having drawn a map of the relative situation of our country on a mat with a piece of coal, detailed the nature and power of the American nation, its desire to preserve harmony between all its red brethren, and its intention of establishing trading-houses for their relief and support. It was not without difficulty, nor till after nearly half the day was spent, that we were able to convey all this information to the Chopunnish, much of which might have been lost or distorted in its circuitous route through a variety of languages; for in the first place, we spoke in English to one of our men, who translated it into French to Chaboneau; he interpreted it to his wife in the Minnetaree language; she then put it into Shoshonee, and the young Shoshonee prisoner explained it to the Chopunnish in their own dialect. At last we succeeded in communicating the impression we wished, and then adjourned the council; after which we amused them by showing the wonders of the compass, spy-glass, magnet, watch, and air-gun, each of which attracted its share of admiration."

The simple-minded Indians, who seemed to think that the white men could heal all manner of diseases, crowded around them next day, begging for medicines and treatment. These were freely given, eye-water being most in demand. There was a general medical powwow. The journal adds:—

"Shortly after, the chiefs and warriors held a council among themselves, to decide on an answer to our speech, and the result was, as we were informed, that they had full confidence in what we had told them, and were resolved to follow our advice. This determination having been made, the principal chief, Tunnachemootoolt, took a quantity of flour of the roots of cow-weed (cowas), and going round to all the kettles and baskets in which his people were cooking, thickened the soup into a kind of mush. He then began an harangue, setting forth the result of the deliberations among the chiefs, and after exhorting them to unanimity, concluded with an invitation to all who acquiesced in the proceedings of the council to come and eat; while those who were of a different mind were requested to show their dissent by not partaking of the feast. During this animated harangue, the women, who were probably uneasy at the prospect of forming this proposed new connection with strangers, tore their hair, and wrung their hands with the greatest appearance of distress. But the concluding appeal of the orator effectually stopped the mouths of every malecontent, and the proceedings were ratified, and the mush devoured with the most zealous unanimity.

"The chiefs and warriors then came in a body to visit us as we were seated near our tent; and at their instance, two young men, one of whom was a son of Tunnachemootoolt, and the other the youth whose father had been killed by the Pahkees, presented to us each a fine horse. We invited the chiefs to be seated, and gave every one of them a flag, a pound of powder, and fifty balls, and a present of the same kind to the young men from whom we had received the horses. They then invited us into the tent, and said that they now wished to answer what we had told them yesterday, but that many of their people were at that moment waiting in great pain for our medical assistance."

It was agreed, therefore, that Captain Clark, who seems to have been their favorite physician, should attend to the sick and lame, while Captain Lewis should conduct a council with the chiefs and listen to what they had to say. The upshot of the powwow was that the Chopunnish said they had sent three of their warriors with a pipe to make peace with the Shoshonees, last summer, as they had been advised to do by the white men. The Shoshonees, unmindful of the sacredness of this embassy, had killed the young warriors and had invited the battle which immediately took place, in which the Chopunnish killed forty-two of the Shoshonees, to get even for the wanton killing of their three young men. The white men now wanted some of the Chopunnish to accompany them to the plains of the Missouri, but the Indians were not willing to go until they were assured that they would not be waylaid and slain by their enemies of the other side of the mountains. The Chopunnish would think over the proposal that some of their young men should go over the range with the white men; a decision on this point should be reached before the white men left the country. Anyhow, the white men might be sure that the Indians would do their best to oblige their visitors. Their conclusion was, "For, although we are poor, our hearts are good." The story of this conference thus concludes:—

"As soon as this speech was concluded, Captain Lewis replied at some length; with this they appeared highly gratified, and after smoking the pipe, made us a present of another fat horse for food. We, in turn, gave Broken-arm a phial of eye-water, with directions to wash the eyes of all who should apply for it; and as we promised to fill it again when it was exhausted, he seemed very much pleased with our liberality. To Twisted-hair, who had last night collected six more horses, we gave a gun, one hundred balls, and two pounds of powder, and told him he should have the same quantity when we received the remainder of our horses. In the course of the day three more of them were brought in, and a fresh exchange of small presents put the Indians in excellent humor. On our expressing a wish to cross the river and form a camp, in order to hunt and fish till the snows had melted, they recommended a position a few miles distant, and promised to furnish us to-morrow with a canoe to cross. We invited Twisted-hair to settle near our camp, for he has several young sons, one of whom we hope to engage as a guide, and he promised to do so. Having now settled all their affairs, the Indians divided themselves into two parties, and began to play the game of hiding a bone, already described as common to all the natives of this country, which they continued playing for beads and other ornaments."

As there was so dismal a prospect for crossing the snow-covered mountains at this season of the year, the captains of the expedition resolved to establish a camp and remain until the season should be further advanced. Accordingly, a spot on the north side of the river, recommended to them by the Indians, was selected, and a move across the stream was made. A single canoe was borrowed for the transit of the baggage, and the horses were driven in to swim across, and the passage was accomplished without loss. The camp was built on the site of an old Indian house, in a circle about thirty yards in diameter, near the river and in an advantageous position. As soon as the party were encamped, the two Chopunnish chiefs came down to the opposite bank, and, with twelve of their nation, began to sing. This was the custom of these people, being a token of their friendship on such occasions. The captains sent a canoe over for the chiefs, and, after smoking for some time, Hohastillpilp presented Captain with a fine gray horse which he had brought over for that purpose, and he was perfectly satisfied to receive in return a handkerchief, two hundred balls, and four pounds of powder.

Here is some curious information concerning the bears which they found in this region. It must be borne in mind that they were still west of the Bitter Root Mountains:—

"The hunters killed some pheasants, two squirrels, and a male and a female bear, the first of which was large, fat, and of a bay color; the second meagre, grizzly, and of smaller size. They were of the species (Ursus horribilis) common to the upper part of the Missouri, and might well be termed the variegated bear, for they are found occasionally of a black, grizzly, brown, or red color. There is every reason to believe them to be of precisely the same species. Those of different colors are killed together, as in the case of these two, and as we found the white and bay associated together on the Missouri; and some nearly white were seen in this neighborhood by the hunters. Indeed, it is not common to find any two bears of the same color; and if the difference in color were to constitute a distinction of species, the number would increase to almost twenty. Soon afterward the hunters killed a female bear with two cubs. The mother was black, with a considerable intermixture of white hairs and a white spot on the breast. One of the cubs was jet black, and the other of a light reddish-brown or bay color. The hair of these variegated bears is much finer, longer, and more abundant than that of the common black bear; but the most striking differences between them are that the former are larger and have longer tusks, and longer as well as blunter talons; that they prey more on other animals; that they lie neither so long nor so closely in winter quarters; and that they never climb a tree, however closely pressed by the hunters. These variegated bears, though specifically the same with those we met on the Missouri, are by no means so ferocious; probably because the scarcity of game and the habit of living on roots may have weaned them from the practices of attacking and devouring animals. Still, however, they are not so passive as the common black bear, which is also to be found here; for they have already fought with our hunters, though with less fury than those on the other side of the mountains.

"A large part of the meat we gave to the Indians, to whom it was a real luxury, as they scarcely taste flesh once in a month. They immediately prepared a large fire of dried wood, on which was thrown a number of smooth stones from the river. As soon as the fire went down and the stones were heated, they were laid next to each other in a level position, and covered with a quantity of pine branches, on which were placed flitches of the meat, and then boughs and flesh alternately for several courses, leaving a thick layer of pine on the top. On this heap they then poured a small quantity of water, and covered the whole with earth to the depth of four inches. After remaining in this state for about three hours, the meat was taken off, and was really more tender than that which we had boiled or roasted, though the strong flavor of the pine rendered it disagreeable to our palates. This repast gave them much satisfaction; for, though they sometimes kill the black bear, they attack very reluctantly the fierce variegated bear; and never except when they can pursue him on horseback over the plains, and shoot him with arrows."

Chapter XXII — Camping with the Nez Perces

Soon after they had fixed their camp, the explorers bade farewell to their good friend Tunnachemootoolt and his young men, who returned to their homes farther down the river. Others of the Nez Perce, or Chopunnish, nation visited them, and the strangers were interested in watching the Indians preparing for their hunt. As they were to hunt the deer, they had the head, horns, and hide of that animal so prepared that when it was placed on the head and body of a hunter, it gave a very deceptive idea of a deer; the hunter could move the head of the decoy so that it looked like a deer feeding, and the suspicious animals were lured within range of the Indians' bow and arrow.

On the sixteenth of May, Hohastillpilp and his young men also left the white men's camp and returned to their own village. The hunters of the party did not meet with much luck in their quest for game, only one deer and a few pheasants being brought in for several days. The party were fed on roots and herbs, a species of onion being much prized by them. Bad weather confined them to their camp, and a common entry in their journal refers to their having slept all night in a pool of water formed by the falling rain; their tent-cover was a worn-out leathern affair no longer capable of shedding the rain. While it rained in the meadows where they were camped, they could see the snow covering the higher plains above them; on those plains the snow was more than a foot deep, and yet the plants and shrubs seemed to thrive in the midst of the snow. On the mountains the snow was several feet in depth. The journalist says: "So that within twenty miles of our camp we observe the rigors of winter cold, the cool air of spring, and the oppressive heat of midsummer." They kept a shrewd lookout for the possibilities of future occupation of the land by white men; and, writing here of country and its character, the journalist says: "In short, this district affords many advantages to settlers, and if properly cultivated, would yield every object necessary for the comfort and subsistence of civilized man." But in their wildest dreams, Captains Lewis and Clark could not have foreseen that in that identical region thrifty settlements of white men should flourish and that the time would come when the scanty remnant of the Chopunnish, whom we now call Nez Perces, would be gathered on a reservation near their camping-place. But both of these things have come to pass.

In describing the dress of the Chopunnish, or Nez Perces, the journal says that tippets, or collars, were worn by the men. "That of Hohastillpilp," says the journal, "was formed of human scalps and adorned with the thumbs and fingers of several men slain by him in battle." And yet the journal immediately adds: "The Chopunnish are among the most amiable men we have seen. Their character is placid and gentle, rarely moved to passion, yet not often enlivened by gayety." In short, the Indians were amiable savages; and it is a savage trait to love to destroy one's enemies.

Here is an entry in the journal of May 19 which will give the reader some notion of the privations and the pursuits of the party while shut up in camp for weary weeks in the early summer of 1806:—

"After a cold, rainy night, during a greater part of which we lay in the water, the weather became fair; we then sent some men to a village above us, on the opposite side, to purchase some roots. They carried with them for this purpose a small collection of awls, knitting-pins, and armbands, with which they obtained several bushels of the root of cows, and some bread of the same material. They were followed, too, by a train of invalids from the village, who came to ask for our assistance. The men were generally afflicted with sore eyes; but the women had besides this a variety of other disorders, chiefly rheumatic, a violent pain and weakness in the loins, which is a common complaint among them; one of them seemed much dejected, and as we thought, from the account of her disease, hysterical. We gave her thirty drops of laudanum, and after administering eye-water, rubbing the rheumatic patients with volatile liniment, and giving cathartics to others, they all thought themselves much relieved and returned highly satisfied to the village. We were fortunate enough to retake one of the horses on which we (Captain Lewis) had crossed the Rocky Mountains in the autumn, and which had become almost wild since that time."

A day or two later, the journal has this significant entry: "On parcelling out the stores, the stock of each man was found to be only one awl, and one knitting-pin, half an ounce of vermilion, two needles, a few skeins of thread, and about a yard of ribbon—a slender means of bartering for our subsistence; but the men have been so much accustomed to privations that now neither the want of meat nor the scanty funds of the party excites the least anxiety among them." To add to their discomfort, there was a great deal of sickness in the camp, owing to the low diet of the men. Sacajawea's baby was ill with mumps and teething, and it is suggested that the two captains would have been obliged to "walk the floor all night," if there had been any floor to walk on; as it was, they were deprived of their nightly rest. Here is an example of what the doctors would call heroic treatment by Captain Clark, who conducted all such experiments:—

"With one of the men (Bratton) we have ventured an experiment of a very robust nature. He has been for some time sick, but has now recovered his flesh, eats heartily, and digests well, but has so great a weakness in the loins that he cannot walk or even sit upright without extreme pain. After we had in vain exhausted the resources of our art, one of the hunters mentioned that he had known persons in similar situations to be restored by violent sweats, and at the request of the patient, we permitted the remedy to be applied. For this purpose a hole about four feet deep and three in diameter was dug in the earth, and heated well by a large fire in the bottom of it. The fire was then taken out, and an arch formed over the hole by means of willow-poles, and covered with several blankets so as to make a perfect awning. The patient being stripped naked, was seated under this on a beach, with a piece of board for his feet, and with a jug of water sprinkled the bottom and sides of the hole, so as to keep up as hot a steam as he could bear. After remaining twenty minutes in this situation, he was taken out, immediately plunged twice in cold water, and brought back to the hole, where he resumed the vapor bath. During all this time he drank copiously a strong infusion of horse-mint, which was used as a substitute for seneca-root, which our informant said he had seen employed on these occasions, but of which there is none in this country. At the end of three-quarters of an hour he was again withdrawn from the hole, carefully wrapped, and suffered to cool gradually. This operation was performed yesterday; this morning he walked about and is nearly free from pain. About eleven o'clock a canoe arrived with three Indians, one of whom was the poor creature who had lost the use of his limbs, and for whose recovery the natives seem very anxious, as he is a chief of considerable rank among them. His situation is beyond the reach of our skill. He complains of no pain in any peculiar limb, and we therefore think his disorder cannot be rheumatic, and his limbs would have been more diminished if his disease had been a paralytic affection. We had already ascribed it to his diet of roots, and had recommended his living on fish and flesh, and using the cold bath every morning, with a dose of cream of tartar or flowers of sulphur every third day."

It is gratifying to be able to record the fact that Bratton and the Indian (who was treated in the same manner) actually recovered from their malady. The journal says of the Indian that his restoration was "wonderful." This is not too strong a word to use under the circumstances, for the chief had been helpless for nearly three years, and yet he was able to get about and take care of himself after he had been treated by Captain (otherwise Doctor) Clark. Two of his men met with a serious disaster about this time; going across the river to trade with some Indians, their boat was stove and went to the bottom, carrying with it three blankets, a blanket-coat, and their scanty stock of merchandise, all of which was utterly lost. Another disaster, which happened next day, is thus recorded:—

"Two of our men, who had been up the river to trade with the Indians, returned quite unsuccessful. Nearly opposite the village, their horse fell with his load down a steep cliff into the river, across which he swam. An Indian on the opposite side drove him back to them; but in crossing most of the articles were lost and the paint melted. Understanding their intentions, the Indians attempted to come over to them, but having no canoe, were obliged to use a raft, which struck on a rock, upset, and the whole store of roots and bread were destroyed. This failure completely exhausted our stock of merchandise; but the remembrance of what we suffered from cold and hunger during the passage of the Rocky Mountains makes us anxious to increase our means of subsistence and comfort, since we have again to encounter the same inconvenience."

But the ingenuity of the explorers was equal to this emergency. Having observed that the Indians were very fond of brass buttons, which they fastened to their garments as ornaments, and not for the useful purpose for which buttons are made, the men now proceeded to cut from their shabby United States uniforms those desired articles, and thus formed a new fund for trading purposes. To these they added some eye-water, some basilicon, and a few small tin boxes in which phosphorus had been kept. Basilicon, of which mention is frequently made in the journal, was an ointment composed of black pitch, white wax, resin, and olive oil; it was esteemed as a sovereign remedy for all diseases requiring an outward application. With these valuables two men were sent out to trade with the Indians, on the second day of June, and they returned with three bushels of eatable roots and some cowas bread. Later in that day, a party that had been sent down the river (Lewis') in quest of food, returned with a goodly supply of roots and seventeen salmon. These fish, although partly spoiled by the long journey home, gave great satisfaction to the hungry adventurers, for they were the promise of a plenty to come when the salmon should ascend the rivers that make into the Columbia. At this time we find the following interesting story in the journal of the expedition:—

"We had lately heard, also, that some Indians, residing at a considerable distance, on the south side of the Kooskooskee, were in possession of two tomahawks, one of which had been left at our camp on Moscheto Creek, and the other had been stolen while we were with the Chopunnish in the autumn. This last we were anxious to obtain, in order to give it to the relations of our unfortunate companion, Sergeant Floyd,(1) to whom it once belonged. We therefore sent Drewyer, with the two chiefs Neeshnepahkeeook and Hohastillpilp (who had returned to us) to demand it. On their arrival, they found that the present possessor of it, who had purchased it of the thief, was at the point of death; and his relations were unwilling to give it up, as they wished to bury it in the grave with the deceased. The influence of Neeshnepahkeeook, however, at length prevailed; and they consented to surrender the tomahawk on receiving two strands of beads and a handkerchief from Drewyer, and from each of the chiefs a horse, to be killed at the funeral of their kinsman, according to the custom of the country."

(1) See page 23.

The Chopunnish chiefs now gave their final answer to the two captains who had requested guides from them. The chiefs said that they could not accompany the party, but later in the summer they might cross the great divide and spend the next winter on the headwaters of the Missouri. At present, they could only promise that some of their young men should go with the whites; these had not been selected, but they would be sent on after the party, if the two captains insisted on starting now. This was not very encouraging, for they had depended upon the Indians for guidance over the exceedingly difficult and even dangerous passages of the mountains. Accordingly, it was resolved that, while waiting on the motions of the Indians, the party might as well make a visit to Quamash flats, where they could lay in a stock of provisions for their arduous journey. It is not certain which of the several Quamash flats mentioned in the history of the expedition is here referred to; but it is likely that the open glade in which Captain Clark first struck the low country of the west is here meant. It was here that he met the Indian boys hiding in the grass, and from here he led the expedition out of the wilderness. For "quamash" read "camass," an edible root much prized by the Nez Perces then and now.

While they lingered at their camp, they were visited by several bands of friendly Indians. The explorers traded horses with their visitors, and, with what they already had, they now found their band to number sixty-five, all told. Having finished their trading, they invited the Indians to take part in the games of prisoners' base and foot-racing; in the latter game the Indians were very expert, being able to distance the fleetest runner of the white men's party. At night, the games were concluded by a dance. The account of the expedition says that the captains were desirous of encouraging these exercises before they should begin the passage over the mountains, "as several of the men are becoming lazy from inaction."

On the tenth of June the party set out for Quamash flats, each man well mounted and leading a spare horse which carried a small load. To their dismay, they found that their good friends, the Chopunnish, unwilling to part with them, were bound to accompany them to the hunting-grounds. The Indians would naturally expect to share in the hunt and to be provided for by the white men. The party halted there only until the sixth of June, and then, collecting their horses, set out through what proved to be a very difficult trail up the creek on which they were camped, in a northeasterly direction. There was still a quantity of snow on the ground, although this was in shady places and hollows. Vegetation was rank, and the dogtooth violet, honeysuckle, blue-bell, and columbine were in blossom. The pale blue flowers of the quamash gave to the level country the appearance of a blue lake. Striking Hungry Creek, which Captain Clark had very appropriately named when he passed that way, the previous September, they followed it up to a mountain for about three miles, when they found themselves enveloped in snow; their limbs were benumbed, and the snow, from twelve to fifteen feet deep, so paralyzed their feet that further progress was impossible. Here the journal should be quoted:—

"We halted at the sight of this new difficulty. We already knew that to wait till the snows of the mountains had dissolved, so as to enable us to distinguish the road, would defeat our design of returning to the United States this season. We now found also that as the snow bore our horses very well, travelling was infinitely easier than it was last fall, when the rocks and fallen timber had so much obstructed our march. But it would require five days to reach the fish-weirs at the mouth of Colt (-killed) Creek, even if we were able to follow the proper ridges of the mountains; and the danger of missing our direction is exceedingly great while every track is covered with snow. During these five days, too, we have no chance of finding either grass or underwood for our horses, the snow being so deep. To proceed, therefore, under such circumstances, would be to hazard our being bewildered in the mountains, and to insure the loss of our horses; even should we be so fortunate as to escape with our lives, we might be obliged to abandon all our papers and collections. It was therefore decided not to venture any further; to deposit here all the baggage and provisions for which we had no immediate use; and, reserving only subsistence for a few days, to return while our horses were yet strong to some spot where we might live by hunting, till a guide could be procured to conduct us across the mountains. Our baggage was placed on scaffolds and carefully covered, as were also the instruments and papers, which we thought it safer to leave than to risk over the roads and creeks by which we came."

There was nothing left to do but to return to Hungry Creek. Finding a scanty supply of grass, they camped under most depressing circumstances; their outlook now was the passing of four or five days in the midst of snows from ten to fifteen feet deep, with no guide, no road, and no forage. In this emergency, two men were sent back to the Chopunnish country to hurry up the Indians who had promised to accompany them over the mountains; and, to insure a guide, these men were authorized to offer a rifle as a reward for any one who would undertake the task. For the present, it was thought best to return to Quamash flats.

Chapter XXIII — Crossing the Bitter Root Mountains

Disasters many kept pace with the unhappy explorers on their way back to Quamash flats after their rebuff at the base of the Bitter Root Mountains. One of the horses fell down a rough and rocky place, carrying his rider with him; but fortunately neither horse nor man was killed. Next, a man, sent ahead to cut down the brush that blocked the path, cut himself badly on the inside of his thigh and bled copiously. The hunters sent out for game returned empty-handed. The fishermen caught no fish, but broke the two Indian gigs, or contrivances for catching fish, with which they had been provided. The stock of salt had given out, the bulk of their supply having been left on the mountain. Several large mushrooms were brought in by Cruzatte, but these were eaten without pepper, salt, or any kind of grease,—"a very tasteless, insipid food," as the journal says. To crown all, the mosquitoes were pestilential in their numbers and venom.

Nevertheless, the leaders of the expedition were determined to press on and pass the Bitter Root Mountains as soon as a slight rest at Quamash flats should be had. If they should tarry until the snows melted from the trail, they would be too late to reach the United States that winter and would be compelled to pass the next winter at some camp high up on the Missouri, as they had passed one winter at Fort Mandan, on their way out. This is the course of argument which Captain Lewis and Clark took to persuade each other as to the best way out of their difficulties:—

"The snows have formed a hard, coarse bed without crust, on which the horses walk safely without slipping; the chief difficulty, therefore, is to find the road. In this we may be assisted by the circumstance that, though generally ten feet in depth, the snow has been thrown off by the thick and spreading branches of the trees, and from round the trunk; while the warmth of the trunk itself, acquired by the reflection of the sun, or communicated by natural heat of the earth, which is never frozen under these masses, has dissolved the snow so much that immediately at the roots its depth is not more than one or two feet. We therefore hope that the marks of the baggage rubbing against the trees may still be perceived; and we have decided, in case the guide cannot be procured, that one of us will take three or four of our most expert woodsmen, several of our best horses, and an ample supply of provisions, go on two days' journey in advance, and endeavor to trace the route by the marks of the Indian baggage on the trees, which we would then mark more distinctly with a tomahawk. When they should have reached two days' journey beyond Hungry Creek, two of the men were to be sent back to apprise the rest of their success, and if necessary to cause them to delay there; lest, by advancing too soon, they should be forced to halt where no food could be obtained for the horses. If the traces of the baggage be too indistinct, the whole party is to return to Hungry Creek, and we will then attempt the passage by ascending the main southwest branch of Lewis' River through the country of the Shoshonees, over to Madison or Gallatin River. On that route, the Chopunnish inform us, there is a passage not obstructed by snow at this period of the year."

On their return to Quamash flats the party met two Indians who, after some parley, agreed to pilot them over the mountains; these camped where they were, and the party went on to the flats, having exacted a promise from the Indians that they would wait there two nights for the white men to come along. When the party reached their old camp, they found that one of their hunters had killed a deer, which was a welcome addition to their otherwise scanty supper. Next day, the hunters met with astonishing luck, bringing into camp eight deer and three bears. Four of the men were directed to go to the camp of the two Indians, and if these were bent on going on, to accompany them and so mark, or blaze, the trees that the rest of the party would have no difficulty in finding the way, later on.

Meanwhile, the men who had been sent back for guides returned, bringing with them the pleasing information that three Indians whom they brought with them had consented to guide the party to the great falls of the Missouri, for the pay of two guns. Accordingly, once more (June 26), they set out for the mountains, travelling for the third time in twelve days the route between Quamash flats and the Bitter Root range. For the second time they ran up against a barrier of snow. They measured the depth of the snow at the place where they had left their luggage at their previous repulse and found it to be ten feet and ten inches deep; and it had sunk four feet since they had been turned back at this point. Pressing on, after they reached their old camp, they found a bare spot on the side of the mountain where there was a little grass for their horses; and there they camped for the night. They were fortunate in having Indian guides with them; and the journal says:—

"The marks on the trees, which had been our chief dependence, are much fewer and more difficult to be distinguished than we had supposed. But our guides traverse this trackless region with a kind of instinctive sagacity; they never hesitate, they are never embarrassed; and so undeviating is their step, that wherever the snow has disappeared, for even a hundred paces, we find the summer road. With their aid the snow is scarcely a disadvantage; for though we are often obliged to slip down, yet the fallen timber and the rocks, which are now covered, were much more troublesome when we passed in the autumn. Travelling is indeed comparatively pleasant, as well as more rapid, the snow being hard and coarse, without a crust, and perfectly hard enough to prevent the horses sinking more than two or three inches. After the sun has been on it for some hours it becomes softer than it is early in the morning; yet they are almost always able to get a sure foothold."

On the twenty-ninth of June the party were well out of the snows in which they had been imprisoned, although they were by no means over the mountain barrier that had been climbed so painfully during the past few days. Here they observed the tracks of two barefooted Indians who had evidently been fleeing from their enemies, the Pahkees. These signs disturbed the Indian guides, for they at once said that the tracks were made by their friends, the Ootlashoots, and that the Pahkees would also cut them (the guides) off on their return from the trip over the mountains. On the evening of the day above mentioned, the party camped at the warm springs which fall into Traveller's-rest Creek, a point now well known to the explorers, who had passed that way before. Of the springs the journal says:—

"These warm springs are situated at the foot of a hill on the north side of Traveller's-rest Creek, which is ten yards wide at this place. They issue from the bottoms, and through the interstices of a gray freestone rock, which rises in irregular masses round their lower side. The principal spring, which the Indians have formed into a bath by stopping the run with stone and pebbles, is about the same temperature as the warmest bath used at the hot springs in Virginia. On trying, Captain Lewis could with difficulty remain in it nineteen minutes, and then was affected with a profuse perspiration. The two other springs are much hotter, the temperature being equal to that of the warmest of the hot springs in Virginia. Our men, as well as the Indians, amused themselves with going into the bath; the latter, according to their universal custom, going first into the hot bath, where they remain as long as they can bear the heat, then plunging into the creek, which is now of an icy coldness, and repeating this operation several times, but always ending with the warm bath."

Traveller's-rest Creek, it will be recollected, is on the summit of the Bitter Root Mountains, and the expedition had consequently passed from Idaho into Montana, as these States now exist on the map; but they were still on the Pacific side of the Great Divide, or the backbone of the continent. Much game was seen in this region, and after reaching Traveller's-rest Creek, the hunters killed six deer; great numbers of elk and bighorn were also seen in this vicinity. On the thirtieth of July the party were at their old camp of September 9 and 10, 1805, having made one hundred and fifty-six miles from Quamash flats to the mouth of the creek where they now camped. Here a plan to divide and subdivide the party was made out as follows:—

"Captain Lewis, with nine men, is to pursue the most direct route to the falls of the Missouri, where three of his party (Thompson, Goodrich, and McNeal) are to be left to prepare carriages for transporting the baggage and canoes across the portage. With the remaining six, he will ascend Maria's River to explore the country and ascertain whether any branch of it reaches as far north as latitude 50'0, after which he will descend that river to its mouth. The rest of the men will accompany Captain Clark to the head of Jefferson River, which Sergeant Ordway and a party of nine men will descend, with the canoes and other articles deposited there. Captain Clark's party, which will then be reduced to ten men and Sacajawea, will proceed to the Yellowstone, at its nearest approach to the Three Forks of the Missouri. There he will build canoes, go down that river with seven of his party, and wait at its mouth till the rest of the party join him. Sergeant Pryor, with two others, will then take the horses by land to the Mandans. From that nation he will go to the British posts on the Assiniboin with a letter to Mr. Alexander Henry, to procure his endeavors to prevail on some of the Sioux chiefs to accompany him to the city of Washington. . .
.

"The Indians who had accompanied us intended leaving us in order to seek their friends, the Ootlashoots; but we prevailed on them to accompany Captain Lewis a part of his route, so as to show him the shortest road to the Missouri, and in the mean time amused them with conversation and running races, on foot and with horses, in both of which they proved themselves hardy, athletic, and active. To the chief Captain Lewis gave a small medal and a gun, as a reward for having guided us across the mountains; in return the customary civility of exchanging names passed between them, by which the former acquired the title of Yomekollick, of White Bearskin Unfolded."

Chapter XXIV — The Expedition Subdivided

On the third of July, accordingly, Captain Lewis, with nine of his men and five Indians, proceeded down the valley lying between the Rocky and the Bitter Root ranges of mountains, his general course being due northwest of Clark's fork of the Columbia River. Crossing several small streams that make into this river, they finally reached and crossed the Missoula River from west to east, below the confluence of the St. Mary's and Hell-gate rivers, or creeks; for these streams hardly deserve the name of rivers. The party camped for the night within a few miles of the site of the present city of Missoula, Montana. Here they were forced to part from their good friends and allies, the Indians, who had crossed the range with them. These men were afraid that they would be cut off by their foes, the Pahkees, and they wanted to find and join some band of the Indian nation with whom they were on terms of friendship. The journal gives this account of the parting:—

"We now smoked a farewell pipe with our estimable companions, who expressed every emotion of regret at parting with us; which they felt the more, because they did not conceal their fears of our being cut off by the Pahkees. We also gave them a shirt, a handkerchief, and a small quantity of ammunition. The meat which they received from us was dried and left at this place, as a store during the homeward journey. This circumstance confirms our belief that there is no route along Clark's River to the Columbian plains so near or so good as that by which we came; for, though these people mean to go for several days' journey down that river, to look for the Shalees (Ootlashoots), yet they intend returning home by the same pass of the mountains through which they have conducted us. This route is also used by all the nations whom we know west of the mountains who are in the habit of visiting the plains of the Missouri; while on the other side, all the war-paths of the Pahkees which fall into this valley of Clark's River concentre at Traveller's-rest, beyond which these people have never ventured to the west."

During the next day or two, Captain Lewis kept on the same general course through a well-watered country, the ground gradually rising as he approached the base of the mountains. Tracks of Indians, supposed to be Pahkees, became more numerous and fresh. On the seventh of July, the little company went through the famous pass of the Rocky Mountains, now properly named for the leaders of the expedition. Here is the journal's account of their finding the Lewis and Clark Pass:—

"At the distance of twelve miles we left the river, or rather the creek, and having for four miles crossed two ridges in a direction north fifteen degrees east, again struck to the right, proceeding through a narrow bottom covered with low willows and grass, and abundantly supplied with both deer and beaver. After travelling seven miles we reached the foot of a ridge, which we ascended in a direction north forty-five degrees east, through a low gap of easy ascent from the westward; and, on descending it, were delighted at discovering that this was the dividing ridge between the waters of the Columbia and those of the Missouri. From this gap Fort Mountain is about twenty miles in a northeastern direction. We now wound through the hills and mountains, passing several rivulets which ran to the right, and at the distance of nine miles from the gap encamped, having made thirty-two miles. We procured some beaver, and this morning saw tracks of buffalo, from which it appears that those animals do sometimes penetrate a short distance among the mountains."

Next day the party found themselves in clover, so to speak. Game was plenty, and, as their object now was to accumulate meat for the three men who were to be left at the falls (and who were not hunters), they resolved to strike the Medicine, or Sun, River and hunt down its banks. On that river the journal, July 10, has this to say:—

"In the plains are great quantities of two species of prickly-pear now in bloom. Gooseberries of the common red kind are in abundance and just beginning to ripen, but there are no currants. The river has now widened to one hundred yards; it is deep, crowded with islands, and in many parts rapid. At the distance of seventeen miles, the timber disappears totally from the river-bottoms. About this part of the river, the wind, which had blown on our backs, and constantly put the elk on their guard, shifted round; we then shot three of them and a brown bear. Captain Lewis halted to skin them, while two of the men took the pack-horses forward to seek for a camp. It was nine o'clock before he overtook them, at the distance of seven miles, in the first grove of cottonwood. They had been pursued as they came along by a very large bear, on which they were afraid to fire, lest their horses, being unaccustomed to the gun, might take fright and throw them. This circumstance reminds us of the ferocity of these animals, when we were last near this place, and admonishes us to be very cautious. We saw vast numbers of buffalo below us, which kept up a dreadful bellowing during the night. With all our exertions we were unable to advance more than twenty-four miles, owing to the mire through which we are obliged to travel, in consequence of the rain."

The Sun, or Medicine, River empties into the Missouri just above the great falls of that stream; and near here, opposite White Bear Islands, the expedition had deposited some of their property in a cache dug near the river bank, when they passed that way, a year before. On the thirteenth of the month, having reached their old camping-ground here, the party set to work making boat-gear and preparing to leave their comrades in camp well fixed for their stay. The journal adds:—

"On opening the cache, we found the bearskins entirely destroyed by the water, which in a flood of the river had penetrated to them. All the specimens of plants, too, were unfortunately lost: the chart of the Missouri, however, still remained unhurt, and several articles contained in trunks and boxes had suffered but little injury; but a vial of laudanum had lost its stopper, and the liquid had run into a drawer of medicines, which it spoiled beyond recovery. The mosquitoes were so troublesome that it was impossible even to write without a mosquito bier. The buffalo were leaving us fast, on their way to the southeast."

One of the party met with an amusing adventure here, which is thus described:—

"At night M'Neal, who had been sent in the morning to examine the cache at the lower end of the portage, returned; but had been prevented from reaching that place by a singular adventure. Just as he arrived near Willow run, he approached a thicket of brush in which was a white bear, which he did not discover till he was within ten feet of him. His horse started, and wheeling suddenly round, threw M'Neal almost immediately under the bear, which started up instantly. Finding the bear raising himself on his hind feet to attack him, he struck him on the head with the butt end of his musket; the blow was so violent that it broke the breech of the musket and knocked the bear to the ground. Before he recovered M'Neal, seeing a willow-tree close by, sprang up, and there remained while the bear closely guarded the foot of the tree until late in the afternoon. He then went off; M'Neal being released came down, and having found his horse, which had strayed off to the distance of two miles, returned to camp. These animals are, indeed, of a most extraordinary ferocity, and it is matter of wonder that in all our encounters we have had the good fortune to escape. We are now troubled with another enemy, not quite so dangerous, though even more disagreeable-these are the mosquitoes, who now infest us in such myriads that we frequently get them into our throats when breathing, and the dog even howls with the torture they occasion."

The intention of Captain Lewis was to reach the river sometimes known as Maria's, and sometimes as Marais, or swamp. This stream rises near the boundary between Montana and the British possessions, and flows into the Missouri, where the modern town of Ophir is built. The men left at the great falls were to dig up the canoes and baggage that had been cached there the previous year, and be ready to carry around the portage of the falls the stuff that would be brought from the two forks of the Jefferson, later on, by Sergeant Ordway and his party. It will be recollected that this stuff had also been cached at the forks of the Jefferson, the year before. The two parties, thus united, were to go down to the entrance of Maria's River into the Missouri, and Captain Lewis expected to join them there by the fifth of August; if he failed to meet them by that time, they were to go on down the river and meet Captain Clark at the mouth of the Yellowstone. This explanation is needed to the proper understanding of the narrative that follows; for we now have to keep track of three parties of the explorers.

Captain Lewis and his men, having travelled northwest about twenty miles from the great falls of the Missouri, struck the trail of a wounded buffalo. They were dismayed by the sight, for that assured them that there were Indians in the vicinity; and the most natural thing to expect was that these were Blackfeet, or Minnetarees; both of these tribes are vicious and rascally people, and they would not hesitate to attack a small party and rob them of their guns, if they thought themselves able to get away with them.

They were now in the midst of vast herds of buffalo, so numerous that the whole number seemed one immense herd. Hanging on the flanks were many wolves; hares and antelope were also abundant. On the fourth day out, Captain Lewis struck the north fork of Maria's River, now known as Cut-bank River, in the northwest corner of Montana. He was desirous of following up the stream, to ascertain, if possible, whether its fountain-head was below, or above, the boundary between the United States and the British possessions. Bad weather and an accident to his chronometer prevented his accomplishing his purpose, and, on the twenty-sixth of July, he turned reluctantly back, giving the name of Cape Disappointment to his last camping-place. Later in that day, as they were travelling down the main stream (Maria's River), they encountered the Indians whom they had hoped to avoid. Let us read the story as it is told in the journal of the party:—

"At the distance of three miles we ascended the hills close to the river-side, while Drewyer pursued the valley of the river on the opposite side. But scarcely had Captain Lewis reached the high plain when he saw, about a mile on his left, a collection of about thirty horses. He immediately halted, and by the aid of his spy-glass discovered that one-half of the horses were saddled, and that on the eminence above the horses several Indians were looking down toward the river, probably at Drewyer. This was a most unwelcome sight. Their probable numbers rendered any contest with them of doubtful issue; to attempt to escape would only invite pursuit, and our horses were so bad that we must certainly be overtaken; besides which, Drewyer could not yet be aware that the Indians were near, and if we ran he would most probably be sacrificed.

We therefore determined to make the most of our situation, and advance toward them in a friendly manner. The flag which we had brought in case of any such accident was therefore displayed, and we continued slowly our march toward them. Their whole attention was so engaged by Drewyer that they did not immediately discover us. As soon as they did see us, they appeared to be much alarmed and ran about in confusion; some of them came down the hill and drove their horses within gunshot of the eminence, to which they then returned, as if to await our arrival. When we came within a quarter of a mile, one of the Indians mounted and rode at full speed to receive us; but when within a hundred paces of us, he halted. Captain Lewis, who had alighted to receive him, held out his hand and beckoned to him to approach; he only looked at us for some time, and then, without saying a word, returned to his companions with as much haste as he had advanced. The whole party now descended the hill and rode toward us. As yet we saw only eight, but presumed that there must be more behind us, as there were several horses saddled. We however advanced, and Captain Lewis now told his two men that he believed these were the Minnetarees of Fort de Prairie, who, from their infamous character, would in all probability attempt to rob us; but being determined to die rather than lose his papers and instruments, he intended to resist to the last extremity, and advised them to do the same, and to be on the alert should there be any disposition to attack us. When the two parties came within a hundred yards of each other, all the Indians, except one, halted. Captain Lewis therefore ordered his two men to halt while he advanced, and after shaking hands with the Indian, went on and did the same with the others in the rear, while the Indian himself shook hands with the two men. They all now came up; and after alighting, the Indians asked to smoke with us. Captain Lewis, who was very anxious for Drewyer's safety, told them that the man who had gone down the river had the pipe, and requested that as they had seen him, one of them would accompany R. Fields, to bring him back. To this they assented, and Fields went with a young man in search of Drewyer."

Captain Lewis now asked them by signs if they were Minnetarees of the north, and he was sorry to be told in reply that they were; he knew them to be a bad lot. When asked if they had any chief among them, they pointed out three. The captain did not believe them, but, in order to keep on good terms with them, he gave to one a flag, to another a medal, and to the third a handkerchief. At Captain Lewis' suggestion, the Indians and the white men camped together, and in the course of the evening the red men told the captain that they were part of a big band of their tribe, or nation. The rest of the tribe, they said, were hunting further up the river, and were then in camp near the foot of the Rocky Mountains. The captain, in return, told them that his party had come from the great lake where the sun sets, and that he was in hopes that he could induce the Minnetarees to live in peace with their neighbors and come and trade at the posts that would be established in their country by and by. He offered them ten horses and some tobacco if they would accompany his party down the river below the great falls. To this they made no reply. Being still suspicious of these sullen guests, Captain Lewis made his dispositions for the night, with orders for the sentry on duty to rouse all hands if the Indians should attempt to steal anything in the night. Next morning trouble began. Says the journal:—

"At sunrise, the Indians got up and crowded around the fire near which J. Fields, who was then on watch, had carelessly left his rifle, near the head of his brother, who was still asleep. One of the Indians slipped behind him, and, unperceived, took his brother's and his own rifle, while at the same time two others seized those of Drewyer and Captain Lewis. As soon as Fields turned, he saw the Indian running off with the rifles; instantly calling his brother, they pursued him for fifty or sixty yards; just as they overtook him, in the scuffle for the rifles R. Fields stabbed him through the heart with his knife. The Indian ran about fifteen steps and fell dead. They now ran back with their rifles to the camp. The moment the fellow touched his gun, Drewyer, who was awake, jumped up and wrested it from him. The noise awoke Captain Lewis, who instantly started from the ground and reached for his gun; but finding it gone, drew a pistol from his belt, and turning saw the Indian running off with it. He followed him and ordered him to lay it down, which he did just as the two Fields came up, and were taking aim to shoot him; when Captain Lewis ordered them not to fire, as the Indian did not appear to intend any mischief. He dropped the gun and was going slowly off when Drewyer came out and asked permission to kill him; but this Captain Lewis forbade, as he had not yet attempted to shoot us. But finding that the Indians were now endeavoring to drive off all the horses, he ordered all three of us to follow the main party, who were chasing the horses up the river, and fire instantly upon the thieves; while he, without taking time to run for his shot-pouch, pursued the fellow who had stolen his gun and another Indian, who were driving away the horses on the left of the camp. He pressed them so closely that they left twelve of their horses, but continued to drive off one of our own.

"At the distance of three hundred paces they entered a steep niche in the river-bluffs, when Captain Lewis, being too much out of breath to pursue them any further, called out, as he had done several times before, that unless they gave up the horse he would shoot them. As he raised his gun one of the Indians jumped behind a rock and spoke to the other, who stopped at the distance of thirty paces. Captain Lewis shot him in the belly. He fell on his knees and right elbow; but, raising himself a little, fired, and then crawled behind a rock. The shot had nearly proved fatal; for Captain Lewis, who was bareheaded, felt the wind of the ball very distinctly. Not having his shot-pouch, he could not reload his rifle; and, having only a single charge also for his pistol, he thought it most prudent not to attack them farther, and retired slowly to the camp. He was met by Drewyer, who, hearing the report of the guns, had come to his assistance, leaving the Fields to follow the other Indians. Captain Lewis ordered him to call out to them to desist from the pursuit, as we could take the horses of the Indians in place of our own; but they were at too great a distance to hear him. He therefore returned to the camp, and while he was saddling the horses the Fields returned with four of our own, having followed the Indians until two of them swam the river and two others ascended the hills, so that the horses became dispersed."

The white men were gainers by this sad affair, for they had now in their possession four of the Indians' horses, and had lost one of their own. Besides these, they found in the camp of the Indians four shields, two bows and their quivers, and one of their two guns. The captain took some buffalo meat which he found in the camp, and then the rest of their baggage was burned on the spot. The flag given to one of the so-called chiefs was retaken; but the medal given to the dead man was left around his neck. The consequences of this unfortunate quarrel were far-reaching. The tribe whose member was killed by the white men never forgave the injury, and for years after there was no safety for white men in their vicinity except when the wayfarers were in great numbers or strongly guarded.

A forced march was now necessary for the explorers, and they set out as speedily as possible, well knowing that the Indians would be on their trail. By three o'clock in the afternoon of that day they had reached Tansy River, now known as the Teton, having travelled sixty-three miles. They rested for an hour and a half to refresh their horses, and then pushed on for seventeen miles further before camping again. Having killed a buffalo, they had supper and stopped two hours.

Then, travelling through vast herds of buffalo until two o'clock in the morning, they halted again, almost dead with fatigue; they rested until daylight. On awaking, they found themselves so stiff and sore with much riding that they could scarcely stand. But the lives of their friends now at or near the mouth of Maria's River were at stake, as well as their own. Indeed, it was not certain but that the Indians had, by hard riding and a circuitous route, already attacked the river party left at the falls. So Captain Lewis told his men that they must go on, and, if attacked, they must tie their horses together by the head and stand together, selling their lives as dearly as possible, or routing their enemies. The journal now says:—

"To this they all assented, and we therefore continued our route to the eastward, till at the distance of twelve miles we came near the Missouri, when we heard a noise which seemed like the report of a gun. We therefore quickened our pace for eight miles farther, and, being about five miles from Grog Spring, now heard distinctly the noise of several rifles from the river. We hurried to the bank, and saw with exquisite satisfaction our friends descending the river. They landed to greet us, and after turning our horses loose, we embarked with our baggage, and went down to the spot where we had made a deposite. This, after reconnoitring the adjacent country, we opened; but, unfortunately, the cache had caved in, and most of the articles were injured. We took whatever was still worth preserving, and immediately proceeded to the point, where we found our deposits in good order. By a singular good fortune, we were here joined by Sergeant Gass and Willard from the Falls, who had been ordered to come with the horses here to assist in procuring meat for the voyage, as it had been calculated that the canoes would reach this place much sooner than Captain Lewis's party. After a very heavy shower of rain and hail, attended with violent thunder and lightning, we started from the point, and giving a final discharge to our horses, went over to the island where we had left our red pirogue, which, however, we found much decayed, and we had no means of repairing her. We therefore took all the iron work out of her, and, proceeding down the river fifteen miles, encamped near some cottonwood trees, one of which was of the narrow-leafed species, and the first of that kind we had remarked in ascending the river.

"Sergeant Ordway's party, which had left the mouth of Madison River on the thirteenth, had descended in safety to White Bear Island, where he arrived on the nineteenth, and, after collecting the baggage, had left the falls on the twenty-seventh in the white pirogue and five canoes, while Sergeant Gass and Willard set out at the same time by land with the horses, and thus fortunately met together."

Sergeant Ordway's party, it will be recollected, had left Captain Clark at the three forks of the Missouri, to which they had come down the Jefferson, and thence had passed down the Missouri to White Bear Islands, and, making the portage, had joined the rest of the party just in time to reinforce them. Game was now abundant the buffalo being in enormous herds; and the bighorn were also numerous; the flesh of these animals was in fine condition, resembling the best of mutton in flavor. The reunited party now descended the river, the intention being to reach the mouth of the Yellowstone as soon as possible, and there wait for Captain Clark, who, it will be recalled, was to explore that stream and meet them at the point of its junction with the Missouri. The voyage of Captain Lewis and his men was without startling incident, except that Cruzatte accidentally shot the captain, one day, while they were out hunting. The wound was through the fleshy part of the left thigh, and for a time was very painful. As Cruzatte was not in sight when the captain was hit, the latter naturally thought he had been shot by Indians hiding in the thicket.

He reached camp as best he could, and, telling his men to arm themselves, he explained that he had been shot by Indians. But when Cruzatte came into camp, mutual explanations satisfied all hands that a misunderstanding had arisen and that Cruzatte's unlucky shot was accidental. As an example of the experience of the party about this time, while they were on their way down the Missouri, we take this extract from their journal:—

"We again saw great numbers of buffalo, elk, antelope, deer, and wolves; also eagles and other birds, among which were geese and a solitary pelican, neither of which can fly at present, as they are now shedding the feathers of their wings. We also saw several bears, one of them the largest, except one, we had ever seen; for he measured nine feet from the nose to the extremity of the tail. During the night a violent storm came on from the northeast with such torrents of rain that we had scarcely time to unload the canoes before they filled with water. Having no shelter we ourselves were completely wet to the skin, and the wind and cold air made our situation very unpleasant."

On the twelfth of August, the Lewis party met with two traders from Illinois. These men were camped on the northeast side of the river; they had left Illinois the previous summer, and had been coming up the Missouri hunting and trapping. Captain Lewis learned from them that Captain Clark was below; and later in that day the entire expedition was again united, Captain Clark's party being found at a point near where Little Knife Creek enters the Missouri River. We must now take up the narrative of Captain Clark and his adventures on the Yellowstone.

Chapter XXV — Adventures on the Yellowstone

The route of Captain Clark from the point where he and Captain Lewis divided their party, was rather more difficult than that pursued by the Lewis detachment. But the Clark party was larger, being composed of twenty men and Sacajawea and her baby. They were to travel up the main fork of Clark's River (sometimes called the Bitter Root), to Ross's Hole, and then strike over the great continental divide at that point by way of the pass which he discovered and which was named for him; thence he was to strike the headwaters of Wisdom River, a stream which this generation of men knows by the vulgar name of Big Hole River; from this point he was to go by the way of Willard's Creek to Shoshonee Cove and the Two Forks of the Jefferson, and thence down that stream to the Three Forks of the Missouri, up the Gallatin, and over the divide to the Yellowstone and down that river to its junction with the Missouri, where he was to join the party of Captain Lewis. This is the itinerary that was exactly carried out. The very first incident set forth in the journal is a celebration of Independence Day, as follows:—

"Friday, July 4. Early in the morning three hunters were sent out. The rest of the party having collected the horses and breakfasted, we proceeded at seven o'clock up the valley, which is now contracted to the width of from eight to ten miles, with a good proportion of pitch-pine, though its low lands, as well as the bottoms of the creeks, are strewn with large stones. We crossed five creeks of different sizes, but of great depth, and so rapid that in passing the last several of the horses were driven down the stream, and some of our baggage was wet. Near this river we saw the tracks of two Indians, whom we supposed to be Shoshonees. Having made sixteen miles, we halted at an hour for the purpose of doing honor to the birthday of our early country's independence. The festival was not very splendid, for it consisted of a mush made of cows and a saddle of venison; nor had we anything to tempt us to prolong it. We therefore went on till at the distance of a mile we came to a very large creek, which, like all those in the valley, had an immense rapidity of descent; we therefore proceeded up for some distance, in order to select the most convenient spot for fording. Even there, however, such was the violence of the current that, though the water was not higher than the bellies of the horses, the resistance made in passing caused the stream to rise over their backs and loads. After passing the creek we inclined to the left, and soon after struck the road which we had descended last year, near the spot where we dined on the 7th of September (1805). Along this road we continued on the west side of Clark's River, till at the distance of thirteen miles, during which we passed three more deep, large creeks, we reached its western branch, where we camped; and having sent out two hunters, despatched some men to examine the best ford across the west fork of the river. The game to-day consisted of four deer; though we also saw a herd of ibex, or bighorn."

Two days later they were high up among the mountains, although the ascent was not very steep. At that height they found the weather very cool, so much so that on the morning of the sixth of July, after a cold night, they had a heavy white frost on the ground. Setting out on that day, Captain Clark crossed a ridge which proved to be the dividing line between the Pacific and the Atlantic watershed. At the same time he passed from what is now Missoula County, Montana, into the present county of Beaver Head, in that State. "Beaver Head," the reader will recollect, comes from a natural elevation in that region resembling the head of a beaver. These points will serve to fix in one's mind the route of the first exploring party that ever ventured into those wilds; descending the ridge on its eastern slope, the explorers struck Glade Creek, one of the sources of the stream then named Wisdom River, a branch of the Jefferson; and the Jefferson is one of the tributaries of the mighty Missouri. Next day the journal has this entry:—

"In the morning our horses were so much scattered that, although we sent out hunters in every direction to range the country for six or eight miles, nine of them could not be recovered. They were the most valuable of all our horses, and so much attached to some of their companions that it was difficult to separate them in the daytime. We therefore presumed that they must have been stolen by some roving Indians; and accordingly left a party of five men to continue the pursuit, while the rest went on to the spot where the canoes had been deposited. We set out at ten o'clock and pursued a course S. 56'0 E. across the valley, which we found to be watered by four large creeks, with extensive low and miry bottoms; and then reached (and crossed) Wisdom River, along the northeast side of which we continued, till at the distance of sixteen miles we came to its three branches. Near that place we stopped for dinner at a hot spring situated in the open plain. The bed of the spring is about fifteen yards in circumference, and composed of loose, hard, gritty stones, through which the water boils in great quantities. It is slightly impregnated with sulphur, and so hot that a piece of meat about the size of three fingers was completely done in twenty-five minutes."

Next day, July 8, the party reached the forks of the Jefferson River, where they had cached their goods in August, 1805; they had now travelled one hundred and sixty-four miles from Traveller's-rest Creek to that point. The men were out of tobacco, and as there was some among the goods deposited in the cache they made haste to open the cache. They found everything safe, although some of the articles were damp, and a hole had been made in the bottom of one of the canoes. Here they were overtaken by Sergeant Ordway and his party with the nine horses that had escaped during the night of the seventh.

That night the weather was so cold that water froze in a basin to a thickness of three-quarters of an inch, and the grass around the camp was stiff with frost, although the month of July was nearly a week old. The boats taken from the cache were now loaded, and the explorers were divided into two bands, one to descend the river by boat and the other to take the same general route on horseback, the objective point being the Yellowstone. The story is taken tip here by the journal in these lines:—

"After breakfast (July 10) the two parties set out, those on shore skirting the eastern side of Jefferson River, through Service (-berry) Valley and over Rattlesnake Mountain, into a beautiful and extensive country, known among the Indians by the name of Hahnahappapchah, or Beaverhead Valley, from the number of those animals to be found in it, and also from the point of land resembling the head of a beaver. It (the valley) extends from Rattlesnake Mountain as low as Frazier's Creek, and is about fifty miles in length in direct line; while its width varies from ten to fifteen miles, being watered in its whole course by Jefferson River and six different creeks. The valley is open and fertile; besides the innumerable quantities of beaver and otter with which its creeks are supplied, the bushes of the low grounds are a favorite resort for deer; while on the higher parts of the valley are seen scattered groups of antelopes, and still further, on the steep sides of the mountains, are observed many bighorns, which take refuge there from the wolves and bears. At the distance of fifteen miles the two parties stopped to dine; when Captain Clark, finding that the river became wider and deeper, and that the canoes could advance more

156

rapidly than the horses, determined to go himself by water, leaving Sergeant Pryor with six men to bring on the horses. In this way they resumed their journey after dinner, and camped on the eastern side of the river, opposite the head of Three-thousand-mile Island. The beaver were basking in great numbers along the shore; there were also some young wild geese and ducks. The mosquitoes were very troublesome during the day, but after sunset the weather became cool and they disappeared."

Three-thousand-mile Island was so named by the explorers, when they ascended these streams, because it was at a point exactly three thousand miles from the mouth of the Missouri. But no such island exists now; it has probably been worn away by the swift-rushing current of the river. The route of Captain Clark and his party, up to this time had been a few miles west of Bannock City, Montana. As the captain was now to proceed by land to the Yellowstone, again leaving the canoe party, it is well to recall the fact that his route from the Three Forks of the Missouri to the Yellowstone follows pretty nearly the present line of the railroad from Gallatin City to Livingston, by the way of Bozeman Pass. Of this route the journal says:—

"Throughout the whole, game was very abundant. They procured deer in the low grounds; beaver and otter were seen in Gallatin River, and elk, wolves, eagles, hawks, crows, and geese at different parts of the route. The plain was intersected by several great roads leading to a gap in the mountains, about twenty miles distant, in a direction E.N.E.; but the Indian woman, who was acquainted with the country, recommended a gap more to the southward. This course Captain Clark determined to pursue."

Let us pause here to pay a little tribute to the memory of "the Indian woman," Sacajawea. She showed that she was very observant, had a good memory, and was plucky and determined when in trouble. She was the guide of the exploring party when she was in a region of country, as here, with which she was familiar. She remembered localities which she had not seen since her childhood. When their pirogue was upset by the carelessness of her husband, it was she who saved the goods and helped to right the boat. And, with her helpless infant clinging to her, she rode with the men, guiding them with unerring skill through the mountain fastnesses and lonely passes which the white men saw for the first time when their salient features were pointed out to them by the intelligent and faithful Sacajawea. The Indian woman has long since departed to the Happy Hunting-Grounds of her fathers; only her name and story remain to us who follow the footsteps of the brave pioneers of the western continent. But posterity should not forget the services which were rendered to the white race by Sacajawea.

On the fifteenth of July the party arrived at the ridge that divides the Missouri and the Yellowstone, nine miles from which they reached the river itself, about a mile and a half from the point where it issues from the Rocky Mountains. Their journey down the valley of the Yellowstone was devoid of special interest, but was accompanied with some hardships. For example, the feet of the horses had become so sore with long travel over a stony trail that it was necessary to shoe them with raw buffalo hide. Rain fell frequently and copiously; and often, sheltered at night only by buffalo hides, they rose in the morning drenched to the skin. The party could not follow the course of the river very closely, but were compelled often to cross hills that came down to the bank, making the trail impassable for horses. Here is the story of July 18 and 19:—

157

"Gibson, one of the party, was so badly hurt by falling on a sharp point of wood that he was unable to sit on his horse, and they were obliged to form a sort of litter for him, so that he could lie nearly at full length. The wound became so painful, however, after proceeding a short distance, that he could not bear the motion, and they left him with two men, while Captain Clark went to search for timber large enough to form canoes. He succeeded in finding some trees of sufficient size for small canoes, two of which he determined to construct, and by lashing them together hoped to make them answer the purpose of conveying the party down the river, while a few of his men should conduct the horses to the Mandans. All hands, therefore, were set busily to work, and they were employed in this labor for several days. In the mean time no less than twenty-four of their horses were missing, and they strongly suspected had been stolen by the Indians, for they were unable to find them, notwithstanding they made the most diligent search."

"July 23. A piece of a robe and a moccasin," says the journal, "were discovered this morning not far from the camp. The moccasin was worn out in the sole, and yet wet, and had every appearance of having been left but a few hours before. This was conclusive that the Indians had taken our horses, and were still prowling about for the remainder, which fortunately escaped last night by being in a small prairie surrounded by thick timber. At length Labiche, one of our best trackers, returned from a very wide circuit, and informed Captain Clark that he had traced the horses bending their course rather down the river towards the open plains, and from their tracks, must have been going very rapidly. All hopes of recovering them were now abandoned. Nor were the Indians the only plunderers around our camp; for in the night the wolves or dogs stole the greater part of the dried meat from the scaffold. The wolves, which constantly attend the buffalo, were here in great numbers, as this seemed to be the commencement of the buffalo country. . . .

"At noon the two canoes were finished. They were twenty-eight feet long, sixteen or eighteen inches deep, and from sixteen to twenty-four inches wide; and, having lashed them together, everything was ready for setting out the next day, Gibson having now recovered. Sergeant Pryor was directed, with Shannon and Windsor, to take the remaining horses to the Mandans, and if he should find that Mr. Henry (a trading-post agent) was on the Assiniboin River, to go thither and deliver him a letter, the object of which was to prevail on the most distinguished chiefs of the Sioux to accompany him to Washington."

On a large island near the mouth of a creek now known as Canyon Creek, the party landed to explore an extensive Indian lodge which seems to have been built for councils, rather than for a place of residence. The lodge was shaped like a cone, sixty feet in diameter at the base and tapering towards the top. The poles of which it was constructed were forty-five feet long. The interior was strangely decorated, the tops of the poles being ornamented with eagles' feathers, and from the centre hung a stuffed buffalo-hide. A buffalo's head and other trophies of the chase were disposed about the wigwam. The valley, as the explorers descended the river, was very picturesque and wonderful. On the north side the cliffs were wild and romantic, and these were soon succeeded by rugged hills, and these, in turn, by open plains on which were descried herds of buffalo, elk, and wolves. On the twenty-seventh of July, having reached the Bighorn, one of the largest tributaries of the Yellowstone, the party have this entry in their journal:—

"They again set out very early, and on leaving the Bighorn took a last look at the Rocky Mountains, which had been constantly in view from the first of May. The (Yellowstone) river now widens to the extent of from four hundred to six hundred yards; it is much divided by islands and sandbars; its banks are generally low and falling in; it thus resembles the Missouri in many particulars, but its islands are more numerous, its waters less muddy, and the current is more rapid. The water is of a yellowish-white, and the round stones, which form the bars above the Bighorn, have given place to gravel. On the left side the river runs under cliffs of light, soft, gritty stone, varying in height from seventy to one hundred feet, behind which are level and extensive plains. On the right side of the river are low extensive bottoms, bordered with cottonwood, various species of willow, rose-bushes, grapevines, redberry or buffalo-grease bushes, and a species of sumach; to these succeed high grounds supplied with pine, and still further on are level plains. Throughout the country are vast quantities of buffalo, which, as this is the running-season, keep up a continued bellowing. Large herds of elk also are lying on every point, so gentle that they may be approached within twenty paces without being alarmed. Several beaver were seen in the course of the day; indeed, there is a greater appearance of those animals than there was above the Bighorn. Deer, however, are by no means abundant, and antelopes, as well as bighorns, are scarce."

It is noticeable that the explorers, all along their route, gave to streams, rocks, mountains, and other natural features of the country many names that appear to us meaningless and trifling. It would appear that they used up all the big names, such as Jefferson, Gallatin, Philosophy, Philanthropy, and the like, and were compelled to use, first, the names of their own party, and then such titles as were suggested by trifling incidents. For example, when they reached a difficult shoal on the Yellowstone River, they named that Buffalo Shoal because they found a buffalo on it; and Buffalo Shoal it remains unto this day. In like manner, when they reached a dangerous rapid, twenty miles below that point, they saw a bear standing on a rock in the stream; and Bear Rapid the place was and is named. Bear and buffalo were pretty numerous all the way along that part of the river which they navigated in July. They had now rejoined the boats, and on the last day of July, when camped at a point two miles above Wolf Rapid (so called from seeing a wolf there), the buffalo were continually prowling about the camp at night, exciting much alarm lest they should trample on the boats and ruin them. In those days, buffalo were so numerous that they were a nuisance to travellers; and they were so free from fear of man that they were too familiar with the camps and equipage. On the first of August we find this entry in the journal of the party:—

"The buffalo now appear in vast numbers. A herd happened to be on their way across the river. Such was the multitude of these animals that, though the river, including an island over which they passed, was a mile wide, the herd stretched, as thickly as they could swim, from one side to the other, and the party was obliged to stop for an hour. They consoled themselves for the delay by killing four of the herd; and then having proceeded for the distance of forty-five miles (in all to-day) to an island, below which two other herds of buffalo, as numerous as the first, soon after crossed the river."

Again, on the very next day, we find this entry:—

"The river was now about a mile wide, less rapid, and more divided by islands, and bars of sand and mud, than heretofore; the low grounds, too, were more extensive, and contained a greater quantity of cottonwood, ash, and willows. On the northwest was a low, level plain, and on the southeast some rugged hills, on which we saw, without being able to approach them, some bighorns. Buffalo and elk, as well as their pursuers, the wolves, were in great numbers. On each side of the river there were several dry beds of streams, but the only one of any considerable size

159

was one to which they gave the name of Ibex River, on the right, about thirty yards wide, and sixteen miles from their encampment of the preceding night. The bear, which had given them so much trouble at the head of the Missouri, they found equally fierce here. One of these animals, which was on a sand-bar as the boat passed, raised himself on his hind feet, and after looking at the party for a moment, plunged in and swam towards them; but, after receiving three balls in the body, he turned and made for the shore. Towards evening they saw another enter the water to swim across; when Captain Clark directed the boat towards the shore, and just as the animal landed shot it in the head. It proved to be the largest female they had ever seen, and was so old that its tusks were worn quite smooth. The boats escaped with difficulty between two herds of buffalo that were crossing the river, and came near being again detained by them. Among the elk of this neighborhood they saw an unusual number of males, while higher up the herds consisted chiefly of females."

It is almost incredible that these wild animals should have been so nearly exterminated by hunters and other rovers of the plains, very soon after travel set in across the continent. The writer of these lines, who crossed the plains to California so lately as 1856, saw buffalo killed for the sake of their tongues, or to give rifle practice to the wayfarers. After the overland railroad was opened, passengers shot buffalo from the car-windows, well knowing that they could not get their game, even if they should kill as they flew by a herd. There are no buffalo nor elk where millions once roamed almost unmolested.

Early in the afternoon of August 3, the party reached the junction of the Yellowstone and the Missouri, and camped on the same spot where they had pitched their tents on the 26th of April, 1805. They were nearing the end of their long journey.

But their troubles thickened as they drew near the close of their many miles of travel. The journal for August 4 has this record:—

"The camp became absolutely uninhabitable in consequence of the multitude of mosquitoes; the men could not work in preparing skins for clothing, nor hunt in the timbered low grounds; there was no mode of escape, except by going on the sand-bars in the river, where, if the wind should blow, the insects do not venture; but when there is no wind, and particularly at night, when the men have no covering except their worn-out blankets, the pain they suffer is scarcely to be endured. There was also a want of meat, for no buffalo were to be found; and though elk are very abundant, yet their fat and flesh is more difficult to dry in the sun, and is also much more easily spoiled than the meat or fat of either deer or buffalo.

"Captain Clark therefore determined to go on to some spot which should be free from mosquitoes and furnish more game. Having written a note to Captain Lewis, to inform him of his intention, and stuck it on a pole at the confluence of the two rivers, he loaded the canoes at five in the afternoon, proceeded down the river to the second point, and camped on a sand-bar; but here the mosquitoes seemed to be even more numerous than above. The face of the Indian child was considerably puffed up and swollen with their bites; the men could procure scarcely any sleep during the night, and the insects continued to harass them next morning, as they proceeded. On one occasion Captain Clark went on shore and ascended a hill after one of the bighorns; but the mosquitoes were in such multitudes that he could not keep them from the barrel of his rifle long enough to take aim. About ten o'clock, however, a light breeze sprung up from the northwest, and dispersed them in some degree. Captain Clark then landed on a sand-bar, intending to wait for Captain Lewis, and went out to hunt. But not finding any buffalo, he again proceeded in the afternoon; and having killed a large white bear, camped under a high bluff exposed to a light breeze from the southwest, which blew away the mosquitoes. About eleven o'clock, however, the wind became very high and a storm of rain came on, which lasted for two hours, accompanied with sharp lightning and loud peals of thunder.

"The party rose, next day, very wet, and proceeded to a sand-bar below the entrance of Whiteearth River. Just above this place the Indians, apparently within seven, or eight days past, had been digging a root which they employ in making a kind of soup. Having fixed their tents, the men were employed in dressing skins and hunting. They shot a number of deer; but only two of them were fat, owing probably to the great quantities of mosquitoes which annoy them while feeding."

On the eleventh of August the Clark party came up with the two white traders from Illinois, of whom we have already made mention as having been met by the Lewis party on their way down the river. These were the first white men they had seen (except themselves) since they parted with the three French trappers, near the Little Missouri, in April, 1805, From them the wayworn voyagers received the latest news from the United States. From them they also had some unfavorable tidings. The journal says:—

"These men had met the boat which we had despatched from Fort Mandan, on board of which, they were told, was a Ricara chief on his way to Washington; and also another party of Yankton chiefs, accompanying Mr. Durion on a visit of the same kind. We were sorry to learn that the Mandans and Minnetarees were at war with the Ricaras, and had killed two of them. The Assiniboins too are at war with the Mandans. They have, in consequence, prohibited the Northwestern Company from trading to the Missouri, and even killed two of their traders near Mouse River; they are now lying in wait for Mr. McKenzie of the Northwestern Company, who has been for a long time among the Minnetarees. These appearances are rather unfavorable to our project of carrying some of the chiefs to the United States; but we still hope that, by effecting a peace between the Mandans, Minnetarees, and Ricaras, the views of our Government may be accomplished."

Next day, August 12, 1806, the party, slowly descending the river, were overjoyed to see below them the little flotilla of Captain Lewis and his men. But they were alarmed when they discovered that Lewis was not with them; as the boats landed at the shore, the captain was not to be seen. Captain Clark's party, on coming up with their friends, were told that Lewis was lying in the pirogue, having been accidentally wounded. The whole party were now happily reunited, and they were soon joined by the two Illinois traders whom they had met up the river; these men wished to accompany the expedition down the river as far as the Mandan nation, for the purpose of trading; they were more secure with a large party of white men than they would be if left to themselves.

Chapter XXVI — The End of a Long Journey

The reunited party now set out for the lower river and proceeded rapidly down-stream, favored with a good wind. They made eighty-six miles on the first day, passing the mouth of the Little Missouri early in the forenoon, and camping at Miry River, on the northeast side of the Missouri. On the second day they arrived at the principal village of the Minnetarees, where they were received with cordial welcome by their old friends. The explorers fired their blunderbuss several times by way of salute, and the Indian chiefs expressed their satisfaction at the safe return of the white men. One of the Minnetaree chiefs, however, wept bitterly at the sight of the whites, and it was explained by his friends that their coming reminded him of the death of his son, who had been lately killed by the Blackfoot Indians.

Arriving at the village of the Mandans, of which Black Cat was the chief, a council was called, and the chiefs of the expedition endeavored to persuade some of the leading men of the tribe to accompany them to Washington to see "the Great Father." Black Cat expressed his strong desire to visit the United States and see the Great Father, but he was afraid of the Sioux, their ancient enemies, through whose territory they must pass on their way down to the white man's country. This chief, it will be recollected, was given a flag and a medal by the two captains when they passed up the river on their way to the Rocky Mountains and the Pacific coast. The flag was now brought on and hoisted on the lodge of Black Cat. On that occasion, also, the commanders of the expedition had given the Indians a number of useful articles, among them being a portable corn-mill. But the Indians had other uses for metal, and they had taken the mill apart and used the iron for the purpose of making barbs for their arrows. From the Omahas, who were located here, the white men received a present of as much corn as three men could carry. Black Cat also gave them a dozen bushels of corn.

Their days of starvation and famine were over. They were next visited by Le Borgne, better known as One-eye, the head chief of all the Minnetarees, to whom Lewis and Clark also extended an invitation to go to Washington to see the Great Father. The journal says:—

"Le Borgne began by declaring that he much desired to visit his Great Father, but that the Sioux would certainly kill any of the Mandans who should attempt to go down the river. They were bad people, and would not listen to any advice. When he saw us last, we had told him that we had made peace with all the nations below; yet the Sioux had since killed eight of his tribe, and stolen a number of their horses. The Ricaras too had stolen their horses, and in the contest his people had killed two of the Ricaras. Yet in spite of these dispositions he had always had his ears open to our counsels, and had actually made a peace with the Chayennes and the Indians of the Rocky Mountains. He concluded by saying, that however disposed they were to visit the United States, the fear of the Sioux would prevent them from going with us."

The truth was that One-eye had no notion of going to Washington; he was afraid of nobody, and his plea of possible danger among the Sioux was mere nonsense to deceive the white men. Captain Clark visited the village of Black Cat, and that worthy savage made the same excuse that Le Borgne (One-eye) had already put forth; he was afraid of the Sioux. The journal adds:—

"Captain Clark then spoke to the chiefs and warriors of the village. He told them of his anxiety that some of them should see their Great Father, hear his good words, and receive his gifts; and requested them to fix on some confidential chief who might accompany us. To this they made the same objections as before; till at length a young man offered to go, and the warriors all assented to it. But the character of this man was known to be bad; and one of the party with Captain Clark informed him that at the moment he (this Indian) had in his possession a knife which he had stolen. Captain Clark therefore told the chief of this theft, and ordered the knife to be given up. This was done with a poor apology for having it in his possession, and Captain Clark then reproached the chiefs for wishing to send such a fellow to see and hear so distinguished a person as their Great Father. They all hung down their heads for some time, till Black Cat apologized by saying that the danger was such that they were afraid of sending any one of their chiefs, as they considered his loss almost inevitable."

Although there was so much reluctance on the part of the Indians to leave their roving life, even for a few months, there were some white men among the explorers who were willing to give up their home in "the States." The journal says:—

"In the evening Colter applied to us for permission to join the two trappers who had accompanied us, and who now proposed an expedition up the river, in which they were to find traps and to give him a share of the profits. The offer was a very advantageous one; and as he had always performed his duty, and his services could be dispensed with, we consented to his going upon condition that none of the rest were to ask or expect a similar indulgence. To this they all cheerfully assented, saying that they wished Colter every success, and would not apply for liberty to separate before we reached St. Louis. We therefore supplied him, as did his comrades also, with powder and lead, and a variety of articles which might be useful to him, and he left us the next day. The example of this man shows how easily men may be weaned from the habits of civilized life to the ruder, though scarcely less fascinating, manners of the woods. This hunter had now been absent for many years from the frontiers, and might naturally be presumed to have some anxiety, or at least curiosity, to return to his friends and his country; yet, just at the moment when he was approaching the frontiers, he was tempted by a hunting scheme to give up all those delightful prospects, and to go back without the least reluctance to the solitude of the wilds."

The two captains learned here that the Minnetarees had sent out a war-party against the Shoshonees, very soon after the white men's expedition had left for the Rocky Mountains, notwithstanding their promise to keep peace with the surrounding tribes. They had also sent a war-party against the Ricaras, two of whom they killed. Accordingly, the white chiefs had a powwow with the Indian chiefs, at which the journal says these incidents occurred:—

"We took this opportunity of endeavoring to engage Le Borgne in our interests by a present of the swivel, which is no longer serviceable, as it cannot be discharged from our largest pirogue. It was loaded; and the chiefs being formed into a circle round it, Captain Clark addressed them with great ceremony. He said that he had listened with much attention to what had yesterday been declared by Le Borgne, whom he believed to be sincere, and then reproached them with their disregard of our counsels, and their wars on the Shoshonees and Ricaras. Little Cherry, the old Minnetaree chief, answered that they had long stayed at home and listened to our advice, but at last went to war against the Sioux because their horses had been stolen and their companions killed; and that in an expedition against those people they met the Ricaras, who were on their way to strike them, and a battle ensued. But in future he said they would attend to our words and live at peace. Le Borgne added that his ears would always be open to the words of his Good Father, and shut against bad counsel. Captain Clark then presented to Le Borgne the swivel, which he told him had announced the words of his Great Father to all the nations we had seen, and which, whenever it was fired, should recall those which we had delivered to him. The gun was discharged, and Le Borgne had it conveyed in great pomp to his village. The council then adjourned.''

After much diplomacy and underhand scheming, one of the Mandan chiefs, Big White, agreed to go to Washington with the expedition. But none of the Minnetarees could be prevailed upon to leave their tribe, even for a journey to the Great Father, of whose power and might so much had been told them. The journal, narrating this fact, says further:—

"The principal chiefs of the Minnetarees now came down to bid us farewell, as none of them could be prevailed on to go with us. This circumstance induced our interpreter, Chaboneau, to remain here with his wife and child, as he could no longer be of use to us, and, although we offered to take him with us to the United States, he declined, saying that there he had no acquaintance, and no chance of making a livelihood, and preferred remaining among the Indians. This man had been very serviceable to us, and his wife was particularly useful among the Shoshonees: indeed, she had borne with a patience truly admirable the fatigues of so long a route, encumbered with the charge of an infant, who was then only nineteen months old. We therefore paid him his wages, amounting to five hundred dollars and thirty-three cents, including the price of a horse and a lodge purchased of him, and soon afterward dropped down to the village of Big White, attended on shore by all the Indian chiefs, who had come to take leave of him.

"We found him surrounded by his friends, who sat in a circle smoking, while the women were crying. He immediately sent his wife and son, with their baggage, on board, accompanied by the interpreter and his wife, and two children; and then, after distributing among his friends some powder and ball which we had given him, and smoking a pipe, he went with us to the river side. The whole village crowded about us, and many of the people wept aloud at the departure of their chief.''

Once more embarked, the party soon reached Fort Mandan, where they had wintered in 1804. They found very little of their old stronghold left except a few pickets and one of the houses. The rest had been destroyed by an accidental fire. Eighteen miles below, they camped near an old Ricara village, and next day, as they were about to resume their voyage, a brother of Big White, whose camp was farther inland, came running down to the beach to bid Big White farewell. The parting of the two brothers was very affectionate, and the elder gave the younger a pair of leggings as a farewell present. The Indian chief was satisfied with his treatment by the whites, and interested himself to tell them traditions of localities which they passed. August 20 they were below the mouth of Cannon-ball River, and were in the country occupied and claimed by the Sioux. Here, if anywhere, they must be prepared for attacks from hostile Indians. At this point, the journal sets forth this interesting observation:—

"Since we passed in 1804, a very obvious change has taken place in the current and appearance of the Missouri. In places where at that time there were sandbars, the current of the river now passes, and the former channel of the river is in turn a bank of sand. Sandbars then naked are now covered with willows several feet high; the entrance of some of the creeks and rivers has changed in consequence of the quantity of mud thrown into them; and in some of the bottoms are layers of mud eight inches in depth."

The streams that flow into the Missouri and Mississippi from the westward are notoriously fickle and changeable. Within a very few years, some of them have changed their course so that farms are divided into two parts, or are nearly wiped out by the wandering streams. In at least one instance, artful men have tried to steal part of a State by changing the boundary line along the bed of the river, making the stream flow many miles across a tract around which it formerly meandered. On this boundary line between the Sioux and their upper neighbors, the party met a band of Cheyennes and another of Ricaras, or Arikaras. They held a palaver with these Indians and reproached the Ricara chief, who was called Gray-eyes, with having engaged in hostilities with the Sioux, notwithstanding the promises made when the white men were here before. To this Gray-eyes made an animated reply:—

"He declared that the Ricaras were willing to follow the counsels we had given them, but a few of their bad young men would not live in peace, but had joined the Sioux and thus embroiled them with the Mandans. These young men had, however, been driven out of the villages, and as the Ricaras were now separated from the Sioux, who were a bad people and the cause of all their misfortunes, they now desired to be at peace with the Mandans, and would receive them with kindness and friendship. Several of the chiefs, he said, were desirous of visiting their Great Father; but as the chief who went to the United States last summer had not returned, and they had some fears for his safety, on account of the Sioux, they did not wish to leave home until they heard of him. With regard to himself, he would continue with his nation, to see that they followed our advice. . . . .

"After smoking for some time, Captain Clark gave a small medal to the Chayenne chief, and explained at the same time the meaning of it. He seemed alarmed at this present, and sent for a robe and a quantity of buffalo-meat, which he gave to Captain Clark, and requested him to take back the medal; for he knew that all white people were 'medicine,' and was afraid of the medal, or of anything else which the white people gave to the Indians. Captain Clark then repeated his intention in giving the medal, which was the medicine his great father had directed him to deliver to all chiefs who listened to his word and followed his counsels; and that as he (the chief) had done so, the medal was given as a proof that we believed him sincere. He now appeared satisfied and received the medal, in return for which he gave double the quantity of buffalo-meat he had offered before. He seemed now quite reconciled to the whites, and requested that some traders might be sent among the Chayennes, who lived, he said, in a country full of beaver, but did not understand well how to catch them, and were discouraged from it by having no sale for them when caught. Captain Clark promised that they should be soon supplied with goods and taught the best mode of catching beaver.

"Big White, the chief of the Mandans, now addressed them at some length, explaining the pacific intentions of his nation; the Chayennes observed that both the Ricaras and Mandans seemed to be in fault; but at the end of the council the Mandan chief was treated with great civility, and the greatest harmony prevailed among them. The great chief, however, informed us that none of the Ricaras could be prevailed on to go with us till the return of the other chief; and that the Chayennes were a wild people, afraid to go. He invited Captain Clark to his house, and gave him two carrots of tobacco, two beaver-skins, and a trencher of boiled corn and beans. It is

165

the custom of all the nations on the Missouri to offer to every white man food and refreshment when he first enters their tents."

Resuming their voyage, the party reached Tyler's River, where they camped, on the twenty-seventh of August. This stream is now known as Medicine River, from Medicine Hill, a conspicuous landmark rising at a little distance from the Missouri. The voyagers were now near the lower portion of what is now known as South Dakota, and they camped in territory embraced in the county of Presho. Here they were forced to send out their hunters; their stock of meat was nearly exhausted. The hunters returned empty-handed.

"After a hunt of three hours they reported that no game was to be found in the bottoms, the grass having been laid flat by the immense number of buffaloes which recently passed over it; and, that they saw only a few buffalo bulls, which they did not kill, as they were quite unfit for use. Near this place we observed, however, the first signs of the wild turkey; not long afterward we landed in the Big Bend, and killed a fine fat elk, on which we feasted. Toward night we heard the bellowing of buffalo bulls on the lower island of the Big Bend. We pursued this agreeable sound, and after killing some of the cows, camped on the island, forty-five miles from the camp of last night." . . . .

"Setting out at ten o'clock the next morning, at a short distance they passed the mouth of White River, the water of which was nearly of the color of milk. As they were much occupied with hunting, they made but twenty miles. The buffalo," says the journal, "were now so numerous, that from an eminence we discovered more than we had ever seen before at one time; and though it was impossible accurately to calculate their number, they darkened the whole plain, and could not have been, we were convinced, less than twenty thousand. With regard to game in general, we have observed that wild animals are usually found in the greatest numbers in the country lying between two nations at war."

They were now well into the Sioux territory, and on the thirtieth of August they had an encounter with a party of Indians. About twenty persons were seen on the west side of the river, proceeding along a height opposite the voyagers. Just as these were observed, another band, numbering eighty or ninety, came out of the woods nearer the shore. As they had a hostile appearance, the party in the canoes made preparations to receive them; they were suspected to be Teton-Sioux, although they might be Yanktons, Pawnees, or Omahas. The journal adds:—

"In order, however, to ascertain who they were, without risk to the party, Captain Clark crossed, with three persons who could speak different Indian languages, to a sand-bar near the opposite side, in hopes of conversing with them. Eight young men soon met him on the sand-bar, but none of them could understand either the Pawnee or Maha interpreter. They were then addressed in the Sioux language, and answered that they were Tetons, of the band headed by Black Buffaloe, Tahtackasabah. This was the same who had attempted to stop us in 1804; and being now less anxious about offending so mischievous a tribe, Captain Clark told them that they had been deaf to our councils, had ill-treated us two years ago, and had abused all the whites who had since visited them. He believed them, he added, to be bad people, and they must therefore return to their companions; for if they crossed over to our camp we would put them to death. They asked for some corn, which Captain Clark refused; they then requested permission to come and visit our camp, but he ordered them back to their own people. He then returned, and all our arms were prepared, in case of an attack; but when the Indians reached their comrades, and informed their chiefs of our intention, they all set out on their way to their own camp; though some of them halted on a rising ground and abused us very copiously, threatening to kill us if we came across. We took no notice of this for some time, till the return of three of our hunters, whom we were afraid the Indians might have met. But as soon as they joined us we embarked; and to see what the Indians would attempt, steered near their side of the river. At this the party on the hill seemed agitated; some set out for their camp, others walked about, and one man walked toward the boats and invited us to land. As he came near, we recognized him to be the same who had accompanied us for two days in 1804, and was considered a friend of the whites.

"Unwilling, however, to have any intercourse with these people, we declined his invitation, upon which he returned to the hill, and struck the earth three times with his gun, a great oath among the Indians, who consider swearing by the earth as one of the most solemn forms of imprecation. At the distance of six miles we stopped on a bleak sand-bar, where we thought ourselves secure from any attack during the night, and also safe from the mosquitoes. We had made but twenty-two miles, but in the course of the day had killed a mule-deer, an animal we were very anxious to obtain. About eleven in the evening the wind shifted to the northwest, and it began to rain, accompanied by thunder and lightning, after which the wind changed to the southwest, and blew with such violence that we were obliged to hold fast the canoes, for fear of their being driven from the sand-bar: still, the cables of two of them broke, and two others were blown quite across the river; nor was it till two o'clock that the whole party were reassembled, waiting in the rain for daylight."

The party now began to meet white men in small detachments coming up the river. On the third of September, for example, they met the first men who were able to give them news of home. This party was commanded by a Mr. James Airs (or Ayres), from Mackinaw, by the way of Prairie du Chien and St. Louis. He had two canoes loaded with merchandise which he was taking up the river to trade with the Indians. Among the items of news gathered from him, according to the private journal of one of the Lewis and Clark party, was that General James Wilkinson was now Governor of Louisiana Territory, and was stationed at St. Louis. This is the Wilkinson who fought in the American Revolution, and was subsequently to this time accused of accepting bribes from Spain and of complicity with Aaron Burr in his treasonable schemes. Another item was to this effect: "Mr. Burr & Genl. Hambleton fought a Duel, the latter was killed." This brief statement refers to the unhappy duel between Aaron Burr and Alexander Hamilton, at Weehawken, New Jersey, July 11, 1804. This interesting entry shows with what feelings the long-absent explorers met Mr. Airs:—

"After so long an interval, the sight of anyone who could give us information of our country was peculiarly delightful, and much of the night was spent in making inquiries into what had occurred during our absence. We found Mr. Airs a very friendly and liberal gentleman; when we proposed to him to purchase a small quantity of tobacco, to be paid for in St. Louis, he very readily furnished every man of the party with as much as he could use during the rest of the voyage, and insisted on our accepting a barrel of flour. This last we found very agreeable, although we have still a little flour which we had deposited at the mouth of Maria's River. We could give in return only about six bushels of corn, which was all that we could spare."

Three days later, the voyagers met a trading-boat belonging to Mr. Augustus Chouteau, the founder of a famous trading-house in St. Louis. From this party the captains procured a gallon of whiskey, and with this they served out a dram to each of their men. "This," says the journal, "is the first spirituous liquor any of them have tasted since the Fourth of July, 1805." From this time forward, the returning explorers met trading parties nearly every day; and this showed that trade was following the flag far up into the hitherto unexplored regions of the American continent.

The explorers, hungry for news from home, would have tarried and talked longer with their new-found friends, but they were anxious to get down to civilization once more. Their journal also says: "The Indians, particularly the squaws and children, are weary of the long journey, and we are desirous of seeing our country and friends." This quotation from the journal gives us our first intimation that any Indians accompanied Big White to the United States. He appears to have had a small retinue of followers men, women, and children—with him.

Below the mouth of the Platte, September 12, Lewis and Clark met Gravelines, the interpreter who was sent to Washington from Fort Mandan, in 1805, with despatches, natural history specimens, and a Ricara chief. The chief had unfortunately died in Washington, and Gravelines was now on his way to the Ricaras with a speech from President Jefferson and the presents that had been given to the chief. He also had instructions to teach the Ricaras in agriculture.

It is interesting to note how that the explorers, now tolerably well acquainted with the Indian character since their long experience with the red men, had adopted a very different bearing from that which they had when coming up the river, in 1805. Here is an extract from their journal, September 14:—

"We resumed our journey. This being a part of the river to which the Kansas resort, in order to rob the boats of traders, we held ourselves in readiness to fire upon any Indians who should offer us the slightest indignity; as we no longer needed their friendship, and found that a tone of firmness and decision is the best possible method of making proper impressions on these freebooters. However, we did not encounter any of them; but just below the old Kansas village met three trading-boats from St. Louis, on their way to the Yanktons and Mahas."

Thirty miles below the island of Little Osage village, the party met Captain McClellan, formerly of the United States army. He informed Captain Lewis that the party had been given up for lost, people generally believing that they would never again be heard from; but, according to the journal of one of the party, "The President of the U. States yet had hopes of us." The last news received in "the U. States" from the explorers was that sent from Fort Mandan, by Gravelines, in 1805.

Scarcity of provisions once more disturbed the party, so that, on the eighteenth of September, the journal sets forth the fact that game was very scarce and nothing was seen by the hunters but a bear and three turkeys, which they were unable to reach. The men, however, were perfectly satisfied, although they were allowed only one biscuit per day. An abundance of pawpaws growing along the banks sufficed as nutritious food. The pawpaw is native to many of the Western States of the Republic. It is a fruit three or four inches long, growing on a small tree, or bush. The fruit is sweet and juicy and has several bean-shaped seeds embedded in the pulp. The voyagers now began to see signs of civilization on the banks of the river. Near the mouth of the Gasconade, above St. Louis, they beheld cows grazing in the meadows. The journal says: "The whole party almost involuntarily raised a shout of joy at seeing this image of civilization and domestic life." Men who have been wandering in pathless wildernesses, remote from man, for more than two years, might well be moved by the sights of a homelike farm and a settled life. Soon after this the party reached the little French village of La Charette which they saluted with four guns and three hearty cheers. Then, according to the journal, they landed and were warmly received by the people, who had long since abandoned all hope of ever seeing these far-voyaging adventurers return. Here are the last entries in the journal that has been our guide so long across the continent and back again to the haunts of men:—

"Sunday, September 21st, we proceeded; and as several settlements have been made during our absence, we were refreshed with the sight of men and cattle along the banks. We also passed twelve canoes of Kickapoo Indians, going on a hunting-excursion. At length, after coming forty-eight miles, we saluted, with heartfelt satisfaction, the village of St. Charles, and on landing were treated with the greatest hospitality and kindness by all the inhabitants of that place. Their civility detained us till ten o'clock the next morning.

"September 22d, when the rain having ceased, we set out for Coldwater Creek, about three miles from the mouth of the Missouri, where we found a cantonment of troops of the United States, with whom we passed the day; and then,

"September 23d, descended to the Mississippi, and round to St. Louis, where we arrived at twelve o'clock; and having fired a salute, went on shore and received the heartiest and most hospitable welcome from the whole village."

The two captains were very busily employed, as soon as they arrived in St. Louis, with writing letters to their friends and to the officers of the government who were concerned to know of their safe return to civilization. Captain Lewis' letter to the President of the United States, announcing his arrival, was dated Sept. 23, 1806. President Jefferson's reply was dated October 20 of that year. In his letter the President expressed his "unspeakable joy" at the safe return of the expedition. He said that the unknown scenes in which they had been engaged and the length of time during which no tidings had been received from them "had begun to be felt awfully." It may seem strange to modern readers familiar with the means for rapid travel and communication that no news from the explorers, later than that which they sent from the Mandan country, was received in the United States until their return, two years and four months later. But mail facilities were very scanty in those far-off days, even in the settled portions of the Mississippi Valley, and few traders had then penetrated to those portions of the Lower Missouri that had just been travelled by Lewis and Clark. As we have seen, white men were regarded with awe and curiosity by the natives of the regions which the explorers traversed in their long absence. The first post-office in what is now the great city of St. Louis was not established until 1808; mails between the Atlantic seaboard and that "village" required six weeks to pass either way.

The two captains went to Washington early in the year following their arrival in St. Louis. There is extant a letter from Captain Lewis, dated at Washington, Feb. 11, 1807. Congress was then in session, and, agreeably to the promises that had been held out to the explorers, the Secretary of War (General Henry Dearborn), secured from that body the passage of an act granting to each member of the expedition a considerable tract of land from the public domain. To each private and non-commissioned officer was given three hundred acres; to Captain Clark, one thousand acres, and to Captain Lewis fifteen hundred acres. In addition to this, the two officers were given double pay for their services during the time of their absence. Captain Lewis magnanimously objected to receiving more land for his services than that given to Captain Clark.

Captain Lewis resigned from the army, March 2, 1807, having been nominated to be Governor of Louisiana Territory a few days before. His commission as Governor was dated March 3 of that year. He was thus made the Governor of all the territory of the United States west of the Mississippi River. About the same time, Captain Clark was appointed a general of the territorial militia and Indian agent for that department.

Originally, the territory acquired from France was divided into the District of New Orleans and the District of Louisiana, the first-named being the lower portion of the territory and bounded on the north by a line which now represents the northern boundary of the State of Louisiana; and all above that line was known as the District of Louisiana. In 1812, the upper part, or Louisiana, was named the Territory of Missouri, and Captain Clark (otherwise General), was appointed Governor of the Territory, July 1, 1813, his old friend and comrade having died a few years earlier.

The end of Captain (otherwise Governor) Lewis was tragical and was shadowed by a cloud. Official business calling him to Washington, he left St. Louis early in September, 1809, and prosecuted his journey eastward through Tennessee, by the way of Chickasaw Bluffs, now Memphis, of that State. There is a mystery around his last days. On the eleventh of October, he stopped at a wayside log-inn, and that night he died a violent death, whether by his own hand or by that of a murderer, no living man knows. There were many contradictory stories about the sad affair, some persons holding to the one theory and some to the other. He was buried where he died, in the centre of what is now Lewis County, Tennessee. In 1848, the State of Tennessee erected over the last resting-place of Lewis a handsome monument, the inscriptions on which duly set forth his many virtues and his distinguished services to his country.

The story of the expedition of Lewis and Clark is the foundation of the history of the great Northwest and the Missouri Valley. These men and their devoted band of followers were the first to break into the world-old solitudes of the heart of the continent and to explore the mountain fastnesses in which the mighty Columbia has its birth. Following in their footsteps, the hardy American emigrant, trader, adventurer, and home-seeker penetrated the wilderness, and, building better than they knew, laid the foundations of populous and thriving States. Peaceful farms and noble cities, towns and villages, thrilling with the hum of modern industry and activity, are spread over the vast spaces through which the explorers threaded their toilsome trail, amid incredible privations and hardships, showing the way westward across the boundless continent which is ours. Let the names of those two men long be held in grateful honor by the American people!

Printed in Great Britain
by Amazon

21143551R00099